LEARNING FROM
BRYANT PARK

LEARNING FROM BRYANT PARK

Revitalizing Cities, Towns, and Public Spaces

ANDREW M. MANSHEL

RUTGERS UNIVERSITY PRESS
NEW BRUNSWICK, CAMDEN, AND NEWARK, NEW JERSEY,
AND LONDON

The opinions expressed herein are solely those of the author and not of the City of New York.

Library of Congress Cataloging-in-Publication Data

Names: Manshel, Andrew M., author.
Title: Learning from Bryant Park : revitalizing cities, towns, and public spaces / Andrew M. Manshel.
Description: New Brunswick, New Jersey : Rutgers University Press, [2020] | Includes bibliographical references and index.
Identifiers: LCCN 2019027885 | ISBN 9781978802438 (hardback) | ISBN 9781978802452 (epub) | ISBN 9781978802490 (mobi) | ISBN 9781978802544 (pdf)
Subjects: LCSH: Urban renewal—New York (State)—New York. | Public spaces—New York (State)—New York. | City planning—New York (State)—New York. | Parks—New York (State)—New York. | Civic improvement—New York (State)—New York. | Economic development—New York (State)—New York. | Bryant Park (New York, N.Y.) | Jamaica (New York, N.Y.)
Classification: LCC HT177.N5 M36 2020 | DDC 307.3/416097471—dc23
LC record available at https://lccn.loc.gov/2019027885

A British Cataloging-in-Publication record for this book is available from the British Library.

♾ The paper used in this publication meets the requirements of the American National Standard for Information Sciences—Permanence of Paper for Printed Library Materials, ANSI Z39.48-1992.

www.rutgersuniversitypress.org

Manufactured in the United States of America

For Heidi, who has taken me to many great places

CONTENTS

LEARNING FROM BRYANT PARK

CHAPTER 1

JACOBS, WHYTE, BRYANT PARK, JAMAICA, QUEENS, AND THE RETURN TO THE CENTER

In the 1990s, the tide changed in how Americans perceived their country's cities. I use the metaphor of the tide rather than saying that a "revolution occurred" because this change in perception took place over an extended period of time. It came about because a series of small, calculated changes over a number of years shifted the perception of safety by residents of urban centers.

It is widely acknowledged that many American cities, particularly the older ones of the Northeast and Midwest, began to decline in the early 1960s. They were perceived at that time to be places that one moved out of if one could. In the American public imagination, cities were thought to be unsafe and physically decaying. For New York City, the low points were the 1975 municipal fiscal crisis and the 1990 *New York Post* headline "Dave, Do Something," which begged then mayor David N. Dinkins to take action after a series of particularly violent events.

But then the tide began to turn. In the mid-1990s, perceptions of city centers began to change, and by the end of the decade, cities—and New York City, in particular—were thought of as safe, clean, and vibrant. People began moving back downtown, and real estate prices, which hit bottom in New York City after the market crash of 1987, began a steady increase, climbing to today's dizzying prices of as much as $6,000 per square foot of residential space in new buildings in Manhattan.

This book makes the case that the ideas that played a critical role in this sea change were first incubated in the 1950s, crept into the minds of those managing urban public spaces in the 1960s, were refined in the 1970s, and started being implemented by the early 1990s. By the end of that decade, principally as a result of the practice of these ideas, the urban tide came back in.

The relevant strategies revolved around reversing the negative perceptions of public spaces by making them feel safe, comfortable, and interesting instead of frightening. After decades of post–World War II development that focused on cars (designing public infrastructure to increase their capacity and speed) and new buildings (glass and steel towers with only one ground-floor entrance), planners, developers, and public officials began instead to center their thinking about public spaces on people. The showpiece in this change of practice was Bryant Park in New York City, at Forty-Second Street and Sixth Avenue, one block from Times Square. Bryant Park is a highly visible public space that for decades was deemed to be dangerous and unpleasant. It was "restored" in 1992 to widespread praise and, more important, wonder. The success of Bryant Park was a signal that public spaces in dense urban centers could be managed in such a way as to make them thought of as safe and inviting. Bryant Park became a model for similar projects around the country as well as a sign of urban possibility. Later, I employed those same strategies and tactics in Jamaica, Queens, to similar effect. Jamaica is becoming a model of a modern, diverse, vibrant downtown in a neighborhood that had previously experienced severe disinvestment and had a dreadful reputation for a lack of safety and violence in its public spaces. It is the next great New York placemaking success story.

One individual catalyzed this slow but massive change in managing public spaces in the United States. William Hollingsworth "Holly" Whyte was an author of a best-selling book[1] and a longtime editor at *Fortune* magazine. At *Fortune*, Whyte published the work of Jane Jacobs, America's most recognized urbanist. Jacobs went on to write *The Death and Life of Great American Cities* (1961), which is widely regarded as the seminal work in the history of thinking about how cities work. Although Jacobs became the high-profile leader of new thinking about urban places, Whyte's work on public spaces, while less recognized, is foundational to the changes that occurred in American cities. The new strategies described by Whyte centered on designing and managing public spaces with the goal of making them attractive to people rather than having them serve as throughways for cars or grand statements of design. Whyte was a careful observer of urban spaces, and he made time-lapse photography a key observational tool. Whyte was given to Yogi Berra–like aphorisms such as "You can see a lot by looking." The conclusions he drew from his hands-on research resulted in the books *City: Rediscovering the Center*[2] and *The Social Life of Small Urban Spaces.*[3] Whyte became involved in the restoration of Bryant Park in 1979, and his principles laid the foundation for the park's tremendous success and widespread impact.

Although it gets used a great deal, different people employ the term *placemaking* in different ways. Recently, some have begun to use the term *tactical urbanism* to mean approximately the same thing.[4] In this book, when I use the term *placemaking*, I am referring to a practice of activating public spaces through programming, high-quality maintenance, and attention to detail. Central to placemaking is the monitoring of space users in real time in order to fine-tune the programming and management of streets, sidewalks, parks, and plazas to draw people to them. Placemaking is about improving public spaces through small moves and adjustments rather than through planning on a grand scale. Over the last thirty years, those of us involved in improving downtowns and public spaces have gained a great deal of practical information about what kinds of things bring people into public spaces and revitalize them. The goal of this book is to describe that knowledge. These aren't big ideas. They are the small ones that make a difference.

THE BEGINNING OF THE BRYANT PARK RESTORATION

The story of the Bryant Park restoration began in 1979 with Andrew Heiskell, the chairman of both Time Inc. and the New York Public Library (NYPL). It is very hard now to imagine the physical and operational decrepitude of NYPL in the 1970s, but the once-elegant central library building at Forty-Second Street and Fifth Avenue, built in 1911 and designed by Carrère and Hastings, had become a run-down and antiquated facility. Heiskell set out to change that and began raising funds for its renovation and improvement. One of his fundraising calls was to William Deitel, the president of the Rockefeller Brothers Fund, a charitable foundation established in 1940 by the sons of John D. Rockefeller Jr.[5] While Deitel was receptive to this appeal for funds for NYPL, he told Heiskell that he thought no revival of the central library building would be possible without doing something about the dangerous eyesore that surrounded it, Bryant Park.

For nearly its entire history, Bryant Park had been an unsuccessful public space. Edith Wharton refers to it in *The House of Mirth* (1905) as "that melancholy pleasure ground."[6] The site of the park, two full blocks bounded by Fifth and Sixth Avenues and West Fortieth and Forty-Second Streets, was first used as a parade ground and an open space. It became a park, referred to as "Reservoir Square," in 1847. The Croton Distributing Reservoir was located on the eastern half of the block. It was a gigantic structure, said to be Egyptian in design, with a popular promenade on top of its walls. In 1853, the Crystal Palace was built in the park as part of the Exhibition of the Industry of All Nations, based on the model of the Crystal Palace in London. That structure burned down in 1858. In 1884, the park's name was changed to honor the editor, abolitionist, and terrible poet William Cullen Bryant. In 1899, the reservoir was demolished to make way for the new main building of the New York Public Library, and a new park was created. That park (Wharton's "melancholy" spot) was never popular, and during the Depression, it became a Hooverville. In 1933–1934, one of the young Robert Moses's first capital projects as parks commissioner

Figure 1. Bryant Park after its Lusby Simpson redesign in about 1936.

was the elimination of the encampment of the poor and unemployed and the implementation of a new design. This 1933 design—the result of a competition won by a landscape architect, Lusby Simpson of the New York City Parks Department—in large part remains today.

But Simpson's design also proved unsuccessful, particularly with the Sixth Avenue El running alongside, casting a shadow and generating considerable noise and smoke. By the 1970s, Bryant Park was principally known as a haunt for drug dealers, prostitutes, and homeless people. There was only one long block separating it from the seediness of Times Square and the Deuce, the block of Forty-Second Street between Seventh and Eighth Avenues that was dominated by pornographic movie theaters. (That slightly scary but also exciting walk between the Port Authority Bus Terminal and Broadway was a memorable part of my youth.)

Deitel told Heiskell about William H. Whyte, who had left his editorship at *Fortune* magazine to spend his time investigating how people behaved in public spaces under the auspices of the Brothers Fund. Whyte had been studying the success of Paley Park on Fifty-Third Street and Greenacre

Park on Fifty-First Street (the site of which was a gift from the Rockefeller family). These were successful "vest-pocket parks" in Midtown Manhattan that featured movable chairs, shade, and water features. For NYPL, the Brothers Fund commissioned Whyte to perform a study of Bryant Park and make recommendations.[7] After the completion of Whyte's study, the Brothers Fund, along with NYPL and the New York City Department of Parks and Recreation (DPR), then led by Commissioner Gordon Davis, decided to establish the Bryant Park Restoration Corporation (now called the Bryant Park Corporation, but it will be referred to here as BPRC) as a private, nonprofit entity to spearhead the implementation of Whyte's recommendations. Dan Biederman, a graduate of Princeton, a couple of years out of Harvard Business School, and the chair of local Community Board Five, was hired to head the operation, with small grants from the Brothers Fund and the library. The initial staff was Biederman and an assistant. Biederman was charged with raising capital funds for the park's improvement, creating programs to activate the space, and developing a restaurant, the rent from which was proposed to support BPRC's operations. However, it would be a long road from those plans to their actual implementation, and BPRC struggled for a decade.

While the Restoration Corporation was founded in 1980, capital improvements to the park didn't begin until 1988. Those improvements, as it turned out, were mostly paid for out of city capital dollars allocated to the NYPL. The situation at the NYPL improved through the 1980s as a result of the leadership and fundraising prowess of Heiskell and Vartan Gregorian, the library's president, and the library knew that it needed modern storage space for its collection. Before the advent of the internet, the amount of printed material that libraries needed to maintain for researchers was growing exponentially. The storage facilities at the main library were far from up to date and lacked basic modern archive features like climate control and compact storage.

NYPL's vice chairman at the time was Marshall Rose, a creative real estate developer, advisor, and investor who also actively served on the board of BPRC. It was Rose's idea to use the land under Bryant Park to build a two-story extension of the library stacks. He essentially created new land for the library. That 120,000-square-foot, two-story facility was planned with all the modern archival amenities.[8] The project also accomplished another important library goal: it jump-started the physical restoration of the park. The plan was to dig up the park's great lawn, build the stack extension under it, and then, when the stack extension project was complete, restore the site—not to its original condition, but to an improved design implementing Holly Whyte's recommendations regarding the park's physical layout. The firm of Hannah Olin Design created the plans in accordance with Whyte's suggestions. This was all to be paid for using $25 million of New York City capital dollars, raised through the city's general obligation borrowing. These funds proved much easier to secure than the private philanthropic dollars BPRC had spent almost a decade trying to raise. BPRC did raise several million dollars to pay for noninfrastructural amenities, which included the restoration of the landmark comfort station (paid for by the J. M. Kaplan Fund), lamp stanchions copied from those on the north entrance to the NYPL (paid for by Celeste Bartos), lighting on top of the New York Telephone Company Building, perennial gardens (designed by Lyndon Miller), and concession kiosks.

After four years of construction, during which it was closed to the public by a cyclone fence, the park reopened informally on April 21, 1992.[9] It included new entrances from Forty-Second Street; openings in the balustrades to allow visitors to cross the park; a working Josephine Shaw Lowell Fountain, which hadn't functioned for decades; and a cleaned-up monument to William Cullen Bryant, which had previously been scarred by graffiti. There were brand-new, high-quality trash receptacles; the rear wall of the library had been cleaned of its perpetual yellow stain; and the boxwood parterres, which had grown to more than seven feet tall and made the park particularly forbidding, had been eliminated. The Sixth Avenue steps were reconfigured to be less steep, with better sight lines from the bottom. The corner at Sixth Avenue and Forty-Second Street (now called Andrew

Figure 2. The construction of the New York Public Library Stack Extension under Bryant Park.

Heiskell Plaza) was completely opened up and reconfigured. The narrow stairs were eliminated and replaced by a broad entrance and two concession kiosks. The restaurant still remained only in the planning stages. Paul Goldberger celebrated the reopening in the *New York Times* and credited the restoration as a tribute to Whyte, whom he called "our prophet of urban space."[10]

The stack extension was attached to the library by a 120-foot tunnel (the tunnel included an exit door that led to the not-yet-built restaurant pavilion). There was a fire door in the lawn that was designed to release smoke that now is covered by a panel listing the original donors to the capital improvements. The lower level of the two-story structure was planned for future needs and was not built out. Unfortunately, after construction was complete, it was discovered that the lower level was built in the path of a historic and latent underground stream—and it began to flood. It was therefore effectively unusable. However, the current plan for the storage of

books, the result of a tremendous controversy about the future programming of the library, calls for the waterproofing of the lower level and its fit
out for storage.

I Enter the Picture

While construction on the park was underway, in 1991, during the continuing economic downturn, I answered a classified ad in the *New York
Times* and soon went to work for the BPRC[11] and its sister organization
and business improvement district (BID), Grand Central Partnership
(GCP),[12] as associate director and counsel. Biederman hired me to create arts programming for the then closed and under construction Bryant
Park, among a number of other assignments. Some of those assignments
drew on my experience as an attorney, but most, at least at the outset, did
not. I worked with BPRC and GCP (as well as the 34th Street Partnership,
which was formed in 1992) for ten years. While there, I had the opportunity to learn from Holly Whyte and to analyze and address a wide range of
urban problems then found in Midtown Manhattan using his lens. By the
time I had left working for the BIDs, Bryant Park had become the symbol
of urban revitalization across the country.

Change in Jamaica

The strategies and tactics we developed in Bryant Park are highly transfer-
rable to other places. They are certainly not unique to Forty-Second Street
and Sixth Avenue—or even to Manhattan, as I hope to demonstrate in this
book. In 2004, a few years after leaving Bryant Park, I had an opportunity to
take my placemaking skills to a disinvested community of color in the borough of Queens. I wanted to see if those skills were relevant to a completely
different set of circumstances from Midtown Manhattan. I was particularly
interested in the challenge of doing placemaking with substantially fewer
resources than we had at BPRC and the other Midtown BIDs.

Figure 3. Bryant Park, early twentieth century. The original design. Note the structures on the lower right.

In Jamaica, I worked as a vice president for the local economic-development entity Greater Jamaica Development Corporation (GJDC). I was attracted to GJDC in part by the prospect of working with Carlisle Towery, its longtime president. Towery, an architect who grew up in Birmingham, Alabama, had a reputation for crossing cultural boundaries as a white southerner working in a black community. I hoped to learn both from his economic-development experience as well as from his leadership, which had earned the respect of community leaders and elected officials. The impact of placemaking on Jamaica is much more recent and far less well known than that in Bryant Park, but it was equally dramatic and important.

Europeans first settled Jamaica, Queens, in 1656. A few of the religious institutions in the community date back almost that far. The railroad came early to Jamaica, and it became a terminal for a number of lines reaching out into Long Island, bringing produce and other goods to be distributed to Queens and the rest of New York City. Later, with the construction of a rail tunnel under the East River, the Long Island Rail Road (LIRR), now headquartered in Jamaica, brought Long Island residents to jobs in Midtown Manhattan. Hundreds of thousands of commuters pass through the station daily. The station is now also served by two subway lines, the AirTrain to John F. Kennedy International Airport, which is minutes away, and several dozen bus lines serving all of Queens and some of adjoining Nassau County. Jamaica is truly a transportation center, and Kennedy Airport is also a major contributor to the local economy. Aviation is the borough's most important business sector, and JetBlue is its largest private employer.

As one of the five original towns in Queens County, Jamaica became, in effect, the capital of Long Island, with many government, business, and social institutions located there. Jamaica was a thriving civic and commercial center for centuries, and it was a particularly vital community just before World War II, with department stores, local banks, and daily newspapers. It has a large number of attractive art deco structures. Its main thoroughfare, Jamaica Avenue, became a mile-long central shopping district for the surrounding middle-class communities. The courthouses for Queens County were located in its downtown area, as was the central branch of the county's extensive public library system. It was also an entertainment center: Jamaica Avenue had half a dozen large movie theatres, including the Valencia, one of the famous Loew's "Wonder Theaters."

Immediately after the war, Jamaica was one of the few places in the region where African American families could purchase single-family homes. A large and dynamic community of middle-class African American families became established with a number of high-profile individuals living there; Count Basie, Lena Horne, Illinois Jacquet, and Lester Young called Jamaica home. Jamaica's influence on the music world continued into the twenty-first century, with performers like Russell Simmons, LL Cool J, and Nicki Minaj all having grown up in the community.

But like so many other northeastern downtowns, depopulation and disinvestment followed the war. White residents took to their cars and moved
to the suburbs on Long Island, changing the character of Jamaica's retail
offerings. White businesses were also leaving. In one year in the 1970s,
Downtown Jamaica lost its three department stores, its remaining daily
newspaper, and its headquarters bank. At the same time, in its *The Second Regional Plan*, the Regional Plan Association (RPA), a respected civic
organization, advised that Jamaica should become a commercial adjunct
to Manhattan, taking advantage of its extensive transportation infrastructure.[13] In the plan, Jamaica was designated as a "satellite" center of
economic activity (along with Newark, Stamford, and Brooklyn). The central idea was to encourage office development around the transit hub in
Jamaica. Toward that end, GJDC would work to ensure that the AirTrain
to Kennedy Airport terminated in Jamaica (requiring a change of trains
in Jamaica) and also began to acquire key properties around the train station with the idea of creating sites for office towers. In 2007 (which was
unfortunate economic timing), the area was dramatically up-zoned to
permit this kind of development. Particular effort was expended in several
unsuccessful attempts to attract jetBlue to the station area for its office
headquarters. But the private market thought differently.

GJDC was not only concerned with transportation, however. It was established in the late 1960s as an outgrowth of the second plan by the RPA, the
Jamaica Chamber of Commerce, and the office of Mayor John Lindsey to
lead development efforts in southeast Queens and to attempt to prevent
the neighborhood's downward slide. In 1971, Towery, who had worked on the
second plan while employed by RPA, was recruited to become GJDC's
first full-time staff member; he would serve as its president until 2015. But
Jamaica's economic decline continued, and with the new scourge of crack
cocaine affecting perceptions of safety in public spaces, Jamaica gained a
reputation for violence and drug trafficking.

In the early 1980s, GJDC's mission shifted to working for the downtown's revitalization. It converted the landmarked former County Hall

of Records into an Afrocentric community arts center, tried to convert an abandoned firehouse into an artist's live/work space, and lobbied for and obtained major public projects for Jamaica, including York College (a senior college of the city university system), the Food and Drug Administration's Northeast Regional Laboratory, and a one-million-square-foot office facility for the Social Security Administration. But private investment remained difficult to attract, and GJDC remained committed to the development of Jamaica as an office center.

After my arrival at GJDC in 2004, I worked to include public-space-improvement strategies into GJDC's efforts. Eventually becoming GJDC's executive vice president, I was afforded the opportunity to manage large-scale real estate development projects as well as a range of programs that were geared toward improving the quality of life and the perception of Jamaica. The implementation of placemaking strategies in Jamaica, as in Bryant Park, had a dramatic impact, playing a part in the revitalization of Jamaica's downtown after decades of decline and decay. More than one billion dollars is now being invested there in private development projects. Jamaica has become another success story of people-oriented programming changing the perception of place, leading to improved quality of life for its residents and its economic revitalization.

Learning from Bryant Park—What Works

Our work in Bryant Park was carefully considered, with each element of the restoration being designed or implemented as a means of making the public more comfortable in returning to the park. Every day, I was able to engage in placemaking practice, seeing what worked and what didn't. The basic idea behind our efforts was to change the perception of the park by manipulating subtle visual cues that visitors read as indicating that the park was safe. The programs we implemented were designed to make clear that the space had returned to social control and visitors could expect no threatening or uncomfortable experiences. From movable chairs, to a

Figure 4. By moving from an outside contractor to an in-house operation, Greater Jamaica Development Corporation expanded and improved its downtown security operation.

perfectly maintained lawn, to immaculate restroom facilities, each element made a contribution to our effort. By presenting a daily array of enjoyable programming, we made the park worth visiting and transformed a place that was long deserted into a place where people wanted to be.

Central to the success of Bryant Park was that it was a triumph of small ideas. It was not the product of grand design. Its restoration was about excellent maintenance and programming rather than extensive capital improvements. Iteration—making small changes building on one another over time—was our basic operating practice. Our success was based on close observation of how people behaved in the park, once it was reopened, and building on what worked and dropping or reengineering what didn't. Using the information gathered from our observations, my team and I implemented carefully designed and monitored programming and maintenance efforts. We provided detailed control over how Bryant Park was managed.

These strategies have proved to be highly transferable to other places, and indeed I brought them with me to Jamaica, where they were equally successful. We learned from our Bryant Park work that no place has problems so unique that it can't benefit from learning from the successes of other places. By writing this book, I hope to share with others what I learned in Bryant Park—as well as in Jamaica and elsewhere—and provide a deep understanding of how people-oriented thinking about downtowns and public spaces can produce measurable improvements in economic activity and the quality of life for urban residents and visitors. The book will discuss both strategy and tactics of "what works."

Taking Placemaking beyond the Big Cities

While many public places, from Campus Martius Park in Detroit to Discovery Green in Houston, have benefited from people-oriented revitalization, and many big cities, particularly on the coasts, have returned to being places where people now choose to live and work, there are still many important public spaces and a number of major cities where automobiles continue to take precedence over pedestrians, where public officials and private developers impose grand architectural statements on the landscape, and where political dysfunction has prevented downtown revitalization. While this book is for people in those places, I intend it also to be for people in smaller cities and towns that have found themselves in economic distress and are losing population—who I believe also can "learn from Bryant Park." I firmly believe that the ideas discussed here are of particular utility in reengaging residents of those small places, creating lively public spaces there and the potential for revitalization on Main Streets across the country. In my view, the "next wave" of placemaking will be in those smaller places.

CHAPTER 2

THE BASIC STRATEGIES
OF PLACEMAKING

I have identified a number of fundamental strategies and tactics that inform placemaking practice. This chapter will lay out basic public-space-improvement project strategies and provide some "parables" that illustrate those strategies. The balance of the book will explore a wide range of successful placemaking tactics and applications for public space revitalization.

I have found that most people feel that the strategies and tactics of placemaking are counterintuitive. That is why the kind of revitalization work that I am describing here is not as widespread as it ought to be and why many public officials, private developers, and urban designers (including architects and landscape architects) remain skeptical about placemaking. But these *are* the ideas that drove the country's most successful and visible public space revitalization project. They are based on not only what I learned from Holly Whyte (and others) but also what I learned from observation and experience of what works.

MAKE NO GRAND PLANS

Daniel Burnham was wrong when he famously said, "Make no small plans." I learned this from making a $600,000 decision that turned out to be a mistake. *Basic to placemaking is that it is an "iterative" process.* An iterative process is one that is based on making small changes and taking small steps. You learn as you go. *It is essential in effectively improving public space to take risks*—but those risks need to be small, manageable ones, risks you can back out of with minimal damage. This is an entirely different approach from creating a grand vision, master plans, and the construction of megaprojects—the kind of thing for which Jane Jacob's bête noire, Robert Moses, became infamous.[1] In practice, very few of those large-scale projects, like the now-under-construction Hudson Yards in Manhattan, end up being successful. This is because there are so many variables involved in the human interactions with the physical manifestations of such developments. Designers and engineers are unable to anticipate even a small portion of the impacts of the many decisions that go into planning a megaproject. The results are unintended effects and places that don't draw people. Add a priority of maximizing automobile volume and velocity to that mix, and you are likely to have an outcome that is inhospitable to people as pedestrians, residents, and workers. For example, the wind tunnel effect on the sidewalks created by the dense, supertall buildings of the not-yet-completed Hudson Yards is already considerable and makes walking through and around the project difficult and unpleasant.

In placemaking, when you see that ideas aren't working out and aren't effective in drawing people into a space, then you need to reverse course. That is an important part of putting people first in public space design and operations—admitting that what you've done isn't working when those people are voting with their feet—in the wrong direction. This is much more difficult to do when a Giorgio de Chirico–like master plan and grand design has been implemented, as at Hudson Yards. The developers can't

just go back and rip the millions and millions of dollars in capital investment out to improve the project.

MAKE SMALL MISTAKES: THE PARABLE OF THE BAD PLANTERS

For example, at the GCP and 34th Street Partnership BIDs, we created a
sidewalk horticulture program. Our horticultural team, led by Lyndon B.
Miller, had already scored a great success with the perennial gardens in
Bryant Park. So we went to work trying to figure out how to extend that
success to the streets around Grand Central Terminal and Penn Station.
We were doing something new here because, while some smaller American towns (like Cooperstown, New York) had hanging baskets, we weren't
aware of any major city where baskets and planters had been implemented
on a large scale. (It would be several years before Chicago's Mayor Richard M. Daley, who sent his staff to spend time with us in Bryant Park to
take notes, implemented the spectacular Chicago State Street streetscape
redesign, with its beautiful horticulture. That successful program eventually expanded all over the Loop.) We did our research and found a catalog
source for the hanging baskets and coco-mat liners. Our fantastic Long
Island–based horticultural supplier, Starkie Brothers, helped us select
plants and buy a truck with a water tank and a long wand for watering. But
we were stumped in finding a source for high-quality, attractive planters
of the scale we were looking for. So we decided to create our own model.

Lyndon suggested a young architect friend of hers who had a classical
sensibility and refined taste and was a pleasure to work with. The architect
created a lovely square-based design that tapered up to a fluted rim that
had the raised logo of GCP on its four sides. Once the design had been
agreed upon by our staff, we went searching for a fabricator who could cast
the planter in high-quality concrete. We were looking for a material that
would have sufficient weight to hold the planter in its place on the sidewalk
and would be of the best craftsmanship in the casting of the detail and the
quality of the surface. It took months working with the fabricator to get a

prototype—which looked spectacular when delivered to our offices. The planter had an elegant shape and a gorgeous, rich surface.

We loved it, and we ordered half a dozen of them for our streetscape prototype block on Vanderbilt Avenue. The various agencies that had authority to approve the project came to look at the prototype and signed off—and we then started mapping out locations around Midtown where planters and hanging baskets would be appropriate. The fabricator quoted us a price of $600,000 for a thousand units. When they were delivered, we installed them, along with the hanging baskets, and sat back and admired them.

And the planters looked great for about six months. Then we noticed that the square corners were being chipped off due to being hit by trucks that were backing up to park and by delivery handcarts. We started to repair them as we noticed the damage. What was originally a trickle of repair work turned into a torrent. Over time, a majority of corners on the planters got knocked off. We also realized that the planters were beginning to discolor. We tried regularly power-washing them, which wasn't terribly effective. They got increasingly dirty, and most acquired a black cast. The beautiful stippled, porous surface effect that we worked hard with the fabricator to create absorbed dirt, grime, and exhaust from the New York streets (particularly in the winter). I had made a $600,000 mistake.

What I learned from this experience was to make smaller bets—and to have a plan B in the event that an idea doesn't work out. It would have been wiser to order a couple of dozen planters and see how they performed over all four seasons, evaluate them, and then decide how to move forward. It is very difficult to predict all the various ways in which an idea will actually work once it gets out on the street. Our brains are just not capable of anticipating and accurately predicting the impact of all of the variables that exist in public spaces. I needed to relearn one of the most basic things I had absorbed from Holly Whyte. The close observation of how people actually act in public spaces also goes for watching how people interact with capital improvements. New ideas for capital investments need to be put into place as incrementally as possible, observing how they work in the real world and then adjusting plans accordingly. That's what I mean when I say that placemaking is an iterative process.

The end of the planter story is also illustrative. We went back to the drawing board and found a *round* planter that was fabricated from extruded PVC and was one-tenth the cost of the concrete planter. The PVC planters were lightweight and much easier to install but when filled with planting material were sufficiently heavy to remain in place.

The round planters, obviously, had no corners, and the plastic didn't chip or discolor. They *worked* when put on the street. Maybe they didn't look as elegant as the concrete planters looked when they were first installed, but they looked way better over time. The hanging baskets have always been a success. The color palette and horticultural materials used in planters in Bryant Park, on Thirty-Fourth Street, as well as in other down-towns around the country have expanded way beyond our original choice of New Zealand impatiens in pink and orange.

What happened to the concrete planters? We sanded off the logos and gave them away to civic improvement groups in other neighborhoods. I still occasionally see them in areas around the city, with the surface painted over, looking derelict and still terrible.

THE ESSENTIAL IMPORTANCE OF THE PERCEPTION OF PUBLIC SAFETY

A second bedrock principle of restoring public space is the requirement of making people feel safe there. Visitors will only return to a downtown or a park if they perceive it to be safe (and, of course, it must actually *be* safe!). The principal reason people avoided Bryant Park before 1990 was because they were afraid to go there. But why did they feel unsafe? What makes people afraid to spend time in certain places? It is a feeling of being unable to predict how other people they see in the space are going to behave, which makes them concerned for their own physical safety. When peo-ple go outside of places where they feel they are in control, they look for markers, visual cues that communicate to them that the other people they encounter in the space will behave in ways that they expect—and make them feel more certain that they will not be physically threatened.

For example, the reason most people avoid spaces where homeless people are present is that they have the sense (often based on actual but limited firsthand experience) that single adult homeless people occupying public spaces behave in ways that are unpredictable. Implicit in that unpredictable behavior (perhaps driven by drugs and mental health issues) is a perception of a possible physical threat from them.

People feel safe with what they know and with people they know. If they don't personally know the people they are going to encounter in a public place, they sense that people who have traits that are as much like theirs as possible are going to behave in ways that they can anticipate. Maybe in prehistoric times, people had circles of trust: one's family and tribe were much less likely to pose a physical threat to that person than those outside the tribe.[2] Perhaps in that environment, we developed carefully honed sensitivities about the cues that told us who was a threat and who wasn't. As a result, we are suspicious of difference (which often leads to prejudice). Sameness generates feelings of predictability and therefore of safety (also a basis of irrational prejudice). In managing public spaces, you have to deal with the reality of the fears of large numbers of people, however irrational or unappealing those fears might be, in order to make public spaces attractive to as broad a cross-section of citizens as possible. Of course, at the same time, public space managers need to be sensitive to both the rights and the social service needs of any individual who chooses to visit the space. Public space managers can't be exclusively driven by elite views of what is "attractive" or desirable in public spaces. As public spaces, they must be accessible by *everyone*. This is part of the complex balancing calculations that are essential to high-quality public space management.

Figure 5. The award-winning but generally deserted Santa Fe Railyard, which lacks programming, shade, and sufficient places to sit. What not to do.

THE PARABLE OF PERCEPTION

Early in my tenure in Jamaica, a business executive from a Fortune 500 company who lived near Downtown Jamaica contacted us. He ran his company's data center, which was then located in an office building in Midtown Manhattan—very expensive space for a bunch of machines. This individual had the idea that he might relocate the data center to industrial space near the transit hub in Jamaica, save his company a ton of money on occupancy costs, and pare his commute time from an hour to ten minutes. Our business services team at Greater Jamaica Development Corporation immediately went to work assembling a list of suitable available spaces. Attracting this major American company to Jamaica would have been a newsworthy event—a big step forward in our revitalization efforts for the downtown.

The executive visited the sites we proposed and selected one as having all the attributes he was seeking. Our team assisted him in assembling a plan to present to his corporate real estate department for their review and approval. A group from that office, which was located in the suburbs, was dispatched to visit the site—and then we heard nothing back for weeks. Finally, we reached out to the executive and inquired about the status of the site selection. He told us that "corporate" had made a determination that Jamaica "was not ready" for their company. We were surprised and disappointed, since the space was inexpensive, was conveniently located, had the structural elements required to host a data center, and had a very cooperative owner who was eager to make a deal.

I spent a good deal of time thinking about what might have occurred and visualized a car full of white guys in suits driving down to Jamaica from their office in the suburbs, getting out at the transit center, and noticing that the other folks on the street didn't look much like them. The social environment was, most likely, entirely unfamiliar. With the street vending, the chaotic retail signs, the lack of national chains, and the poor conditions of the sidewalks, they may have perceived the space to be disordered and out of social control. I speculated that they felt unsure and unsafe, that they were afraid.

The actual crime data at the time for Downtown Jamaica indicated that it was no more unsafe than Midtown Manhattan. But there was a broad perception that the downtown *was* unsafe.[3] The question became how to change that perception—however invalid or even irrational and founded in racial prejudice. The challenge became to find cues that would positively communicate to first-time visitors that the social behavior in the space was actually familiar and therefore predictable. We needed to find physical things that we could control that would send the right subliminal messages. I realized that this project was similar to the changes we made to the Bryant Park environment in 1992 to draw people back into the park and was the first step that needs to be taken in any public-space-improvement project—manipulating the physical environment to encourage visitors to perceive the public space as well ordered and absent of physical threats.

ESTABLISHING THE PERCEPTION OF SAFETY

There are a number of basic placemaking tools that have proven their efficacy in changing people's perception of the safety of public space. Visitors need to see things that are familiar to them. The most basic one is creating more of what Jane Jacobs called "street-corner mayors" or "eyes on the street."[4] These can be visible security staff / ambassadors who, by their presence, convey a sense to the visitor that someone is paying attention and attempting to maintain social control. Counterintuitively, I believe that unarmed staff is more effective in conveying this message than people carrying guns. A well-trained, friendly, outgoing, unarmed staff communicates a sense of calm and sense of order.

That public presence doesn't have to be one that appears to be related directly to security. People engaged in maintenance of public spaces convey a similar message. These can be people doing cleaning or horticultural work. They can be performers, ranging from formal presentations to buskers. A wide range of programmed activities in parks and along sidewalks has the same effect. Plants and flowers are a powerful tool in providing positive social cues, as I discuss in detail in chapter 5. Good physical maintenance is an important tool. Better graphics in both wayfinding and retail presentation can make a positive impression. Well-organized commercial activity, like farmers' markets and night markets are also transformative of perceptions of safety in public spaces. In my experience, media can be valuable in supporting efforts to change perception, particularly community newspaper press coverage and social media activity.

Positive programming in public spaces has the ability to change people's perception of them. The level of intensity of such programming required to reverse negative perceptions is in inverse proportion to the depth of the perception of lack of safety. Whatever preconceived notions people might have about a place can be influenced and changed subliminally, no matter the source of those misperceptions. I will describe in detail our programming in Bryant Park in chapter 6. In Jamaica, we were successful in beginning to move the needle of the public perception of safety through public space programming strategies, leading to new investment and development. Those programs in Downtown Jamaica included deploying "ambassadors," creating an extensive horticulture program, and intensively programming cultural events in public spaces (all described more extensively later in the book). Understanding the feelings that drive people to avoid public space is essential in working to draw them back. Making spaces feel familiar and predictable is at the core of revitalizing them.[5]

Patience Truly Is a Virtue

Placemaking takes patience. As I described in chapter 1, it took fourteen or fifteen years from the founding of BPRC to the recognition that the park had been turned around. Now that we know what the basic successful strategies and tactics for placemaking practice are, change can be induced somewhat more quickly. But in my experience, it generally takes three to five years for a revitalized public space to irreversibly improve. This time frame is longer than most public officials and private developers find tolerable. The time it takes for a public space to turn around is generally longer than the terms of most local elected officials—making it difficult to persuade them to allocate their limited financial resources to make one of these projects a success. But it is far better to have one successful initiative that takes five years than to engage a string of failed two-year projects—which is generally what happens. For example, I often refer to Detroit as a museum of failed urban revitalization ideas, including the People Mover, the Renaissance Center, Trappers Alley, the Washington Boulevard pedestrian mall, riverfront condemnations for casinos, and countless demolitions and urban renewal clearings. But more recently, with the success of the relatively small but well-executed placemaking-based revitalization of Campus Martius Park, the city has clearly reached a positive tipping point and has become a beacon of place-based redevelopment.

THE PARABLE OF PATIENCE—NEWSRACKS

An example of the kind of lead time required for a public-space-improvement project to become successful is our effort to eliminate plastic news boxes from Midtown Manhattan. In the 1990s, metal and plastic containers distributing newspapers, magazines, and ads were scattered all over New York, contributing to the sense of chaos and social disorder in public spaces. While newsracks are no longer the issue they once were in most downtowns, and they certainly weren't the world's most pressing problem at the time, the process by which we organized and informally regulated them is instructive as to how apparently impossible public space problems can be addressed. It takes a deep knowledge of the regulatory and legal environment, creativity, flexibility, and persistence—the last being the most important.

In the 1990s, three types of publications utilized stand-alone containers for the distribution of printed material. Daily newspapers (like the *New York Times* and the *New York Daily News*) sold their publications through coin-operated metal machines. Weekly publications (like the *Village Voice*), most of which were free, also mostly used metal racks, while some also used lighter plastic dispensers. A range of advertisers also used flimsy plastic racks to distribute materials. The most ubiquitous of these was something called the Gotham Writers' Workshop (which ultimately was one of the two or three publishers that chose not to participate in the program).

Racks were mostly located at or near corners; some chained to lampposts, some freestanding. A majority of Midtown corners had a least one rack; some had a dozen or more. A majority of the racks were poorly maintained and often derelict, empty, and/or broken. I did a census of all of the racks within the Bryant Park, Grand Central, and Thirty-Fourth

Figure 6. The newsrack situation before their replacement with the multi-vend unit.

Street Districts in 1993 and counted close to four hundred individual racks at some sixty corners. To address the problem, we initially developed the outline of a program and began to persuade the various stakeholders to participate in it the next year. The preliminary work was about two years. From that point, it took another three years to actually fully implement our program—altogether about five years from beginning to end. This example demonstrates the strategy of patience in solving problems impacting social order in public spaces.

We started with an understanding that the newspapers clearly had the benefit of First Amendment protection for the distribution of their product, which requires that any regulation of that activity be limited to time, place, and manner and is subject to a reasonableness standard under applicable case law.[6] All the other publications using newsracks claimed the same rights. Because newspaper distribution rights were so broadly protected and well defined in the law, we determined that a voluntary, consensual program was the best way to proceed in the long run. We did this in order to avoid years of litigation with a strong possibility of loss, no matter how well our proposed program was structured. The city had already lost more than one lawsuit attempting to control this blight.[7]

We decided that the optimal manner in which to address the problem was to design a better-looking distribution mechanism that required less sidewalk space. We started with the premise that when we implemented the project, the number of available corners and the number of distribution points (racks) would have to be at least as many as were then in existence. In that way, we would not be asking the papers and distributors to be giving anything up in terms of distribution points. At the time, the circulation departments of the daily papers were charged with retaining every single reader and every distribution point. It was their view that if a person regularly purchased a paper from a certain newsstand or newsrack, it was a matter of survival for them to maintain the ability to distribute the paper from that location.

I sat down with GCP's director of capital projects, Arthur Rosenblatt— one of the city's most experienced project managers of public building and public space and also an entertaining, cynical, and curmudgeonly character—to try to design a replacement multivend rack. Sketching on a pad of legal paper, Arthur came up with a schematic design of a multivend rack with two rows of four machines set one on top of the other, standing on a double pedestal. This became the basis for our proposal.

Our idea was to propose to the city and the publications that we put out multivend racks at the sixty corners that currently had single-vend racks—with no more than one rack on each corner. Every publication that had an individual rack on a corner would get a slot in the multivend racks. The multivend racks would be paid for by the BIDs (we had substantial capital capacity as a result of having issued the tax-exempt bonds that are discussed in chapter 4). The publications would stock the racks, and the BIDs would maintain them—relieving them of the expense of doing so (as well as of the capital expense of buying the racks). The quid pro quo would be that any publication that participated in the multivend rack program would agree not to put out single-vend racks within the BID boundaries. As a result, the racks would take up less sidewalk space, appear more organized, and be better maintained. In order to make the deal palatable to the newspapers, we had to do everything we could to make the project as attractive to them as possible. There were substantial financial incentives built into our program—and it certainly involved significant capital and operating expenses for the BIDs. We were, however, determined to solve this problem.

In about 1994, we took the idea to our colleagues in city government: Seth Cummins, general counsel at the Department of Transportation (DOT), which regulates sidewalk use, and Gabe Taussig at the Law Department, the longtime head of its Administrative Law Bureau. Our ally at DOT was Frank Addeo, who was decades ahead of his time, advocating from within DOT for improved sidewalks and art in public spaces. We also had an ally in city hall: Craig Muraskin, who worked for David Klasfeld, chief of staff to Deputy Mayor Fran Reiter, both of whom empowered Craig to smooth the way for us when problems arose. Identifying sympathetic insiders in city government was absolutely essential to our success.

We presented our proposal to them, asking if DOT would grant licenses to attach the proposed multivend racks to the sidewalks if we could get the publishers to agree to use them. We thoroughly discussed both the constitutional issues and the city's rules about sidewalk uses and how our plan was carefully crafted to fit within them. We eventually persuaded Seth and Gabe over a period of months, with assists from Craig and Frank, that our proposal was an improvement over the current chaotic situation. They agreed to allow us to move forward and approach the publications. While Seth and Gabe were highly risk averse and skeptical of new ideas (like most city officials, something I'll discuss in more detail in chapter 12), they liked the idea of getting control of sidewalk use and, I think, didn't believe we'd be able to persuade the publishers to participate anyway and thought we were unlikely to be successful.

We then contacted all of the publishers and invited them to a meeting for a presentation of our proposal. The *New York Times* sent its First Amendment expert, George Freeman, as well as a circulation manager. The *Village Voice* sent its outside counsel, Victor Kovner, a former corporation counsel of the City of New York, a longtime New York political fixture, and an eminent First Amendment attorney. Almost all of the publishers of any size sent someone. George and Victor played a leading role in representing the publishers; Victor in particular understood the public benefit of our proposal. We had many individual meetings with the dailies and weeklies as well as with the more ubiquitous of the organizations that used racks to publicize their services. Again, over a period of months, with many phone calls and several all-hands meetings, and following the lead of the *New York Times*, *New York Daily News*, and *Village Voice*, all but one or two of the publishers agreed to sign on. Again, it was my sense that the papers "supported" our project because they were reasonably sure we wouldn't be able to pull it off.

In 1995, we moved to a two-pronged implementation process—actually creating the multivend rack and doing a more complete census of the existing single-vend racks. The daily papers put us in touch with their fabricator, Sho-Rack of Shiner, Texas. Sho-Rack sent a sales representative to us to discuss our idea. They were distrustful at first. Sho-Rack was concerned about the reaction to the proposal of their big customers—the newspapers. They were also wary of cannibalizing their existing business. It took almost eighteen months to cajole them to produce a prototype multivend rack that they eventually had delivered to our office. At the same time, we needed to secure approval from DOT and the city's Art Commission of the design, which progressed on a parallel track.

When executing projects like this one, I am always conscious of what lies in the critical path: What is the next step in the process of creating the project that will move it forward? In order to get these long-term programs in public spaces implemented, you need to have a laser-like focus on the next step and to not be distracted by other issues that may present themselves but won't become problems until a condition precedent has been satisfied.

Similarly, if when analyzing the critical path for a project, more than one option presents itself, it is essential to determine which of the possible options has the highest probability of being successful. You need to keep taking the highest-probability option as you work your way down the decision tree that represents the critical path. I ascribe much of my success in implementing innovative projects to improve public space like the newsrack program to my ability to calculate those probabilities. You need to keep pushing against the highest probability option that presents itself as the project advances—and keep devoting all your attention and energy to accomplishing that option. Generally, public-space-improvement programs involve multiple regulatory, logistical, and financial steps. It takes great patience and diligence to keep pushing the project along, overcoming each obstacle as it appears. If any one option either fails or becomes more improbable of success, then you go back and reassess the probabilities of your various options.

Once the newsrack prototype was delivered in mid-1996, it was installed on the sidewalk to try it out. The several-month trial run of the prototype persuaded us to put a slanted top on the rack in order to keep people from leaving trash on it. Here again, we were observing how a novel program in a public space has an impact on that space—and adjusting the program to accommodate people's responses. Once everyone had signed off, we ordered about sixty racks from Sho-Rack.

The staff and I performed a census of the district's racks, creating a spreadsheet of all the corners and identifying every location where publishers had racks. I took that spreadsheet home and spent a weekend on the floor of my living room with a detailed, scaled street plan, placing racks on corners (making sure they fit, given city siting criteria for street furniture) and assigning racks to publications. We also decided during this time that since free publications were generally narrower than the dailies and they didn't require a coin mechanism (because they were, well, free), they could be accommodated in a half-rack space. My distribution scheme was circulated first to the city and then to the publications. DOT had to approve the locations we proposed for the racks. There was some back and forth about clearances and bus stops, which was a new wrinkle: while the publishers had put their racks wherever they wanted, we had to follow the rules, one of which was that there could not be racks in bus stops. Eventually we all agreed upon a site plan for the racks and which publications would go in them.

The publishers were then given the opportunity to claim any empty spaces in the racks not taken up by publications that already had racks on those corners, so when all the spaces had been distributed, several publications ended up with additional distribution points. After a bit of negotiation and a lottery among the applicants for the empty spaces—also worked on from the floor of my apartment—a plan was agreed upon. An order was placed with Sho-Rack for the fabrication of the doors—with the logos of the various publications printed on them and the proprietary coin mechanisms of the dailies installed. My colleague Dan Pisark, who worked closely with me on the project (and whose father had worked in a newspaper circulation department), hired Kathy Khang out of one of the newspapers' circulation department to manage the program day to day.

Sho-Rack delivered the sixty-odd racks, and one of the BID contractors installed them in the sidewalks in 1997. The publishers removed their individual racks from corners. There was no adverse effect on adjoining blocks outside of our districts, where publishers might have tried to skirt the rules. We had created a program that continues to this day and has been copied in downtowns all over the country (notably in San Francisco and Chicago). Several designers have improved on the look of our original clunky but functional multivend rack, including the Midtown BIDs' talented in-house industrial designer, Ignacio Ciocchini. New York City later enacted legislation regulating the maintenance of racks and requiring participation in the BIDs' multivend program in the districts where they existed.[8]

Figure 7. The first multivend newsrack design, literally created on a napkin. The program took patience and years to develop.

The purpose of this long narrative on an obscure, twenty-year-old project is to describe how complex and long the process was to solve this highly visible, not-quite-earth-shaking urban problem. The project illustrates the persistence required to implement changes in public spaces as well as the step-by-step process, the analysis of the risk of each decision outcome, and the focus on the critical path that are required to get a program fully implemented.

It is illustrative of the success of the program that once it had proved itself as a voluntary scheme, the city made it mandatory. It helped that the BIDs had the financial capacity to pay for and maintain the racks. It took the assistance of sympathetic city government insiders, the goodwill and seriousness of purpose of the city's attorneys, and the leadership of counsel to the *New York Times* and *Village Voice*. But we were also flexible and worked hard to anticipate and address stakeholders' objections and problems. We tried to be as well informed on the law, the design elements, and the mechanics of distribution as all of the counterparties—because that's what it took to be able to address their concerns. We kept at it for years (more than five in the case of the newsracks)—as we did with sidewalk vending, phone kiosks, newsstands, and automatic public toilets—because that's what it takes to solve these knotty public space problems. The result was worth it.

Improving the New York City vending situation, even today, proves to be complex and difficult.[9] In Jamaica, Queens, for example, it remains a serious problem—the large numbers of vendors spread out on and dominating the sidewalks, selling from beat-up carts and stands, communicate to visitors that the downtown is not well ordered. Creating a better regulatory and enforcement scheme for sidewalk vending is by no means hopeless if the kind of persistence described earlier was applied to it by an organization with a stake in public space improvement. If someone were to take on the task and had the capacity to keep at it over a period of years and some resources to contribute to whatever solution might be worked out, eventually that person is likely to be successful.[10] Folks can say no a million times, but you only need them to say yes once. This was certainly the case with all of the streetscape issues we faced at the Midtown Manhattan business improvement districts in the 1990s.

———

This chapter has attempted to lay out in detail the essential strategies I used in successful public space revitalization. Keeping projects small and manageable, making changes to the project as you hit obstacles or observe how people interact with them, and having the patience to see the project through to the end over multiple years have been the foundation for every successful innovative public-space-improvement project with which I have been involved. Subsequent chapters are detailed discussions of specific tactics to be used in making great downtowns and parks, all of which rely on exercising these basic, underlying strategies. Operating in the manner described provides the way in which complex and solution-resistant sources of danger, chaos, and disorder in public places can be reversed.

CHAPTER 3

WHY BRYANT PARK IS IMPORTANT

For anyone who lived in New York City during the 1970s and 1980s, the reopening of Bryant Park in 1992 seemed nothing short of miraculous. The general perception of the city as chaotic and unsafe reached its nadir in about 1991. Times Square, one block away from the park, was the symbol and epicenter of that urban chaos. Forty-Second Street was lined with former movie palaces showing porn; you walked down it away from the Port Authority Bus Terminal toward Midtown along West Forty-Second Street as fast as you could. When I arrived in the city for graduate school at New York University (NYU) in 1978, I was warned away from Bryant Park, being told that it was crime ridden and drug infested (and was advised by classmates to stick to buying my drugs in the much safer Washington Square Park). By design, Bryant Park was raised from street level and had one narrow entrance from Forty-Second Street. The stairs up from Sixth Avenue were steep and forbidding. The place wasn't maintained; the hedgerows hadn't been pruned for decades, and their height created dark shadows and good places to engage in antisocial behavior. The restrooms and the fountain, dedicated to the interesting but forgotten

Josephine Shaw Lowell,[1] hadn't functioned for as long as anyone could remember.

In 1992, the construction fence around the park was taken down, and the resident drug dealers moved across the street and then disappeared forever. A daily schedule of lunchtime concerts began to draw huge crowds into the park, which now boasted two immaculately maintained three-hundred-foot-long perennial beds and a well-kept two-acre lawn. Two thousand movable French bistro chairs were scattered around the park—and were left out overnight. The park was lit at night from the top of an adjacent office building with a lovely moon glow. It was maintained by a highly visible, hardworking crew who regularly emptied the trash cans and a team of friendly, well-trained, unarmed security guards who patrolled the park twenty-four hours a day.

The impact of the park's reopening and success quickly became a symbol of urban possibility and a case study for people-oriented placemaking. Bryant Park demonstrated that the very heart of Manhattan could be—and was—safe, inviting, and lively. The fact that it was conveniently situated a block away from the offices of the New York Times helped broadcast the image of the park around the city, country, and even the world. It was the park's reopening that was the catalyst for a changed perception of New York City and was part of a national trend of downtown revitalization that included a striking demographic change of a dramatic movement of some college-educated individuals back to center cities across the country, mostly from the suburbs.[2] The park's success was the stimulus for similar efforts in other places, most notably in Chicago but also in Houston, Detroit, and San Francisco. The park's triumphant reopening took on a life of its own, and every year in the mid-1990s, the perception of the park improved and its power as a symbol gained momentum with new activities and innovations.

The 1992 reopening was followed by the completion of construction and the opening of the restaurant four years later, the creation of an outdoor movie series, and the semiannual presentation of the New York

Figure 8. A photo taken in 1980 from the northwest quadrant of the park.
The bare ground, broken light, and overgrown hedgerows are obvious.

Fashion Week shows in the park. The weekly televised announcement by
supermodel and celebrity Heidi Klum that the prize for winning *Project
Runway*, the cable reality TV sensation, would be the incredible opportunity to show the winners' designs in Bryant Park cemented the park's
national reputation. Such a thing would have been unthinkable a decade
before.

The park's success was equally important in establishing the efficacy
of placemaking for public space administrators, designers, and planners
across the United States. The park's reopening was all about changing the
perception of an urban public space by activating it, following Holly Whyte's
recommendations. While the park's reopening occurred after some major
physical changes were implemented (as recommended by Whyte in his
study), more important to Bryant Park's new impact were the intensive
programming and high-quality maintenance that began in 1992. Whyte's
placemaking strategies gained currency throughout the 1990s around the

country and around the world, and they were much emulated. Whyte carefully observed people's behavior in public spaces and drew conclusions about the elements that drew people to parks and plazas—as well as those that repelled them. He made wise recommendations based on those observations—which were incorporated into a 1979 study of Bryant Park—and he became the guru to the park's management until his death in 2009.[3] The park's international reputation is a tribute and testament to Whyte and his work.

Fixing Broken Windows

Dan Biederman, the original and continuing executive of Bryant Park Restoration Corporation, the entity established to manage the park's rebuilding, was intrigued by a March 1982 article in the *Atlantic Monthly* that ultimately provided one of the intellectual frameworks for our efforts. That article, "Broken Windows: The Police and Neighborhood Safety," written by James Q. Wilson and George L. Kelling, introduced the idea of "fixing broken windows."[4] Kelling became a longtime advisor to the park's leaders. The broken-windows theory, later adopted by the New York City Police Department under Commissioner William Bratton, employed the analogy of a deserted building to describe a process of growing public disorder. Wilson and Kelling argued that once a single window in an abandoned building appeared to be broken, all of the other windows would rapidly be broken as well. Their idea was that quickly repairing the first damaged window, thus restoring the perception of order, would prevent the other windows from being trashed. In public safety, this meant that by paying attention to public disorder violations—public drinking, turnstile jumping, graffiti, petty thefts—a police department could get into the unprecedented, revolutionary business of *preventing crime* rather than solving (or merely documenting) criminal activity after it occurred.[5] Richard Dillon, the vice president of security for Bryant Park and its affiliated BIDs, called police officers "historians of crime."

Figure 9. A photo taken from the same location in 1996. The many small-scale improvements are evident, from lights to trash baskets.

BPRC carried these ideas over into public space management by implementing high-quality physical maintenance in Bryant Park after 1992 and using a security staff employed by BPRC to maintain the perception of high standards for behavior in the park. Graffiti was immediately removed, stolen plants were quickly replaced, trash was efficiently picked up, and trash baskets never, ever were allowed to overflow. An immaculately maintained restroom became part of the park's physical restoration, powerfully communicating a sense of stability to park users and establishing a perception of safety. *Conscientious maintenance is one of the two basic pillars of public space revitalization through placemaking* (the other being programming, of which will be discussed later).

These ideas defied (and to a certain extent continue to defy) the conventional wisdom about how people behave in public space. The usual thinking at that time held that the movable chairs would be stolen, the restrooms would be vandalized, and the gardens would be impossible to maintain. In 1991, the idea that there could be successful horticultural amenities amid the Wild West atmosphere of Forty-Second Street was regarded as absolutely insane by just about everyone. The park's managerial philosophy was based not on folk wisdom and urban legends but rather on the careful observation of how people *actually behaved* in the park and other urban spaces, using Whyte's detailed ideas about managing public plazas drawn from his observations in the Paley and Greenacre Parks in Midtown in the 1960s and 1970s. It was this data-driven approach that formed the intellectual foundation for Bryant Park's success.

The Chair: The Symbol of Success

The best example of the kind of change upon which Bryant Park's success is built is Holly Whyte's requirement of movable chairs, which have become the park's trademark. Whyte first set out movable chairs in Paley and Greenacre Parks. His time-lapse photography showed that people preferred movable chairs to benches and that the chairs themselves drew people into empty public places. Putting movable chairs in public settings allows visitors to control their space, unlike a bench, which is in a fixed position. People can arrange the chairs so they can chat with each other. They can face the chair in a way that makes them feel secure with respect to whatever else is going on in the public space. They can move the chair into the sun or the shade. The fact that the chair isn't attached to something also conveys a message of safety and social order—it's not tied down and it hasn't been stolen. The very existence of the chair in the space demonstrates that someone has put it there, cares about the space, and is taking care of it. *The movable chair delivers a powerful message about the character of the place where it can be found.* Its use has been copied, and it is being deployed in plazas and parks all across America.

There is no magic, by the way, to the particular chair that is used in Bryant Park. Whyte actually preferred another chair, which had been used in Paley and Greenacre Parks. That chair was constructed of welded white metal, with a mesh seat and back. BPRC had used the mesh chair on the front terrace of the New York Public Library (which it also managed under its management agreement with the city's DPR) before and during the time the rest of the park was under construction. We found that after about a year, the welds tended to give way under, shall we say, larger people. Also, the mesh seats left an unappealing checkerboard pattern on people's butts when they stood up.

There is a story behind that particular green French bistro chair. In 1991, in preparation for the park's spring 1992 reopening, I was tasked with finding alternative chair models. I spent months visiting showrooms and department stores and reviewing home furnishings catalogs. This was not my usual reading material. About a dozen chair candidates were eventually selected and lined up along the wall outside my office. Staff and visitors were invited to sit in the chairs and place a pencil mark on the wall above their preferred chair. Holly came to the office to participate and placed a mark above the Paley/Greenacre chair. I preferred a white plastic chair that was the most comfortable to sit in. Both of us were outvoted in a landslide in favor of the chair that is now used.

We had found the preferred chair in a garden supply catalog. It was very expensive and available only in sets of two. Sourcing the chair before the internet was a project, but we found out that it was manufactured by a company called FERMOB, which was located in Beaune, France. My colleague Lloyd Zuckerberg was a fluent French speaker. He got on the phone and called the factory early one morning New York time and ordered a shipping container loaded with two thousand chairs. Many weeks later, the chairs came in a trailer truck and were unloaded in the park. They were an immediate hit, conjuring up an image of Parisian sophistication in the once forbidding park. They became a sensation. And, of course, they were rarely stolen. FERMOB now has a major distribution facility in Georgia. You're welcome.

I insist that there is no particular magic to the much-copied green FERMOB chair. In the wake of the Bryant Park chair, a number of site

furniture companies (yes, that's a thing) have come up with their own interesting designs. I encourage public space managers to select and use *their
own* signature movable chair to brand their place. Tables and umbrellas are
great and inexpensive as well! Putting out tables, umbrellas, and chairs is
one of the easiest, least expensive, and most transformative tactics that can
be employed in beginning a public space revitalization. They are particularly
effective on downtown streets—even those with narrow sidewalks.

The skeptics about the chairs as well as our other programming initiatives were many and vocal. The results were by no means inevitable
and were the outcome of years of planning and persuasion. BPRC was
founded in 1980. The physical restoration of the park wasn't completed
until 1992, and the restaurant—originally the key element in the plans for
the restoration[6]—didn't open until 1996. Advocacy groups and elected
officials objected to the "privatization" and "commercialization" of the
park. Public officials were threatened by the loss of control of city land
and the risks entailed by the implementation of untested and unconventional programs. Working on park property—on city-owned land
that was the subject of scenic landmark designation—required years of
approvals and processes. Even today, there are some public officials who
regard Bryant Park as a failure and a mistake because of its "privatization"
and "commercialization."

THE "PRIVATIZATION" OF PUBLIC SPACE

The most vocal critics of the Bryant Park project were principally concerned with turning over the management of the space to a nongovernmental organization (NGO). BPRC was a private, conservancy-like entity
established to take on the responsibility of managing the park. This was at
about the same time that the Central Park Conservancy was founded to
raise the funds required to restore the landscape in the city's flagship park.
Gordon Davis, who was then serving as parks commissioner under Mayor
Ed Koch, was particularly progressive in assisting in the establishment of

BPRC and the conservancy. These two organizations demonstrated the effectiveness of the nongovernmental, private nonprofit model for public space revitalization—and both BPRC and the Central Park Conservancy became much-copied examples around New York City and across the country. Policy makers took note and realized that city government did not have the political capacity or the financial resources to maintain highly used and highly visible public spaces in dense urban neighborhoods.

City parks departments exist in a political environment where every neighborhood and every park has to be treated equally. But what we've learned is that parks in dense downtowns (like Bryant Park) are much more intensely used than parks found outside of downtowns in residential neighborhoods (say in Queens) and as a result require significantly more maintenance and programming—which demands substantially more resources. This is generally politically impossible for city parks departments to provide without the criticism from city legislators (who represent the neighborhoods) that money is unfairly being spent "downtown" or in the wealthier parts of town. The establishment of a private nonprofit to generate additional resources for park maintenance and to provide more intense management and programming has proven to be a success in addressing this political problem. Significantly, private nonprofit park management organizations have been able to both generate additional resources (through charitable donations, concessions, sponsorships, and a diverse range of other sources) and provide more intensive maintenance and programming employing dedicated staff.

BID BASICS

Bryant Park used another novel vehicle to generate funds for maintenance and programming. In 1985, a business improvement district was established to support the park. While three or four BIDs already existed in New York City (in Jamaica, Queens, and Downtown Manhattan and on Fourteenth Street), the use of the BID structure was both creative and key to being a reliable source of operating resources for Bryant Park. The BID structure's prior use had been exclusively linear—that is, each BID served the block fronts along a length of a particular commercial corridor. There were no BIDs that maintained public spaces or operated in a nonlinear area prior to BPRC.

A BID is a geographical area upon which an assessment is levied at the time property taxes are paid on all the properties within that area. The New York statute allows for great flexibility as to how an assessment may be levied.[7] Assessments can be done on the basis of front footage (how long a building is on one side), square footage, or assessed value for real estate tax purposes. Our BIDs charged an assessment based on square footage. The bulk of a structure as measured by its square footage was determined by the BIDs' founders to be the best proxy for the amount of benefits that a building would receive from the BID and therefore the fairest and most reliable means of assessment for dense Midtown Manhattan. Most linear BIDs by contrast use a block-front-based formula. The greater the length of the building on the street, the more it pays. At the time BPRC was established, New York City real property taxes for Midtown Manhattan office buildings averaged around nine dollars per square foot. The initial BID assessment was less than twenty-five cents per square foot.

Assessment funds are collected semiannually by the city at the time it collects property taxes. Those proceeds are turned over to the nonprofit BID to provide services additional to those provided by the city in that area (the municipality is required by statute not to decrease its services in the BID area). In 1985, at the time of the creation of the Bryant Park BID, the existing BIDs were focused on street cleaning, retail promotion (holiday lighting), and the maintenance of new capital improvements installed by the city to spur local revitalization. The Bryant Park Management Corporation (BPMC, which was a separate entity from BPRC but had the same board as BPRC and turned over the BID funds to BPRC under a simple memorandum of understanding) was the first BID established to exclusively support a park and was the first to offer a much wider range of services and programming—including security, horticulture, and public events.

The success of the model—even before the restored park was opened—led to the establishment of two much larger organizations. Grand Central Partnership covered fifty blocks around Grand Central Terminal along Forty-Second Street adjacent to Bryant Park. The 34th Street Partnership covered thirty-five blocks around Penn Station and along Thirty-Fourth Street. The three BIDs were operated together, with the same senior management team, myself included, and Dan Biederman as executive director / president. Their striking success drew attention to the BID vehicle. In the decade to follow, hundreds of BIDs were formed around the country. New York City alone now has more than seventy such organizations. The Bryant Park BID was the first BID to draw national attention, and it paved the way for what became the principal tool across North America (and later Europe and Australia) for downtown revitalization.

Maintenance and Programming First!

Bryant Park also proved that high-quality maintenance and programming are the keys to creating successful public spaces. The conventional wisdom before the park's reopening was that great design and expensive capital improvements were the first step to making great public spaces. This is still a widely held view—unsurprisingly, particularly among landscape architects and architects but also in city halls and parks departments across the country. And while a great deal of energy, time, and money were spent on physical improvements to Bryant Park, looking back, I have come to the conclusion that even without those changes, the quality of maintenance and programming in the park alone could have driven its revival.

Public space revitalization projects must *include a sustainable means of providing the resources for continuing maintenance and programming. It cannot be repeated often enough that ongoing operations of a public space are much, much more important than design.* I contend that just about any public space can be revitalized through excellent maintenance and programming no matter how poorly laid out. By contrast, the best-designed space in the world is highly unlikely to draw a sustained critical mass of visitors consistently over time if there are insufficient resources available for operations. This is a vital strategy that has proven itself at Campus Martius Park in Detroit, Yerba Buena Gardens and Union Square in San Francisco, and Discovery Green in Houston.

While well-designed public space is certainly a very good objective, perhaps the most important thing we learned in Bryant Park was that in planning urban parks, the first thing to consider isn't how the space is going to be designed but rather how it is going to be managed. This is challenging in the current municipal environment because paradoxically, capital dollars (raised through public bond issues) are easier for parks departments to obtain than money for ongoing maintenance that comes out of a city's heavily constrained operating budget. The New York City parks commissioner once told me that the Parks Department would not take on responsibility for any additional open space unless that space came with a guaranteed continuing source of funds for operations. It is a sad state of affairs when a city is unable to take care of its parks and even more unfortunate when, because it has insufficient resources, it is unable to expand access to the outdoors to more city residents.

But this is nonetheless true and an essential reality for park planners to come to grips with. In order to turn around or create a great public space, provisions must be made for continuing, reliable sources of revenue—whether those be from the city's operating budget, from a BID, from concessions,[8] or as at the Central Park Conservancy, from philanthropy. (Generally, private donations are the least consistent form of support. While there are individuals and institutions who have been generous in supporting parks and public spaces, because their contributions are by definition voluntary, they are in no way obliged to give every year—and, particularly in economic downturns, may not give.) This is a problem now facing the high-visibility High Line and Hudson River Parks—two major capital investments in public space that are intensively used and widely celebrated but do not receive operating funds from the government and do not yet have sufficient recurring sources of revenue. They are both scrambling for a sustainable financial model.

No Place Is Unique: Creating Sustainability

Nothing about the success of the restoration of Bryant Park was inevitable. I like to tell the story of my first two paychecks from Bryant Park Restoration Corporation—which bounced. Part of my job in the early years was to twice a year (while waiting for assessment funds to arrive from the city) walk across Forty-Second Street from our offices to those of Republic National Bank (which had its headquarters offices overlooking the park) to request a $25,000 increase in our line of credit. This was necessary for BPRC at the time in order to be able to meet payroll. I made this pilgrimage semiannually for a few years. In the early 1990s, BPRC was cash strapped. But after a few tough years, the project became self-sustaining.

The park's ultimate success, both financially and as a public place, was due to careful calculation, close observation, and intense day-to-day management, and it is a transferable model for others to follow. I firmly believe that many public spaces in larger cities across the country have the potential to generate pedestrian traffic sufficient to ultimately make the space financially self-sustaining from concessions and other earned income with the right business acumen and level of activity. It has been my experience that success in public space management undergoes what Jim Collins, the author of *Good to Great*, called the "flywheel effect." He says, "Then, at some point—breakthrough! The momentum of the thing kicks in in your favor, hurling the flywheel forward, turn after turn . . . whoosh! . . . its own heavy weight working for you. You're pushing no harder than during the first rotation, but the flywheel goes faster and faster. Each turn of the flywheel builds upon work done earlier, compounding your investment of effort. A thousand times faster, then ten thousand, then a hundred thousand. The huge heavy disk flies forward, with almost unstoppable momentum."[9] Once you reach that breakthrough point, success often can become self-sustaining.

Over and over again, we were told that our plans and ideas, many of which were based on things we had observed in other places, wouldn't work in New York or on Forty-Second Street. What we found is that *good ideas are transferable*. This kind of sustainability shouldn't be unique to Bryant Park. There is nothing exceptional about the corner of Sixth Avenue and Forty-Second Street that makes the park's success nonreplicable. In the 1980s and 1990s, people said that the special conditions at that location made the park's revitalization singularly impossible. That turned out to be equally untrue.

Today, I hear the comment when I speak with groups trying to revitalize public spaces in other cities about how their town or space is different: "Oh, that may have worked in New York—but it will never work in [fill in the blank]." What we learned in restoring and managing Bryant Park is broadly applicable and useful. Movable chairs work in public space revitalization everywhere. Outdoor movies are successful in small and big public spaces in small and big cities across the country. Providing food service is key to attracting people to empty public spaces no matter where. No place is unique, and while not every idea we employed in Bryant Park will be successful in every environment, many if not most of them are likely to prove to be useful.

The most important thing we learned from Holly Whyte was to closely observe how ideas work in real places in real time and to adjust programming based on how people actually respond to them. You need to be flexible and creative. You need to stop doing the things that people don't like and tweak the things that look promising but aren't fulfilling their potential, expanding on the things that draw people. Park managers need to say yes to potential users (as discussed in chapter 6). These are the tactics that drove the Bryant Park turnaround. These tactics are broadly applicable and are set out in detail in this book. This is how great places are made, and my hope is that by describing the process by which Bryant Park was revitalized and the ideas that were the foundations for our work, others will be inspired to bring the best in placemaking practice to their communities. Great downtowns and public spaces are important parts of every community's social infrastructure. They are the places where citizens of all backgrounds and beliefs meet and engage each other. They provide the key to revitalizing cities and towns of all sizes and reengaging their residents.

CHAPTER 4

THE ROLE OF BUSINESS IMPROVEMENT DISTRICTS IN URBAN REVITALIZATION

BIDs have been around since the late 1970s. They have different names in different states and in Canada. They can be known as special assessment districts (SAD), business improvement areas, business revitalization zones, community improvement districts, special services areas, or special improvement districts. The general concept is that a fee is charged to property owners within a defined geographical area, collected by local government, and then generally turned over to a private, nonprofit special-purpose entity that expends those funds within the geographic area for district improvement.

In New York State (with which I am most familiar and about which I will generally be speaking in this chapter), each of the first SADs, dating back to the 1970s, required a special act of the legislature to be formed. The concept proved to be so popular in the 1980s that the New York State legislature adopted a new, blanket statute setting out a procedure allowing local governments to approve the formation of new BIDs.[1] That process is very much like New York City's Uniform Land Use Review Procedure, with review by the City Planning Commission and the city council and the final sign-off by the mayor. The formation of a BID can be stopped if more than 50 percent of the property owners in a district sign a form and file it with the city clerk after the vote of the council and before mayoral approval.

As private nonprofits, BIDs have their own boards of directors and their own staffs. The statute requires that a majority of the board be elected by property owners and that at least one board member be elected by commercial tenants. An interesting fact is that given the way most office and retail leases are structured, tenants tend to pay a pro rata share of the BID assessment or of increases in the assessment over a base—so in dense business districts, most of the assessments are actually paid for by tenants. The larger BIDs tend to have a substantial minority of board members elected by commercial office tenants. There are also board seats for the mayor, the comptroller, the borough president, and the local city council member.

The mayor is represented on BID boards by staff from the Department of Small Business Services (SBS), an agency with roots in the antipoverty programs of the Johnson administration with funding from the Community Development Block Grant (CDBG) program. With the shrinking of CDBG funds, regulating and supporting BIDs have become major focuses of the agency. After a BID is formed, SBS issues a contract to the local nonprofit that governs the relationship between the BID and the city. When I went to work for BPRC, there were fewer than a dozen BIDs; today there are more than seventy. These BIDs are located in commercial districts in all five boroughs. Most of the newer ones have budgets of less than $500,000.

The way in which BIDs are governed has raised serious policy issues about the amount of discretion and power that BID boards and BID staff have in their districts. All that power is derived from the BID's assessment and the cash it provides. The BIDs have the capacity to determine how those funds are spent. However, nearly all of a BID's work is done on public property and is therefore subject to an overlay of municipal control, beyond the participation of elected officials' representatives on a BID board. Trash pickups must be coordinated with the local sanitation department. Security services are regulated by state licensing authority, and their effectiveness is determined by the quality of their relationship with local police. Much of what BIDs do is advocacy with city government on the hyperlocal issues with which the BID is concerned and that are controlled by local government—like where a crosswalk is painted or how many times a day trash is picked up.

BIDs are private, nonprofit organizations (all have tax-exempt status and some are authorized by the Internal Revenue Service to accept tax-deductible contributions) and are governed by the same rules as other charities. Their boards are responsible to neighborhood stakeholders and to the state attorney general with respect to ensuring that their assets are deployed exclusively in pursuit of their mission. Board members tend to be concerned with those microissues that affect the quality of life in the district—trash, public safety, and the appearance of neighborhood stores. BIDs don't run schools, administer justice, enact legislation, or direct city planning. Their briefs are quite circumscribed; they must act in concert with the government.

THE BRYANT PARK BID

Part of the genesis of the Bryant Park restoration was that a restaurant would be built, and the rent paid by the restaurant would support the operations of BPRC. Many attempts were made through the 1980s to secure a restaurant tenant: Warner LeRoy (Tavern on the Green) and Jerome Kretchmer (Gotham Bar and Grill) both failed in their attempts.[2] The prospect of a restaurant without street frontage—that faced internally on the park—was a difficult sell. During its first five years, BPRC existed solely on philanthropic funds from the Rockefeller Brothers Fund and others, and the staff was essentially Dan Biederman and an assistant. After a number of years passed without the restaurant having been constructed, an alternative recurring source of revenue for BPRC was essential, and the BID vehicle was settled upon to provide it.[3] The initial assessment for the BID was set at $450,000 per year. Those funds allowed BPRC to expand both its staff and its programming efforts. From 1988 to 1992, the park was under construction for the NYPL stack extension and was closed with a fence around it. During this time, BPRC maintained the front terrace of the library and managed the two Hugh Hardy–designed kiosks there. But the regular source of income from the BID allowed BPRC to have sufficient staff to raise capital dollars for the aboveground portion of the stack extension project, which included the lighting, the restroom, and the horticulture—among other features. The assessment was raised when the fence came down in 1992, and it paid for a large maintenance team and twenty-four-hour private security—both of which were managed in-house.

FROM BRYANT PARK TO GRAND CENTRAL

After the apparent success of the Bryant Park BID (described at length in chapters 5 and 6), even before the park opened, the BID model became attractive to others. One was Peter Malkin, who around 1985 became worried about the neighborhood where most of his family's real estate investments were located, particularly those around Grand Central Terminal. As the son-in-law and law partner of Lawrence Wein, Malkin was the steward of a large part of the Helmsley Spear real estate empire, which included the Lincoln Building on Forty-Second Street, the New York Central Building, and the Empire State Building. Mobil Oil, a major office tenant on Forty-Second Street, produced a film that demonstrated the deteriorated conditions around the terminal—trash in the streets, taxi hustling and other antisocial activity in public spaces, homeless people living in and around the terminal, and a lack of activity at night—which they showed to Deputy Mayor Kenneth Lipper during the Koch administration. It was Lipper's idea that perhaps an area-wide (rather than linear) BID might be useful in addressing these problems. Lipper and Malkin approached Biederman with the idea and asked him to create a budget and a program for an area-wide

BID for fifty blocks around Grand Central. The program Biederman devised included supplementary security and sanitation services, a program to serve the homeless, taxi dispatch booths (to deal with the hustling), a tourist-greeter program (to make the neighborhood more welcoming), a capital budget, and funds for promotion and programming in public spaces. Biederman engaged the firm of Ben Thomson and Associates to create a master plan for the district. In 1988, the Grand Central Partnership BID was established, with Malkin as chairman and Biederman as president.[4]

When I arrived at GCP and BPRC in 1991, talks were well underway to set up a third area BID around Pennsylvania Station to provide the same array of services there. The process was made relatively easy because two-thirds of the commercial real estate square footage in the proposed district was held by Malkin's group and a group led by Bernard Mendik, who both enthusiastically supported the plan. In 1992 34th Street Partnership was founded, again with Malkin as chairman and Biederman as president.

WHAT THE BIDs DO

The signature programs and most of the staff of all three BIDs were dedicated to sanitation and security. After the establishment of 34th Street Partnership, the three BIDs had more than three hundred employees performing security and sanitation services. Biederman strongly believed in keeping service delivery and its management in-house. It was his contention, which has proved to be correct, that in-house staff, directly employed by the BID, would provide a higher level of service at a lower cost than would contracting out to a third party. The sanitation program was set up by Thomas Gallagher, a former chief of Manhattan borough operations for the Department of Sanitation (DOS). Gallagher's program, which became the backbone of most BIDs around the country, was to employ workers who would sweep the streets and gutters and bag the trash along defined routes covering the entire district several times a day. They would also empty trash baskets before they became full (overflowing trash baskets having been a prominent feature of the Mobil film). DOS agreed to pick up the bags twice a day. DOS staff no longer had to empty the baskets, as the BID's sanitation crew took on that role. Gallagher also managed the Bryant Park crew.

Richard Dillon, a former Manhattan borough chief of the New York City Police Department (NYPD), was engaged by Biederman to create a private, unarmed security force. The BID obtained a license to provide and train private security employees. Security guards in blue uniforms patrolled fixed beats within the district (and in Bryant Park). They carried walkie-talkies that connected to a base station that had a direct line to NYPD through a program called Operation Interlock. The security team also manned the two taxi dispatch booths around the terminal and reported problematic street conditions, like illegal vending, and suspicious activity to the base. The security employees had no power to make arrests themselves.

Both the security and sanitation staffs constituted the "eyes on the street" and the "street-corner mayors" praised by Jane Jacobs. While the individuals Jacobs discussed as key neighborhood actors were local shopkeepers and residents, these BID paid employees played essentially the same role. They were the most important tool in the execution of the broken-windows strategy that had become central to the BIDs' operations. Biederman was a tough boss who demanded a high level of attention and service. Both crews did visibly outstanding work, contributing to a sense of order in the park and the areas around the two train stations. Once the teams were deployed, one could see the difference immediately. The streets and sidewalks were cleaner. The activity on sidewalks in the districts seemed to be more secure and orderly. The resources of GCP and later the 34th Street Partnership enabled the Bryant Park team to raise its game, with access to the expertise of Gallagher, Dillon, and other staff (including me), which it would have been unable to afford as a stand-alone operation.

In General, there has been little controversy over BIDs' sanitation and security operations, the impacts of which have been at worst benign, particularly given the security staffs' lack of enforcement power. Those uncontroversial services are the ones that have most been emulated by

BIDs everywhere. Other BID activities have seemed to raise a higher level of scrutiny and skepticism, particularly with respect to GCP's decision to provide services to the homeless and to issue bonds to pay for capital improvements.

BID Public Financings

One unusual aspect of GCP was that it had a $2.5 million provision in its original operating budget of debt service for capital improvements. Later, 34th Street Partnership had a similar $1.7 million allocation. The Thomson master plan had some vague ideas on how that money might be spent, but there was no firm idea as to how the debt might be issued. Biederman had explored using the city's Industrial Development Authority (IDA) as a conduit for issuing tax-exempt bonds, but the IDA's attorneys determined that it was not within their authority to issue bonds on behalf of BIDs and would require state-authorizing legislation. Local assemblyman Richard Gottfried opposed the idea of BIDs issuing debt, which became an insurmountable roadblock to that vehicle. Biederman also explored "piggybacking" on a Metropolitan Transportation Authority (MTA) bond issue in exchange for GCP putting a couple of million dollars into amenities for the MTA's North End Access project, which created entrances to Grand Central on blocks north of it. The piggybacking would involve the MTA issuing a somewhat larger bond issue, with GCP covering the additional debt service using assessment funds. GCP and the MTA were not able to come to terms on an agreement for such an arrangement. As with a dozen other projects on which Biederman had reached a dead end, the project was handed off to me when I came on board in 1991.

Working with my Oberlin friend Liam Stokes, who had gone to work in municipal finance at J. P. Morgan, we figured out a novel legal structure that worked. Liam had developed a relationship with a small group of attorneys who had left the well-established public finance practice at Hawkins Delafield & Wood to create a New York beachhead for the San

Francisco firm of Orrick, Herrington and Sutcliffe (the New York office is now that megafirm's largest). Orrick attorneys Albert Simons and Richard Chirls worked out that under an underused provision of the tax code, the BID itself could issue bonds for capital improvements if the city would agree to take title to the improvements. With J. P. Morgan as underwriter and Orrick as bond counsel, GCP issued its first bonds in 1992, ultimately raising more than $70 million for the three BIDs through the same structure. Those funds were used to pay for new streetlights,[5] distinctive pink granite corners, and high-design trash baskets purchased from the Victor Stanley Company (which like the Bryant Park chairs became ubiquitous around the country after being deployed by GCP). All those streetscape elements required extensive review as to both design and siting by the city's Art Commission (now called the Public Design Commission) and Department of Transportation.

When I first got involved in this work in the early 1990s, all of the city's trash baskets (that were not repurposed thirty-gallon oil drums) were really ugly wire-mesh baskets. They got banged up pretty regularly when they were being emptied into trucks, were poorly maintained, and often overflowed. They were the first elements of street furniture we tried to upgrade, mostly because they didn't need any expensive installation and we could just get permission from the city to use them, get rid of the old ones, and put them out. Arthur Rosenblatt, GCP's capital projects vice president, looked through a bunch of steel fabricator catalogs and picked one out from Victor Stanley in Maryland. Arthur chose a forest-green color and ordered some at about $600 a can. This was a big advancement from the wire-mesh baskets, which cost the city less than $100. The Victor Stanley baskets were better looking, more durable, and had lids—to keep trash from overflowing onto the sidewalk. We ended up buying hundreds of them and deploying them in Bryant Park and on street corners all around Midtown. Since that time, many manufacturers have entered the market with high-design trash "receptacles." Victor Stanley still makes the workhorse model used by Grand Central Partnership, although they also make a more technologically advanced basket that has a transmitter and sends a message when it is full.

After we bought the basket, it started being used everywhere—like the chair. When I traveled around the country, I would see it in more and more cities throughout the 1990s. I got into the annoying habit of elbowing my spouse whenever the basket turned up in the background of movies that had outdoor location shots in cities. It seemed like the basket appeared in about a quarter of the films we saw during the late 1990s.

This is just another example of the power of really good small ideas. Putting out a better-designed trash basket in Midtown Manhattan and Bryant Park—and not a particularly elegant one—created demand in communities across the country not just for a better garbage can but for an improved design for a lot of the stuff that cities put on sidewalks. The standard of design for bus shelters, streetlights, newsstands, phone booths, and kiosks of all sorts rose dramatically in the middle of the 1990s. This was a very significant improvement in the quality of public space in this country that was driven by the change from the city standard receptacle to a better one.

The Backlash

However, GCP's capital improvement program was one of two or three of our programs that generated hostility from local elected officials. Assemblyman Gottfried was upset at what appeared to him to be a runaround of his objection to the BID's issuing of debt. Later, Mayor Rudy Giuliani was reportedly incensed when Peter Malkin challenged him about the soundness of the issuance of further debt by GCP in connection with the extension of the BIDs' boundaries.[6] The mayor had been advised by his staff that the markets would view BID debt as an obligation of the city. Their view was that the city would be deemed by the markets to be responsible for the obligations of an entity over which it had limited control. We took the position that as a formal legal matter, this was incorrect and the relevant law and the bond documents made clear that the city was not responsible for any debt obligations incurred by the BID. It seemed unlikely to us that, under those circumstances, the tens of millions of dollars of BID debt would have an impact on the hundreds of billions of dollars of city general obligation bonds.

The political and philosophical objections to BIDs grew during the 1990s. Biederman's compensation package became a particular lightning rod and obsession of city government. As recently as 2016, *Crain's New York Business* carried a broadside attack on business improvement districts on its front page, featuring a photo of Biederman.[7] The article raised a range of charges that had already been the subject of dozens of newspaper articles published in the 1990s as well as a half-dozen government inquiries, including those by the New York City Council, the Office of Comptroller of New York City, the Federal Department of Housing and Urban Development, and a forensic audit commissioned by city hall. Given New York's tabloid culture, many casual (and even some well-informed) observers assume that where there is extensive press coverage, there must be some truth to the many stories. In fact, our BIDs were models of good nonprofit governance and transparency, and none of the negative policy arguments have been shown to be of any merit. In my view, BIDs provide essential services without compromise of any important democratic principles.[8]

So why did the BIDs draw and continue to draw such scrutiny? In my estimation, it comes down to two things: distrust of success and distrust of privatization. New York's journalistic culture produces a recurring cycle of intense media attention to success and a subsequent effort to prove that the subject of veneration has feet of clay (e.g., Anthony Weiner). Elected officials are particularly sensitive to media attention and the success of others, given the highly competitive nature of political life in New York City and the difficulty of drawing attention to local matters in one of the world's leading media markets.

What is called in New York City a "progressive" policy perspective always produces some public official reaction and journalistic and academic scrutiny. First, there was the idea that something called a "business" improvement district could not possibly act in the public interest and must be advancing an exclusively private agenda at the expense of the public. Second, there was the notion that because BIDs are private nonprofits, they are not democratically accountable. There was, and is, serious concern by many in government and interested in public policy about the "privatization" of public services, resulting in both a lack of public accountability and the possible exclusion of otherwise underserved populations.

However, the actual evidence demonstrates that BIDs have not advanced a private agenda at the expense of the public good. In my view, these philosophical objections remain hypothetical—and actual facts on the ground refute them. One interesting aspect of the real estate industry is that, except with respect to setting the level of property taxes, the industry's long-term interests actually align closely with those of the public at large. Property owners can't pick up and move their buildings, and so the public realm is essential to the value of their investments. Few things are more public than the success of Bryant Park and other revitalized public spaces. In Bryant Park, all have been welcome, no one has ever complained about having been excluded, and many have benefited.

With particular respect to homeless individuals, their presence in Bryant Park has not raised a public policy concern. The homeless have never been asked to leave the park as a result of their appearance or status. Most homeless individuals choose not to be in places crowded with other people, but those homeless individuals who choose to spend time in the park were such a small percentage of park users at any particular time that their presence wasn't visible.[9]

One advantage of BIDs is that their boards, composed of owners, tenants, residents, and public officials, reflect the microconcerns of neighborhood stakeholders—an area smaller than that of any governmental subdivision. The BID board determines the expenditure of what is essentially its money—and that is the extent of its power. In the 1990s, the sobriquet "mayor of Midtown" was applied to Biederman as a shorthand to reflect a projection of an aggregation of power.[10] But in reality, BIDs are severely constrained in determining the ways and means of the services they provide. BIDs' "power" is even more constrained by the oversight of elected officials, who hold the real power over the public realm and maintain seats on the BIDs' boards.

SBS in particular sees its role as ensuring that BIDs dot their i's and cross their t's. They perform the role of a brake on BIDs' risk taking in order to ensure compliance and to prevent scandal and embarrassment to the city government. The agency has been effective in this mission.[11]

This is not to say that the BID program in New York City is without fault. In the past decade, dozens of small new BIDs have been formed. There is research that demonstrates that smaller BIDs (those with budgets of under $2 million) are generally resource constrained and have limited impact.[12] It is the small BIDs that generally run into governance and financial problems. In addition, it is particularly difficult to get local property owners and retailers in the boroughs to participate in BID governance. Small retail owners work long hours and generally need to be at their stores when they are open, making meeting attendance difficult. Local property owners tend to be highly focused on the immediate challenges facing their businesses and properties. I've generally found it impossible to persuade them (even the reasonably sophisticated owners of many properties in multiple neighborhoods) to take a broader or longer view by getting more involved in community issues. They prefer to stick to managing their properties. Property owners tend to be wary of the government and want to stay on the good side of local elected and appointed officials. As a result, the ex officio board members representing elected officials tend to end up running things at the sixty or so smaller BIDs.

The BID world has changed a lot in the last twenty-five years. When I started working for the Midtown Manhattan BIDs, there were a grand total of around ten BIDs. Today there are more than seventy. While the first few BIDs were of relatively modest capacity, the trend in the 1990s was to take the concept of downtown management organizations onto a larger scale in cities across the country. New organizations with substantial resources were being established in the densest commercial areas. Now the trend is the proliferation of small organizations with limited staffs and funds of less than $500,000, which is about the current mean BID size. In the mid-1990s, there were fewer than a dozen BIDs, and half of those were the BIDs with budgets of more than $5 million. The large BIDs formed in the 1990s are ones with the largest budgets. The BID world in the nineties in New York was all about those larger organizations: GCP, 34th Street Partnership, Bryant Park, Times Square, and the Downtown Alliance.

At first, in the early 1990s, BIDs got lots of positive press, particularly after the reopening of Bryant Park in 1992. But in 1995 journalistic attitudes changed. There were a slew of critical *New York Times* stories about BIDs that appeared between 1995 and 2002.[13] The onslaught was brutal and constant, and not just in the *New York Times*. However, in my view, the bottom line was, and is, that the critical assumptions and projected potential problems were and are ill-founded. Today, if there is any global criticism of BIDs that I might level, it is that BIDS have become overly risk averse, siloed, and sclerotic. City government, in recent years, has gotten slightly more creative and interested in new solutions to problems—for example, the use of streets as public spaces and the deployment of accessible technology in public spaces.

THE ATTACK ON BIDs

In 1992 we were visited by two high-profile advocates for the homeless. They demanded that GCP and 34th Street Partnership take the hundreds of thousands of dollars they had budgeted for homeless services and turn those funds over to the advocates' own organizations. They threatened endless "trouble" if their demands were not met. Their argument was that a "business" organization had no place providing services to the homeless. It was their assertion that profit-making organizations were contributors to the market forces that create homelessness; that their interests, particularly those of the real estate industry, were antithetical to those of the homeless; and that as a result, it would be impossible for them to work to improve the situation of homeless individuals.

In fact, GCP had established its own innovative social service affiliate that ran a drop-in center adjacent to Grand Central Terminal under contract with the city. The center provided a place indoors open twenty-four hours that served three meals a day and that offered shelter for homeless clients in which to spend time. In a very short period of time after the opening of this program, almost all of the six hundred or more homeless individuals left the terminal and its environs, and most migrated to the drop-in center, hence changing the perception of the area around the terminal, which was a critical part of GCP's mission.

But make trouble the homeless advocates did. First, in early 1995, they filed a lawsuit alleging that GCP social service participants in its job readiness program were not being paid in compliance with federal and state wage and hour laws. They were represented in this claim by one of the city's most prestigious law firms. Then it got worse. In the spring of 1995, the *New York Times* ran a five-thousand-word investigative report saying that three former program clients claimed that they had been encouraged by GCP staff to beat up other homeless people in order to force them out of public spaces and bank ATM vestibules in Midtown.[14] The story got traction, and dozens of follow-up stories were printed, seriously damaging the reputations of the GCP and 34th Street Partnership and the BID program more generally. Both the district attorney and the Federal Department of Housing and Urban Development (a funder of the social service program) began investigations.

Another wave of critical stories arose out of an "investigation" into BIDs by the city council. The report purported to look into the "tremendous power" that BIDs allegedly wielded and their lack of responsiveness and transparency.[15] Much of this was focused on our Midtown Manhattan BIDs. In retrospect, many folks, particularly elected officials who viewed publicity as a competitive zero-sum game among participants in the public arena, resented our visibility and the success of our work in revitalizing Bryant Park and the rest of Midtown. Dan Biederman was outspokenly—and often caustically—critical of as well as independent of the government. But in managing the BIDs, he was driven by a results-oriented approach that was meritocratic in hiring and essentially apolitical in its operations. Elected officials found it impossible to believe that Biederman had no aspirations to elected office. But he never had any such ambition and had no interest in party politics or political power. He thought of himself as a new kind of private-sector, technocratic Robert Moses, focused on using private-sector management to improve urban service delivery. This, to say the least, was often not well received by government officials and the leaders of other nongovernmental organizations engaged in similar work. Additional agencies and elected officials piled on, resulting in other audits and "investigations."[16]

In addition, occupants of an apartment building added to the Grand Central District in a geographic expansion filed suit challenging the imposition of the BID assessment on residents. It turned out that one of the apartment owners was a tax attorney! The case went up to the Federal Second Circuit Court of Appeals, which held in GCP's favor.[17] But the city council, followed by SBS, then made it city policy not to include residential buildings in BID assessments.

Finally, another storm arose in 1999, when Mayor Giuliani began a campaign to split up the three BIDs run by Biederman. There were many theories of where this came from. The precipitating event was a request by GCP to close a block of Park Avenue in order to create public spaces adjacent to the new Pershing Square Café. An appeal for reconsideration by GCP after a deputy mayor had denied the request was badly received by the mayor, whose policies generally placed a priority on improving the speed of car traffic rather than on the pedestrian experience.[18] The earlier meeting to ask for reconsideration of a mayoral decision not to allow the issuance of a tax-exempt borrowing to finance capital improvements in extensions to the Grand Central District was also a contributing factor.

That situation ended when the GCP board voted out the BID's officers, including Malkin, Dan, and me. Those officers were replaced with individuals who held the mayor's trust.[19] The city ordered a forensic audit be performed at GCP, with the implication that something untoward had been going on. This effectively marked the end of the era of BIDs' independence of city government. After that, BID boards and staff across the city became more risk averse. The smaller BIDs became even more reliant on SBS, particularly after it began a program of providing discretionary programmatic grants to BIDs with small budgets. In fact, for the last dozen years, New York BIDs have been particularly circumscribed in their activities. They mostly stick to the tried and true of clean and safe and are not the laboratories of civic innovation that they were in the 1990s. With the replacement of our team at GCP in 1999, everyone else in the BID business got the message to maintain a lower profile. In recent years, when choosing leaders for BIDs, their boards have generally chosen to go a political route, seeking former elected officials and former government employees who are trusted by local government. Those individuals do come with knowledge of how to navigate New York City's political and journalistic environment, sensitivity to avoiding the kind of political minefields we so often found ourselves in, and a range of useful relationships both inside and outside of government.

Ultimately, our BIDs were found to have operated in an exemplary fashion by just about every entity that looked into them. Reports on the GCP social service program by an expert on homeless services retained by GCP and one by the Federal Department of Housing and Urban Development (HUD) found no evidence of abuse of homeless people by GCP staff. In fact, the HUD study (obtained after extensive Federal Freedom of Information Act litigation)[20] found the program design to be "exemplary." No evidence of any injured homeless people was ever found—no police reports, no hospital records, and no homeless person ever came forward to say they had been injured (the allegations in the *New York Times* story were by people who were plaintiffs in the wage and hour lawsuit who claimed that *they* had assaulted *other* homeless people). The wage and hour lawsuit was settled after an adverse judicial ruling—by then district court judge Sonia Sotomayor—on whether the trainees in the program were "employees" for purposes of the wage and hour laws.[21] None of the audits found any evidence of anything other than excellent stewardship and transparency by GCP. Nothing was ever heard of the 1999 forensic audit.

The era of big, ambitious BIDs, working independently of (but in partnership with) the government, is over, at least in New York City. The continued level of innovation and high-quality service delivery at the BIDs run by Biederman are to his great credit. Biederman continues to run the Bryant Park and 34th Street BIDs. He has maintained his high standards and innovative programming despite the journalistic and political attacks, with an important positive impact on Midtown. In retrospect, it was an exciting time and place to work. It was a privilege to have had the opportunity to make a demonstrable difference in the quality of life and economic vitality of the city beginning in 1991, a rather dark time (that is difficult to conjure up now) in the city's history.

THE FUTURE OF BIDs

The number of business improvement districts has expanded greatly over the last twenty years, both in New York City and nationally. There are now close to one thousand BIDs in the United States. The focus of most BIDs is what's been labeled "clean and safe"—that is, providing sidewalk and street cleaning and security services. Following the model we set up at GCP, they provide staff to sweep the sidewalks and curbs and empty trash baskets. Larger BIDs also tend to provide unarmed private security services on sidewalks within the district, and often those staff members are trained to provide directions and other tourist information. Most of the small BIDs, and even some larger ones, elect to contract out to third-party providers for this work.

As noted earlier, data from the Furman Center indicate that while larger BIDs have a significant effect on commercial property values, smaller BIDs in New York City lack sufficient resources to make much of an impact.[22] The Furman report questions the efficacy of the creation of small organizations, much of whose budgets are necessarily spent on administration, and in recent years, it has been smaller BIDs that have been started in New York. The challenge of limited resources, which can reduce the effectiveness of smaller BIDs, was certainly my experience in Downtown Jamaica, Queens, which has three BIDs, two of which are quite small. None of the three can afford to maintain a security program, and even the largest of them finds itself with very limited resources, given the magnitude of the challenges with which it has been tasked.

As mentioned previously, it has been my experience that services provided by in-house employees are always higher quality than going to a third party. I found this to be true at Greater Jamaica Development Corporation when we stopped contracting out for security services for our parking facilities and trained and hired our own security staff. By doing so, we were able to improve the quality of staff as well as their compensation. The business model of the outside security service was to charge the customer a premium over the amount paid directly to their employees. That premium covered supervision and profit for the security company. We were able to hire members of the community who were far more committed to our mission than security agency employees and at higher wages than the contractor paid. And we gained a midlevel staff member who was a retired New York City police officer who added a great deal of value beyond his responsibility of supervising his team. Quite frankly, I don't understand the benefit of contracting out security and sanitation services for all but the smallest organizations. A tremendous amount of the benefit of the BID is lost when doing so.

Beyond Clean and Safe

There is, to my mind, one improvement to their service delivery that many BIDs might make. In the twenty-plus years since GCP rolled out the first clean and safe programs, this template has been used in scores of cities

across the country. I think that the time has come to reevaluate these programs and determine whether they remain the best use of the bulk of BID
resources in downtowns that have experienced revitalization. Security programs in particular, which generally absorb a third of larger BID budgets,
may no longer be optimal, given that through broken-windows policing,
order has been perceived to be restored to downtowns everywhere. Why,
with the huge improvement in the perception of public safety in downtowns across the country, do many of the larger BIDs continue to provide
security services at all, and why aren't BIDs challenged to do more?

There is still a need for a safety patrol in many places. In Downtown
Jamaica, the biggest obstacle to private investment and attracting high-
quality commercial tenants continues to be the perception of a lack of
public safety. Jamaica needs more resources to provide private security
services. But with so much having been accomplished in Midtown and
Downtown Manhattan as well as other places, why are those districts still
spending as much as a third of their budgets on security services? Many
successful BIDs may need to rethink their missions and how they expend
their resources. They may want to explore acquiring and repositioning,
leveraging their assessments for the financing of capital improvements, or
more actively supporting the work of artists in their districts.

CHEAP SPACE FOR ARTISTS

My first thought as to where those funds might be better applied is to a
higher level of programming, particularly in supporting artists and artistic endeavors.[23] The cost of space has become the single most significant
impediment to the health of the arts in a number of cities. One of our
most successful projects in Jamaica was a partnership with chashama
(chashama.org), an organization that supports visual artists, creating gallery and studio space in an empty former dentist's office. By providing
free space to artists, who in turn expended "sweat equity" in improving the
space, we animated a dark block, particularly at night. The impact of this

project was far beyond what we had imagined when we first engaged in the partnership: ultimately, an architectural firm bought the building and moved its offices there, which was a major step forward for the downtown. This success was recently repeated in Jamaica with a group called No Longer Empty (nolongerempty.org), which not only provided free space to local artists but also created a brilliant series of programs targeted toward engaging the community in their work. This long-empty space too leased up days after the residency began.

GJDC provided free and low-cost spaces to performing arts groups in downtown underused venues. This activated those spaces and drew the attention of the artistic community to the low-cost space in Jamaica. Frankly, I wish we had expended more resources on this kind of programming because of the substantial benefits it provided to the perception of the downtown, going well beyond enhancing the perception of security. It advertised that the downtown was a vital, lively, and creative place. This is placemaking at its highest level. We also provided essential financial operating support for the local arts center, which had been founded by GJDC decades before and struggled to secure adequate resources to program its spaces in a disinvested community.

Big Car in Indianapolis (bigcar.org) is doing similar work in a smaller city, supporting artists in order to build community and engage in placemaking. They have done a range of creative and impactful projects. There has been a great deal of talk, particularly in the philanthropic community, about creative placemaking, and these folks are demonstrating its efficacy.

Capital Improvements

Support for art and artists is just one example of an area where BIDs might extend their reach. The New York BIDs have the capacity to incur debt secured by the BID assessment. While GCP and 34th Street Partnership used this tool to pay for district capital improvements, city government was resistant to the idea, and as a result, it has proved difficult for others to emulate. Philadelphia's Center City District has also had great success in using its bonding capacity to enhance its effectiveness. I believe this ability has been underexploited and could be used for a range of downtown revitalization projects, from improving parks to adaptively reusing architecturally significant structures. City government and affected property owners need to be persuaded of the tremendous benefits BIDs might provide by taking advantage of their ability to borrow for capital projects. Some places have used tax increment financing in a similar way. In New York, a comparable structure was used to finance the public space improvements required to support the Hudson Yards project.

BIDs do marketing, work on retail and facade improvements and better retail presentation, pay for social services for those without shelter, and engage in research and advocacy for and about their districts. Chaotic retail signs are one of the biggest impediments to downtown improvement, but they have also proved to be one of the most difficult problems to address. More thought needs to go into creating programs that deal with this problem effectively. BIDs might also support coworking spaces, business incubators, and improved street food vending (through capitalizing carts and providing commissary, storage, and sanitary facilities).

BIDs have been a powerful tool for civic renewal, but my sense is that there is much more that they might be doing to improve the quality of life downtown and to foster economic activity. In my experience, they have been most effective around the country when city governments have partnered with them, encourage them to take carefully calculated risks, and provided them with the resources required to catalyze improved quality of life and increased economic activity.

CHAPTER 5

OPERATING PUBLIC
SPACES

Providing the highest possible level of maintenance in a public space is the sine qua non of placemaking. It is job one. There is no substitute for it. It is the foundation for communicating to users that a space is under social control. Doing it right takes constant, sustained attention to detail. When we finally got the management of the Bryant Park lawn right,[1] our excellent landscaping contractor, Butch Starkie, told me that it was now time for BPRC to fly solo and take over maintaining the lawn ourselves. He sold us two precision eighteen-inch lawn mowers (the kind that are used on putting greens), set them to a two-inch height, and discussed with me a watering and mowing regime that would produce a high-quality result. He advised that keeping the lawn in shape would require constant monitoring and that the narrow hand mowers would produce a better result than a riding mower or a wider, self-propelled machine.

I then set up a meeting with our maintenance crew and, at the request of our supervisors, shared Butch's recommendations. One of the supervisors spoke up and told me that the maintenance staff wouldn't have sufficient time to mow the lawn and deal with regulating the watering because they were way too busy picking up trash, emptying trash cans, and attending to their other day-to-day tasks. They were really a great bunch of hardworking, nice people. We had a warm and collegial relationship—and they took ownership of the park with zeal. I didn't want to spoil that relationship by going all authoritarian with them or asking the supervisory team to do that.

So about a week later, on a very warm June day, I wore jeans and a T-shirt to work. I got one of the brand-new mowers out, gassed it up, and started it (thank goodness it had an electric ignition and I didn't have to embarrass myself in front of the staff hopelessly pulling on a cord). I began to mow the two-acre lawn. It was about three hundred feet long—and I went about pushing this little mower back and forth across the grass. It was hot. The wheels weren't motorized, so the thing had to be pushed. I was sweating profusely. After about my tenth pass and a half an hour went by, the supervisor, David Rojas, ran up to me and asked me what I was doing. I said, "David, what does it look like I'm doing?" He said, "It looks like you're mowing the lawn." I said, "You're right. That's exactly what I am doing." He replied, "But that's our job!" I said, "You're right about that too!" He said, "OK, OK, you can stop mowing. We'll do it." I told him that I wanted to have the satisfaction of finishing that job, but after that, I didn't want to do it again. He smiled and walked away. Most of the staff watched for a while and then went back to work. It took me a couple of hours, but I got it done. I had made my point. I did what I needed to do to establish the importance of the fastidious care of the lawn.

The lawn became the park's calling card. Keeping it in top shape was essential to maintaining the perception of the park as a place not only that is safe and orderly but that people were drawn to. Early on I learned that when people said to me that Bryant Park looked great, what they actually meant was "Wow, the lawn is really green." I even got a letter once from the managing editor of the *New York Times* complimenting us on how good the lawn looked and asking if I would come out to Long Island to give him a hand with his yard. Nothing communicates that a public space is well managed and safe better than a verdant, well-kept greensward. It may be high maintenance and not ecologically correct, but it is an essential component of most parks and large public spaces. People want to look at, sit on, play on, and *lie* on a beautiful carpet of grass. And getting a lawn to be beautiful like that isn't easy. At the same time, keeping people *off* the grass sends exactly the wrong message—you want it to be open to use as often as possible. This signals that people are invited and are welcome to use the space.

I paid careful daily attention to the condition of the lawn because that's one of the things that can substantially contribute to making a great public space. A good-looking lawn is about three things—seed, sun, and water. Getting them in balance is what makes for successful turf. Having people on the lawn makes it more complicated to manage. Their feet compact the soil, making it difficult for water to get to the roots. Too much sun and not enough water make for burned-out grass. And folks don't like to sit on wet grass, so you can't solve those problems by overwatering. Every morning, three seasons a year, on my way into Bryant Park in the morning, I would put my hand down and feel the grass. I would determine by feel how wet the turf was and make a determination whether and for how long the grass should be watered that night or whether people should be kept off it that day.

I would also make the decision about when it needed to be mowed. Like the wetness of the turf, its length is a judgment call. Some people like putting green-length grass. That looks manicured and carefully managed. Many folks like to sit on a long cushy bed of grass. Shorter grass burns out more easily during long periods of sun. Longer grass protects the roots from sun and holds moisture. But if the grass gets too long, it looks like no one is paying attention.

Compaction is the enemy of a great greensward. The more people who walk on the lawn, the more compact it gets. That makes it harder to get water to the roots and more difficult for the roots to grow. The longer the roots are, the more water the grass will be able to absorb, and the more abuse it will be able to take. Core aeration can be an important tool in producing a top-notch lawn. Core aeration is a relatively simple process that involves a tractor (even a very small one) and a device pulled behind it with a roller. The roller extracts plugs from the soil and dumps them on the surface. This serves to break up the soil and makes it easier for roots to grow and water to circulate. It's a good thing to do after a big event and at least a couple of times a season. After aeration is complete, it is a good opportunity to lay down seed, as the aerated soil and watered seed creates a particularly receptive environment for successful seed germination. You need to keep people off the lawn for a couple of weeks after seeding to allow the new grass to get established.

And speaking of which, let me put in a good word for seed—as opposed to sod—lawns. Seeded lawns are more resilient because they establish deeper roots. Sod lawns *can* become established over time (sod is a mat of soil with grass with roots already established in it, which, unlike seed, can provide an "instant" lawn). But regular resodding prevents the kind of root establishment that enables a lawn to take a beating. In Bryant Park, when the fashion shows moved from being exclusively on paved areas to also occupying the grass, resodding after events became essential. There is now annual resodding after the removal of the ice rink in the early spring. The sod lawn has never looked quite as great as the seed lawn (once we got it right) of the mid-1990s. It is important to note that Bryant Park management takes great pride in (and keeps track of) how many days a year the lawn is open to the public for use.

Allowing the lawn to recover for a day or two after heavy use is also a good idea and helps keep the turf stay in the best possible condition for as long as possible into the summer. It is good to keep people off the turf when it is very wet, because that is when it is most vulnerable to both compaction and wear. Again, this is part of the balancing act that is essential to maintaining a great-looking patch of green and letting people use it as much as is feasible.

A great example of the challenges that turf creates is the rooftop lawn at Lincoln Center. It was a wonderful idea to create a green panel at this otherwise heavily hardscaped public space. The lawn panel was designed at a steep slope, which forces water toward the bottom (making the top of the lawn drier and the bottom wetter). The bottom of the lawn is narrower and effectively the "entrance" to the space—creating a situation of very heavy use and wear at the bottom of the panel—which is nearly impossible to keep green as a result. There are no ideal solutions to how to manage this turf. Given the way the lawn and roof were designed, there is no way to keep the lawn at the bottom green. But the public does love to look at it and sit on it—and it makes the public spaces at Lincoln Center warmer, more welcoming, and better.

No doubt this is more than any reader really wants to know about lawn maintenance. But in most places, great lawns mark great spaces.

Lighting

Lighting is also important to changing perceptions. The Bryant Park lighting scheme was carefully planned, including moonlighting from rooftops, beautiful historic replica fixtures at entrances, and relatively closely set lamps on historic poles within the park. All of the luminaires shed white light—which we found was much more helpful to creating a perception of safety than the standard orangeish sodium vapor lights that were then widely used. Today, LED lighting is much more efficient and less expensive, and the quality of its light can be precisely controlled. It is essential that lighting be well maintained and that lamps never appear to be out—again, contributing to the sense that the place is well maintained.

Outside of the park, we lit the facade of Grand Central Terminal and on the sidewalks replaced standard-issue sodium vapor streetlights with white, metal halide luminaires. We also tried to light the sidewalks where it was possible to do so—an important pedestrian-friendly amenity. The lamps are monitored daily, and burned-out lamps are quickly replaced. With today's long-lasting LED technology, this has become even easier to maintain.

The Flagship Restroom

One of the most important high-visibility improvements to the restored Bryant Park was the reopened restroom—which may be the most famous toilet in New York. The 1936 design of the park included two rather ornate restroom buildings—a men's and a women's—designed by the architects of the library, Carrère & Hastings. Over the decades, these structures had essentially been abandoned and allowed to deteriorate. Dan Biederman was insistent that for the park to be perceived as being civilized, it had to have high-quality toilet facilities. In his view, if public bathrooms needed to be attended whenever the park was open in order for them to work in a dense urban environment, we had to do it. To him, this was therefore an essential operating expense. He was correct. I have concluded that for restroom facilities in public spaces to be maintained as safe and attractive, they *always* need to be attended. The attendants have to be well trained and highly motivated to keep the place clean and well ordered. There doesn't appear to be a way around this. Without dedicated staff, toilet facilities inevitably get messy. I'm not sure why this has to be the case, but it is.

When the restored restrooms were opened to the public in 1992, they had one male and one female staff member assigned to monitor and clean them. From the beginning, the facility had fresh flowers and later classical music. The positive publicity from the restrooms alone might have changed the perception of the park. It was regarded as nothing short of miraculous. The bathrooms have been renovated at least twice since 1992, with each renovation incorporating yet more improvements. They have become flagship elements of the park and demonstrate the importance to any public space improvement of securing the resources to properly maintain restroom facilities.

SUFFICIENT OPERATING SUPPORT

Having reliable revenue to support maintenance and programming activity is essential. A public space revitalization project must have adequate operating resources from day one in order for it to be successful. This is nonnegotiable. It cannot be done by halves. Hoping that a project will attract enough operating resources over time is a delusion. It doesn't happen. A restored space must be fully funded and well programmed and maintained from its first day. What does happen over time is that successful projects become self-sustaining with revenue derived from activities, sponsorship, and even philanthropy. But in the initial period, the promoters of a new or restored public space must secure ample operating funds with BID, public, or private (often philanthropic) dollars.

Having multiple income sources is one way to ensure long-term reliability. BID assessments are basic, reliable income sources. But in Bryant Park, sponsorships, outdoor advertising, private philanthropy, concessions (including the restaurant), and events all contribute to its operations. None of these existed—other than the BID and some foundation dollars—when I started there in 1991.

RISK TAKING AND PUBLIC SPACE MANAGEMENT

Additional revenue sources were developed in Bryant Park by being open, opportunistic, creative about income generation, and perhaps most importantly, tolerant of a certain level of risk. Calculated risk taking is at the center of good placemaking practice. Making places better involves iterating: trying new things, monitoring how they go, and fine-tuning them—or eliminating them—based on how they are received by real people in real time. This is part of why the private nonprofit management vehicle is so important. The government is highly constrained in its ability to take risks. Failure, even minor failure, can prove to be professionally fatal in the public sector. Private entities and their boards can and should be more tolerant of risk.

This kind of risk taking isn't about wildly taking flyers. It is about carefully weighing the risks involved in a proposal with its potential benefits. It is being willing to create the possibility of failure but limiting those failures to a small scale. When GCP put trash baskets out with its logo on them, we were advised that putting our name on street amenities would draw personal injury lawsuits. The high-design baskets were a great success and the legal liability turned out to be nonexistent. Most of our important initiatives drew concern, particularly from the public sector, about the potential risks involved. Often those risks arise from someone's "common sense" or are something "everyone knows." But those assumptions need to be tested against data from experience. What "everyone knows" about how people behave in public space, it turns out, actually isn't generally the case. That's what Holly Whyte learned through his time-lapse photography.

It is also possible to manage liability risk by buying insurance for it. Every responsible organization carries some level of liability insurance. With each new project, insurers can be asked to price out the cost of additional insurance to cover it. Most risks can be covered, and those in public spaces can be surprisingly inexpensive to buy additional coverage for (and, in fact, are often already covered by insurance; you need to check with your broker about what your policy covers). For example, in order to encourage activity in Bryant Park, when smaller organizations brought to us proposals for creative programs, rather than demand that they provide *us* with insurance, we provided *them* with insurance in order to assist them in their presentations and to generate activity in the park, which we were in the business of promoting.

Having an excellent insurance broker can be a tremendous asset to a public space manager in evaluating risks and purchasing insurance for them. I also tried to establish relationships with the underwriters at the insurance companies themselves in order to give them a high level of confidence in our team's attention to mitigating and minimizing risk. These relationships paid big dividends in *decreased* premiums.

One caveat in creating new nonprofit public space management entities is to avoid taking on municipal risk in establishing a contractual relationship with local government to manage a municipally owned public space. In Bryant Park, under the terms of our agreement with DPR, we took over all the risks associated with the physical plant and became a regular target of slip-and-fall claims arising out of the way in which the paths were paved (in 1936). This became a serious headache.

Careful attention to the operations of a public space is essential—and one of the most important recurring themes of this book is that it is even more important than the quality of its design in making the space successful. Constant attentiveness to detail is key. Fixing what's broken or not working immediately upon discovery is what most powerfully transmits to visitors that a public place is safe and inviting.

POISONING PIGEONS IN THE PARK

As a result of our fastidiousness in park operations, in 1994, I had my fifteen minutes of fame. BPRC's press representative at that time was an experienced theatrical (meaning most of his work was promoting plays and musicals) flack named Bruce Cohen. One day in the spring of 1994, Bruce got a phone call from a reporter at the *New York Daily News* who was working on a story, based on a tip from an animal lover, that BPRC was poisoning the Bryant Park pigeons, which we sort of were. Gigantic flocks of pigeons had become a serious problem with people and food returning to the park after years of being underused. The pigeons seemed to be particularly happy to hang out on the Fifth Avenue terrace of NYPL. Yes, pigeon poop was always a problem, but the operational problem was that they liked to make a meal of impatiens, and in a matter of hours, they destroyed the flower beds we planted in front of the library. Given our problem-solving orientation at BPRC and our concern about managing the most minute details of the park experience, the destruction of the impatiens (and the poop) made the pigeon issue rise very high on my to-do list. I called around to exterminators, and the company we used (which I think I found in a *Real Estate Weekly* ad) put out some stuff called orni-trol, which they told us was totally humane and prevented the pigeons from reproducing. We found that it took a long time to work and that its impact was fleeting from year to year. New avian visitors seemed to turn up each spring with fertile partners and no notion of self-control or contraception.

The "bird-control engineers" suggested a plan B; putting a substance called abitrol in some appealing pigeon cuisine. That stuff *really* worked. Abitrol was actually a behavioral approach to pigeon control. When one or two pigeons had eaten the bait, they developed terrible shakes and after a good while died a highly visible death. The other pigeons in the flock immediately got the idea that the local food source was tainted and went elsewhere for their lunch. The good part was that it only physically affected a couple of birds. The bad part was that the death of those birds was vis-ibly dreadful. Unfortunately, on the day the bait was put out, this horrible death scene was observed by a pigeon lover, who picked up the phone and called the *Daily News*.

Bruce sprang into action. He drafted a press release, quoting Dan Bie-derman as the president of a fictitious organization that had popped into Bruce's mind called Planned Pigeonhood. The release was clever and full of exaggerated statements and puns discussing the park's fictive pigeon birth control program. Dan said there was no way he was going to be used in this ridiculous way and so scratched out his name and put in mine. The release went out to the local media, and the *New York Times* called to schedule an interview on the front steps of the library. Veteran reporter Ellie Blau was assigned to the story along with a photographer, and the *New York Times* went for the bait.[2] The story ran on the front page of what was then called the Metro Section, with a photo of me and some of my feathered buddies in a prominent position above the fold. Bruce's gambit worked. The *Daily News* story never ran. Bruce had made lemonade out of media lemons. But that was only the beginning.

After the *New York Times* story ran, Bruce was deluged with media inquiries. I learned from that experience to never underestimate the power of the *New York Times* with other news outlets. I spent the next several weeks conducting interviews with print, radio, and TV reporters. It must have taken up half of my time for a month. I was on television in Australia and Japan and on the radio in Germany. The stunt generated dozens of features. Eventually the clamor died down. An interesting fact is that despite the huge flurry of attention, after more than twenty years, no one but me remembers the story! The report does illustrate the press coverage we began to generate about the successful redevelopment of the park.

The story does have a happyish ending. We eventually found a superior solution to the flower-eating bird problem—we placed nets over the flowers, which prevented the birds from eating them. It worked perfectly, and BPC still uses that netting. You can see the nets over the beds on Fifth Avenue in front of the library every spring.

Making a Great Visitor Experience

How the people who take care of a public space interact with the public is just as important as the manner in which they perform their duties. Providing a great experience to visitors to public spaces is something we know that Disney *gets* for its parks. It's also essential to the hotel business. Even museums and other cultural institutions are focused today on being responsive to visitor needs—to providing great customer service. They do this because the visitor experience is essential to generating repeat visits and building brand loyalty. At nonprofit institutions, treating visitors well is also part of their development strategy—happy visitors are more likely to become future donors.

In the world of public space management, we don't talk much about the visitor experience—but we should. Most public spaces are operated by government agencies, and the incentive systems of government bureau-cracies are oriented toward different goals—keeping costs down, prevent-ing graft and corruption, minimizing risk, and avoiding political problems (analogous in some ways to good consumer relations, but not exactly the same thing). Those goals can often be in conflict with providing park visi-tors with a positive time. Perhaps those of us in downtown revitalization and public space management ought to think a little more about how the individual visitor is treated in our spaces.

I would argue that creating great user experiences is at the very center of managing public space. It should be our goal, even in public parks, to provide a great visit and get the visitor to feel good about having been there and to want to come back. And in those instances when we are restoring degraded parks or revitalizing disinvested downtowns, we are in the busi-ness of changing individuals' perceptions about that public space, so it is important to that mission to make their visits as pleasant and convenient as possible. A negative experience with a government, BID, or other non-profit employee creates a powerful, difficult-to-reverse perception about the attractiveness of the space; the opposite is true as well—a great interac-tion with staff can leave a strong, lasting positive impression about a space. There is also a moral component to treating visitors with respect. It's just the right thing to do.

Fundamentally, these spaces are *public*. That is, in our democratic soci-ety, they exist to serve every citizen. Every visitor to a park or downtown is entitled to equal treatment, and in my view, their treatment in that place ought to be excellent. One of the best things about well-managed public spaces is that every visitor feels equally welcome and well treated, whether that person is a wealthy philanthropist, a tourist in town for the day, a local resident or office worker, or a homeless person seeking respite from more unpleasant or dangerous places. To me, that is part of what makes a public space successful.

Public managerial systems, in my experience, are generally set up for the convenience and efficiency of the folks who work for the relevant

agency. They often ignore the user experience with the standard procedures. Similar issues seem to arise when a visitor informs public space
managers about a problem. Staff members' first reaction to such information is often to communicate to the visitor that the situation is not the
employee's fault, that the staff member already knew about the problem,
that the issue is "already being addressed," or that it is the responsibility of
some other agency. These kinds of responses simply don't add any value
and are off-putting to the member of the public who is generally trying to
be helpful.

These are situations that I've noticed a lot of public spaces suffer
from. Very few additional resources are required to redesign processes
in public spaces in order to put the experience of the visitor first and for
public space employees to put the visitors' interests ahead of their own.
For example, staff should be encouraged to take the time to answer a visitor's questions rather than replying, "I'm busy here." Similarly, when there
is a visitor complaint, a much better response than "I already knew about
that" is to thank the member of the public for supplying the information and for caring about the park; to tell that person that the problem
will be taken care of; and most importantly, to *give the visitor a date by
which the problem is expected to be remedied* (this is especially easy if the
issue is already in the process of being resolved!). Such a response makes
the member of the public feel appreciated—and part of the team working to make the space better. It also provides the person with a responsive
answer—giving him or her information that enables him or her to follow
up and see that the issue was resolved.

I have noticed that when I think about public space users, I generally
consider them as a group, and I think about providing programs and services to groups, not to individuals. A great horticultural program affects
all users. Detail-oriented maintenance has a group impact. Events in public spaces are for large groups. But we really ought to be putting more
thought and effort into the experiences of individuals. The best BIDs
have always provided some kind of customer service training to their

"ambassadors," even when those employees are presented as more conventional security guards. But all employees ought to be trained to think about their work from the perspective of the visitor, shopper, and office worker. This is harder to do in government—given the constant sense of limited resources, collective bargaining agreements, and other systemic legal restraints—but still it is no less important in the government context.

Placemaking is about enabling visitors to derive the maximum amount of pleasure out of their experiences in downtowns and public spaces. That pleasure comes not just from engaging in activities they enjoy—be they sports, reading, sitting in the sun, or people watching. It also comes from the feeling of being respected and well treated. We ought to think more about how interactions among space users, staff, and administrative systems play into that; providing high-quality customer service training to *all* employees; and designing administrative systems that put the visitor, rather than the staff, first. That encourages people both to think well about the spaces we manage and to make a return visit.

Restaurants: They Are Harder Than They Look

Food service can be a great amenity for park visitors as well as a consistent revenue generator. Over the last three decades, we've come a long way in our view of the impact of restaurants in public spaces. When I began working in Bryant Park in 1991, most park and community advocates viewed restaurants in parks as anathema. They were seen as commercial activity and therefore as forbidden from public spaces. There is certainly a view of urban public spaces as a natural sanctuary from everyday activity—particularly activities that require money. Nature should be a realm that doesn't involve cash or acknowledge economic or social status. Public spaces should be the great democratic leveler where all visitors are equal and where an absence of financial resources shouldn't get in the way of enjoying all of what a park has to offer.

But as the result of what we've seen in successfully revitalized public spaces in the last two decades, we've learned that some kinds of commercial activity can actually be invaluable in animating public spaces—including restaurants, food kiosks, food trucks, craft markets, and most recently, night markets. In fact, in many public space (and downtown) revitalization projects, food service has come to be seen as something of a silver bullet. This is another area of policy making in public spaces that demands a carefully balancing of interests and preferences. While commercial activity can be a great animator of parks and plazas, their operation should be carefully designed and monitored so as not to have a materially exclusionary result. If you can't or don't want to buy a drink, that should not prevent you from being able to enjoy what a public space has to offer.

Unfortunately, selling food in a public space isn't a panacea for the problems of an underutilized place. Restaurants are difficult and expensive to develop. Most restaurants are unsuccessful. In my experience, even the most successful restaurants in formerly underinvested, underused places take years to be cash-flow positive. Food kiosks are even more difficult to make work.

The original financial model for the Bryant Park restoration was that rent from a restaurant would pay for the operation and programming of the park, going back to Holly Whyte's 1979 report. It took more than fifteen years from the time that the idea for a restaurant in Bryant Park was first broached to the day that the Bryant Park Grill and Café opened its doors. Not only was a lengthy process required for approval of the design of the restaurant structure, but financing its construction seemed to be an unsolvable problem.

In the original plan, the restaurant developer was to finance the construction and fit out of the structure. Years were spent trying to gain the state legislative approval required to allow for the imposition of a mortgage on park property that would serve as security for a leasehold mortgage loan to the private operator that would pay for the project. Part of the problem was a lack of confidence in the viability of a restaurant that was in the middle of the park and did not have sidewalk frontage. In the 1980s, the *New York Times* regularly ran a story about how the Bryant Park restaurant was going to open the following spring. But the project simply would not come together.

The plan was to build two mirror-image structures on either side of the Bryant Monument to be designed by architect Hugh Hardy. The idea was to finance the construction of the restaurant using a mortgage against the lease with the operator (in the event of a default by the operator in making loan payments, the rent would go directly to the lender rather than to BPRC). The problem with the mortgage idea was that the property was city-owned parkland, which under the New York State Constitution could not be mortgaged or sold without the approval of the New York State legislature. Getting a bill passed through the legislature and signed by the governor is a very difficult task under the best of circumstances, but given the opposition of many local elected officials to the "privatization of public space," getting approval for a mortgage to build a restaurant in Bryant Park was a herculean task. BPRC employed some of the city's top lobbyists to attempt to persuade the leadership of the state legislature to consider such legislation and after years of trying was ultimately successful in gaining approval. But even with the ability to place a mortgage on the property, financing from banks or private lenders proved impossible to obtain for an untested venture.

When I arrived at BPRC, a determination had been made to try to finance only one of the pavilions—the one on the south side of the monument—in order to lower the amount of money required. Negotiations with Ark Restaurants Corp. were well advanced, but no progress was being made on how to pay for the construction of the building. NYPL had reluctantly pledged to loan $1 million into the project but had also been reticent about entering into an agreement with BPRC about the intersection of the library's interests with those of BPRC and Ark—issues having to do with access to the stack extension, operating hours, exhaust ventilation, fire suppression, and storage space for refrigeration on library property.

At the end of 1992, Dan Biederman got so frustrated with the progress on the lease and financing, he handed off the project to me to try to figure out. One of the initial projects to which I was assigned the year before was finding a way for the BIDs to use the amounts assigned in their budgets for capital projects to generate borrowed capital dollars (which I describe more completely in chapter 4). Once GCP had issued $32 million in tax-exempt debt, secured by the BID assessment, in 1992, I had the idea that the same financing vehicle could be used to secure the $5 million needed to construct the restaurant and do the associated landscaping. We could use the Bryant Park BID's annual assessment as security for the loan; that is, if BPRC defaulted on the loan, the assessment would be paid directly to the lenders to cover the debt service. On an operating basis, the hope was that the rent from the restaurant would cover the debt service.

I then went to work with our bond counsel to persuade Manufacturers Hanover Trust and the library that the loan would be a secure one. During that time, Manny Hanny merged into Chemical Bank, and new representatives from the bank had to be persuaded of the safety of the loan. Ultimately, Marshall Rose made a call to John McGillicuddy, the merged bank's chairman, and then Chemical (now J. P. Morgan Chase) signed on. Both the bank and NYPL were nervous about the loan. Ark, which was putting $1 million into the construction of the kitchen and the decorating of the restaurant, was equally nervous. This made closing the lease and the loan particularly challenging. It is interesting to note that the idea of the mortgage on parkland, permission for which was so difficult to obtain from the state legislature, became unimportant when the lenders became convinced of the viability of the BID assessment as security for the loans.

BPRC borrowed $5 million from what is now J. P. Morgan Chase and the New York Public Library at a taxable, market interest rate for a ten-year term. These funds were used to build the core and shell of the Bryant Park Grill and Café and its associated landscaping. The restaurant developer, in exchange for a long-term lease with a relatively low base rent over a percentage of the gross receipts of the restaurant, fitted out the kitchen and dining room and operated the facility.

The lease negotiation was long and contentious. The city was concerned about public access to certain tables around the building (which were never put in place), and the developer was insistent on an exclusive right to provide food service in the park, to which the city was—quite rightfully, as it turned out—highly resistant. The first issue was worked out by a detailed compromise (which was never implemented) and the second by an eleventh-hour concession by the city and BPRC. The exclusive catering deal turned out to be an ongoing nightmare for us at BPRC when various event sponsors—particularly the fashion shows—wanted to use park facilities and their own caterers.

The most important fact about all of this is that for about the first five years, the rent from the restaurateur to BPRC did not cover the interest and principal payments on its $5 million loan, so rather than supporting the operation of the park, the BID assessment was used to supplement the rent received from the restaurant to cover the debt service. As with all of the similar projects that I have worked on, the Bryant Park Grill and Café took a while to catch on. The popularity of the restaurant was established after four or five years, and the amount of rent paid to BPRC increased to much more than the amount of the debt service. Eventually, in fact, the loan was entirely paid off, so today all of the rent from the Bryant Park Grill and Café goes to park operations.

The planned second restaurant pavilion was never built. Sometime during construction of the restaurant, Michael Weinstein, the president of Ark, brought up the idea of building a deck on the site of the second planned building. Hugh Hardy's office was asked to design a deck that covered exactly the footprint of the planned restaurant, and approvals for the deck were secured from the Parks Department and other city agencies. The deck served food and drink (mostly drink), was called the Bryant Park Café, and was a huge success from the beginning. Fun fact—it was in front of the café that Mayor Giuliani held the press conference announcing to the

Figure 10. The Bryant Park Grill and Café, designed by Hugh Hardy, took almost fifteen years to develop and several years after that to provide significant income for park operations.

world (as well as to his second wife) that he was seeking a divorce. The restaurant operation expanded to include the roof of the Bryant Park Grill and Café and a courtyard to the south of it. In 2017, the Bryant Park Grill and Café did $25 million in business, making it the ninth highest-grossing independent restaurant in the United States.[3]

The lesson for others here is that these projects take a long time—and many fail. We had a similar experience with the Pershing Square Café, where Grand Central Partnership financed the adaptive reuse of an abandoned former trolley barn into restaurant space. GCP paid for the demolition of the space, the creation of a white box for the restaurant, and the installation of an HVAC system for a total of about $2 million. The Pershing Square Café took at least five years to begin to be cash-flow positive. Now like the Bryant Park Grill and Café, it is a huge success, both programmatically and financially. It has revived a formerly dark and deserted strip of street in a key location.

This is why I am wary about rosy projections concerning public space restaurant projects. Approvals take a long time. Financing is difficult. Restaurants are slow to become successful, and success is not certain. I also advise project sponsors that the more financial risk they impose on the developer, the smaller the number of developers who will have the capacity to bid on the project, the less likely the project is to be successful, and the longer it will be before the developer will be able to pay rent to support public space programming and maintenance. The more capital that the nonprofit or government sponsor can put into the project, the more likely it will be to be a winner and the more money it will be able to throw off sooner to support programming and maintenance. I know that sponsors often feel they don't have the capacity to put capital into such developments—and most hope that the private restaurateur will cover all the capital costs. This impulse should be minimized or avoided if at all possible in order to increase the likelihood of success and the ultimate profitability of the restaurant. Nonprofits or governmental entities, if they get creative, can often, as we did, find capital sources.

My experience is that food kiosks are nearly impossible to make economically successful. There have been many food kiosk tenants in Bryant Park, and they have been hard to find and generally haven't lasted very long. Producing food in a constrained space seems to be a challenge. Pricing the offerings properly and then getting the food over the counter quickly both seem to be difficult. Why are food trucks proliferating but stationary kiosks are not? Frankly, I don't know. But kiosks are even riskier as revenue generators than are full-service restaurants.

BALANCING THE LEVEL OF COMMERCIAL ACTIVITY

Because of its potential for animating otherwise dormant public spaces, commercial activity can be a great tool. It also provides for amenities that can make a park visit more enjoyable and revenue to support maintenance and programming. But at the same time, amount and context are

important. A hot dog stand and an advertising billboard next to the Colo-
rado River in the Grand Canyon are obviously terrible ideas. Preserving
the natural or aesthetic integrity of a special place is essential. Overcom-
mercialization can also be a serious problem. An excess of private activity
can turn a public place into an exclusive reserve for those who can afford
it—which is the antithesis of what a park should be. There also is such
a thing as too much activity—making reading, quiet contemplation, or
even a serious chess game impossible. I would also argue that permitting
commercial activity in a park for the sole purpose of generating revenue
without regard to its impact on the program you are trying to achieve is
not good policy. In order to develop a successful public space, the program
needs to come first. At one point we were persuaded to host an event in the
park that involved motorcycles, young women in bikinis, and a good deal
of cash for the park. After the event took place, we realized that it had been
a terrible idea. The event wasn't at all in line with the kind of atmosphere
we were trying to create, and the money wasn't worth it.

Commercial activity is one of the many things that must be balanced
by thoughtful public space managers. Parks can certainly be overly com-
mercialized. However, that is not an argument for *no* commercial activity in public space. The years of wrangling between the City of New York
and Bryant Park Restoration Corporation about the public's access to the
proposed restaurant, the menu prices, and the use and locations of certain specific tables were, in retrospect, unproductive and did not speak
to the actual operating reality of the facility. The restaurant's success in
drawing people to a formerly dangerous public space and the substantial revenue that the facility generates demonstrate the efficacy of a well-
designed, well-managed, appropriate commercial venture in a park. One
of the best ways to get people into an abandoned space certainly is food
and drink, and they are essential tools in a public space manager's arsenal
for activation. A well-planned, well-financed, well-run restaurant can be
both a public space activator and a major income generator for patient
placemakers.

SUCCESS IS SELF-PERPETUATING

Great public spaces become self-perpetuating. We were surprised to find after we reopened Bryant Park that our staff rarely had to pick up paper bags after the lunch crowd had left. I went out one afternoon and sat and watched for a while, and people were policing *each other.* People's lunch bags weren't being left on the ground because other people were asking them to pick them up after they had dropped them or *people were picking up other people's bags!* Visitors quickly took ownership of the space after its four-year closure. The high standards that we set in the maintaining and programming of the park were translating into people having high standards for their own (and for others') conduct. It was, indeed, a remarkable turnaround from when the park was a haven for drug sales and other illicit behavior.

The same became true about revenue generation. The number of people coming to the park over a period of two or three years kept getting larger, particularly with respect to events. Gross revenue at the restaurant increased year after year—increasing the net rent to BPRC. We developed advertising revenue from the newsstands. People with sponsorship deals came to us, and the volume of this increased over time. Ironically, once the park was successful, we even received unsolicited charitable gifts. We went from scrounging together the money to present daily programming to curating proposals for events others wanted to produce. All of this success was built on the foundation of the adequately funded and well-managed maintenance of the park. This kind of management requires not only money and staff but also constant attention to detail in order to communicate to visitors that the park is a safe and pleasant place to spend some time or simply to walk through. Equally important to creating a great public space is the amount and kind of programmed activity in the park, plaza, or downtown. That is the subject of the next chapter.

CHAPTER 6

PROGRAMMING PUBLIC SPACES

The crowning glory of Bryant Park is its programming. From summer concerts to winter ice-skating, the park is always packed with activity. This is by design. A driving principle is that "good uses drive out bad."[1] Heavily programming public spaces is the way to draw people in and push antisocial activity, like drug dealing, out. The beauty is that with programming, we found that the flywheel effect takes over. Successful programming attracts other programs and sponsors—and as a result, programming becomes self-sustaining. You go from being a beggar (for money and in-kind services) to being a curator. When I use the term *programming* here, I am defining it quite broadly to include anything that activates a public space, including horticultural programs and commercial ventures. I break managing public spaces into two categories—maintenance and programming. Programming is everything that management does in the place that isn't maintenance!

Like Yogi Berra, Whyte is often remembered for his tautological aphorisms: "People tend to sit where there are places to sit"; "What attracts people most, it would appear, is other people"; and "If you want to seed a place with activity, put out food." I have one of my own to add: "You can generate activity in a public space by *allowing* activity in a public space."

My background in programming is certainly unconventional. In late 1990, I found myself a recently minted partner in a small law firm in Manhattan—and not as happy about it as I had anticipated being. The firm was a very cultured place, founded by Austrian émigrés. It's the only job I've ever had where when I came into work in the morning, my colleagues wanted to know about the concert or opera I had attended the night before. I made partner in the firm's litigation department, and while I was thought to be an excellent researcher and writer, I was never going to be much of a trial lawyer for a host of reasons, including the fact that I had fully participated in a grand total of one trial at the time I became a partner. Also, when I was invited into the partnership and was shown the firm's books, I went into shock. As has so often become true at law firms, the firm's rent (at 30 Rockefeller Plaza) was absorbing all of its profits. So I started to look around.

I answered a classified ad in the *New York Times* placed by a nonprofit organization looking for someone with a juris doctor or a master of business administration degree. Since I had both, it seemed like a possibility. My interest and knowledge of the arts turned out to be an asset in the interview process, and I got the job in early 1991. My most important major responsibilities were to fundraise for programming in the park and then to organize lunchtime events for the planned reopening of the park in the spring of the next year.

PROGRAMMING BASICS

We planned to attract attention to the reopened Bryant Park by intensively programming the reopened space. Dan Biederman was concerned about making sure people returned to the park after its having been closed for four years. I spent my first year at BPRC doing that fundraising and programming for a hoped for four-month schedule of daily lunchtime events.

It was hard, frustrating work. Eventually, we secured funds and in-kind services from the New York Times Company Foundation (thanks to the late Arthur Gelb, former *New York Times* associate managing editor and foundation president, who was a great friend of the park), HBO, and the Paul Foundation.

The HBO relationship came about because of a lucky break, which was a result of persistence. The HBO offices were on the north side of the park—although the door to the building was on Sixth Avenue. This was no accident. At the time, having an entrance facing Bryant Park was seen as a detriment, so building management changed the orientation of the lobby.

Andrew Heiskell, one of the founders of BPRC, was a legendary figure in American journalism and a person of great charm. One of Andrew's protégées at *Time* was Michael Fuchs, the chairman of *Time*'s HBO subsidiary. Michael was placed high on my list of contacts for event sponsorship—and I called his office regularly during my first year at BPRC without successfully reaching him, leaving a message with whatever assistant answered the phone. I kept a list of fundraising prospects and their phone numbers on a little pad next to the phone on my desk with the last date I had called each listed. I kept going down the list and repeatedly calling people.

In February 1992, I came into the office on a quiet day—as it turned out, it was Presidents' Day, which I guess I hadn't noticed. Since it was quiet, I started working my way down my call list. I called the number I had for Michael's office at HBO—and *he* picked up the phone, to my great amazement. It was a holiday, HBO was closed for the day, and since Michael's assistant was out, he was answering his own phone! I had my elevator pitch down, suggesting to Michael (whom I had never previously met or spoken to—nor had anyone else at BPRC) that HBO's Comedy Central sponsor a weekly comedy series in Bryant Park. Michael's response was something like "Sure. Why not?" and he asked me to call his assistant Susie Sigel to set up a meeting. I called Susie the next day, and we arranged the meeting.

I went to the meeting by myself, and there must have been forty people from HBO there—production, business affairs, programming—I had no idea who all these people were and what they did. It was a little overwhelming. Susie chaired the meeting on Michael's behalf, and it was productive.

The weekly Comedy Central series on Thursdays became the park's best-attended event. Each week's event featured three or four young comics doing a set—several of whom, like Ray Romano and Lewis Black, went on to national fame. Susie became my longtime good friend and colleague, and she eventually left HBO and joined BPRC in its public events department. Michael became a member of the board of BPRC after a couple of years and then became chairman—a position he has held ever since. Had I not kept making those calls to HBO and caught a break on a holiday, none of this is likely to have happened.

In June of 1992, the first summer the restored park was reopened, we presented concerts by students from the Julliard School and the St. Luke's Chamber Ensemble, and HBO presented its comedy series. There was programming at lunchtime from Monday through Thursday. From the beginning, most of these events drew crowds; the comedy series drew audiences in the thousands.

It is important to recognize how wrong the conventional wisdom almost always is when it comes to public spaces. We were told that no one would come to movies on Forty-Second Street at night, that plants and movable chairs would be stolen, and that homeless people would take over the restrooms and benches. How did people "know" these things? I couldn't tell you. But it is essential to push the envelope in managing public spaces and not take the conventional wisdom for granted. This is where iterating and failing on a small scale come in. You can test the validity of the conventional wisdom by putting something out in the public space and seeing how it goes. This is how pétanque,[2] chess, and many other activities came to Bryant Park. We first rolled them out on a small scale, and then when we saw that people enjoyed them, we built a larger, more permanent program.

Public Space Commercialization

The conventional wisdom in the 1980s and 1990s was that commercial activities in public spaces are always a bad thing. Business activity in public spaces most generally involves the selling of food, but it can also include anything from the rental of recreational equipment like ice skates and boats to the sponsorship of promotional events. We learned that the idea that any buying- and selling-related activity in parks and plazas interferes with public use is wrong. The retailing of food almost always enlivens and improves a public space. Markets have proven themselves to be both community builders and essential public space enhancers. Even attractive, well-designed, backlit-panel advertising can brighten and enliven public spaces. It takes money to run a great public space, and concessions are an important way to diversify the income stream supporting maintenance and programming.

There are still people who argue that any commercialization or privatization of public spaces is wrong. The argument goes that private/commercial activity in public spaces excludes people who can't afford to participate and devolves decision-making about the space away from democratically elected leaders to privately selected individuals. It certainly is possible to overly commercialize a park or plaza—and arguably that is the case today in Bryant Park. But managing public spaces is about balance—active as opposed to passive uses, quiet as opposed to loud presentations, and noncommercial versus commercial activities. There is no right answer that applies to all parks, sidewalks, and plazas. In fact, there is no right answer with respect to how much is the right amount of commerce in any particular public space. Making good judgments about these kinds of issues is what makes for great public space management. It has certainly been proven that private management and business activities can improve and enliven a wide range of public spaces. Public spaces with no private or retail activity, like Pershing Square in Los Angeles, are usually dull and empty.

SAYING YES

I've noticed over the years that the first reaction from people who control public spaces to requests to use the space is generally an emphatic no. There appear to be two motivations for this automatic reaction. The first is a fear of risk and the liability that might arise from the proposed activity. The second is a desire not to lose control over the space. People seem to be empowered by control over space and enjoy asserting that power. *Resist the urge!* In retrospect, one of the most important unplanned reasons for the success of Bryant Park in the early years was that I said yes to just about everyone who wanted to do something in the park. Activity in the park created a virtuous cycle. The more stuff we had going on in the space, the more people came to use it, and the more other people wanted to use it and be there or be associated with it.

An odd thing started to happen after the first couple of years of intensive programming. I would get an occasional call from a national public relations firm (often Edelman) asking for permission to do a promotional event, usually a product launch, in the park. I would ask them how much their client was in a position to donate to BPRC in connection with the event. This would generally be a low four-figure number, to which I would say yes and send out a form of license agreement I had come up with. This trickle eventually became a stream and then a torrent, and the general offer got to be about $5,000 per event. In the early years, we almost never turned anyone down, and we took whatever amount he or she offered. We were highly opportunistic. This turned into a major source of revenue for park operations and maintenance, part of the diversified revenue stream for the park.

Saying yes led to events marking the listing of companies on a stock exchange, a glamorous party for MTV after the Grammy Awards, and a party during a Democratic National Convention with a rock group called the Moscow Cowboys, who wore rhinestone-studded suits and performed Beatles covers. Two of our most memorable "asks" were film shoots for

Howard Stern (which was fun and paid $50,000 for the day) and Woody Allen (which was not so fun).

The events we said no to were generally large-scale productions that promoted an exclusively commercial product (often a product launch with a sample giveaway) and that offered us a very small amount of money. We also tended to turn down performances by small theater and dance groups that wanted to take over large amounts of the park for extended periods of time. In those cases, we determined that the productions would exclude too many people from enjoying the park who weren't likely to be interested in the performance. In retrospect, I can't say there was ever an event that we turned down or lost that I ever regretted. We were very fortunate in that way.

In my numerous discussions with potential event sponsors, I learned never to put out the first number. Often, what people were willing to pay was way more than I would have ever thought to ask. The amounts were always voluntary donations to the park in addition to the $25 permit fee required by DPR. If people didn't have a number in mind, I asked how much they had in their budget for a location fee. If I couldn't persuade them to offer something, eventually I generally quoted $5,000 for a two-hour event. We almost never turned anyone down. Either they came up with an acceptable donation or they decided to do their event somewhere else. All of these fees, by the way, were net of any event-related costs to BPRC. If we had to hire additional security or sanitation forces to support the event, the sponsor was required to pay that as well. If the producers broke something, they paid for it—and we carefully reviewed the park's condition after every event. Under BPRC's unique arrangement with the City of New York, the revenue we generated from events went directly to supporting the park's ongoing operations.

7TH COMES TO SIXTH

The fashion shows came to the park because Stan Herman, the president of the Council of Fashion Designers of America (CFDA), had an office overlooking the park and had been a colleague of Dan Biederman's on the local community board for a number of years. Stan came to us after the New York Public Library stopped making its beautifully reno- vated Bartos Forum available to New York designers for fashion shows. We were chatting about how the annual shows might be centralized in one location. Prior to that time, they were held not only all over the Gar- ment District but also all over Manhattan, which was a logistical night- mare for the models, store buyers, and the fashion media. Paris had just opened an event space for its fashion shows near the Louvre, which had proved to be a boon to the French fashion industry. In particular, the media attention to the Parisian runway shows had greatly increased with their centralization.

We took out a scale drawing of the park and began measuring how much space there might be between the fixed features of the park where we might be able to shoehorn tents to house the shows. Initially we did not include the lawn as a possible site for erecting structures. We argued that the lawn was sacrosanct. It was tight, but we figured out a way to fit two large tents onto paved areas in the park. What started out as a $50,000-a-year fee to BPRC ended up generating millions of dollars and national exposure. But nothing contributed more to the park's public profile than the weekly televised announcement by Heidi Klum that the winner of *Project Runway* would have the opportunity to show his or her designs in Bryant Park.

The introduction of the fashion shows to Bryant Park put a spotlight on that last, deal-breaking point resolved in the negotiation of the Bry- ant Park restaurant lease. Ark Restaurants, during the entire course of the negotiation, insisted on the exclusive right to serve food in the park— including the operation of the kiosks. The leadership at the Parks Depart- ment objected to giving such an exclusive right for the entire park to the restaurant operator. We were eager to get a deal after several previous failed attempts and were willing to concede the point, but parks commis- sioner Betsey Gotbaum was firm. By the time we were at the closing, all the other issues had been resolved—except the exclusive right matter. It was only with the direct appeal by Andrew Heiskell and Marshall Rose to Mayor Dinkins, with the mayor overruling the parks commissioner, that the deal got done. The leaders of 7th on Sixth, the organization formed by the Council of Fashion Designers of America to present the fashion shows in Bryant Park, did not want to be bound to use Ark for food service at the shows. They had their own caterers that they wanted to use. Ark insisted on standing on its rights. It had a written agreement, won the point, and provided the catering. The folks at the CFDA were very unhappy about this situation for years.

How the Movies Happened

The movies happened as a result of a chance conversation. While the comedy series was extremely popular, it was also the source of numerous complaints about its volume and scatological language, which carried up to the offices of the *New Yorker* magazine, which faced the park, from whose employees we received (highly literate) complaints. In September 1992, Michael Fuchs, Dan Biederman, and I were standing around waiting for a more-than-two-hours-late Governor Bill Clinton to arrive for a campaign rally in the park. We got to talking about what we were going to do to replace the comedy series, since the complaints had become a serious problem. Someone mentioned (who it was is remembered differently by those present; success has many fathers) the idea of doing a drive-in movie but without cars. Michael immediately jumped on the idea and put Susie Sigel and me to work on creating an outdoor film series to replace the comedy series, for which *he* would personally select the films to be shown. For the first two or three years, only a couple of hundred people turned up on Monday nights for the films. But it quickly became (and remains) a phenomenon attracting thousands. And showing movies outside in public spaces turned out to be another one of those ideas hatched in Bryant Park that went viral.

Figure 11. The Bryant Park Film Series was the pet project of Michael Fuchs, chairman at the time of Home Box Office; the film series has become a huge success and one of the park's signatures.

An interesting aside to that story is that after the Clinton event in the park, I was taken to meet Governor Clinton. I was introduced to Clinton (hyperbolically) as the person responsible for organizing the event. I was thrilled to shake Clinton's hand and walked away starstruck, as most people are when meeting him. As I was leaving, a campaign aide rushed up to me and said, "Governor Clinton is so grateful to you for helping us with what has been our best campaign event. He'd like to invite you and your partner to his fundraising dinner at the Sheraton tonight, if you're available." Of course we were available!

Heidi and I showed up at the Sheraton's grand ballroom for the event and were seated next to the kitchen but at a table made up of members of the family that owns the *New York Times*, who were gracious hosts to us both. As the dessert was being served, there was a commotion at the kitchen doors, and the secret service began to set up a "rope line" between the kitchen and dais for the event. Someone told us to stand up and be at the head of the line. Out came Governor Clinton and his wife, Hillary Clinton, and we were first in the line to shake their hands. As the governor came out of the kitchen, he grabbed my hand and said, "Andy Manshel, I'm so glad you could join us. It's great to see you here. Thanks for your good work on our event this afternoon." And that, I imagine, tells you a lot about how he came to be elected president of the United States.

Curating Programming and Managing Risk

One of the things that made it possible to say yes to a wide range of events was that our excellent insurance brokers, Michael Fishman and Lenore Carasia, were always able to put a price on the additional risk created by new or unusual uses, and the cost of that additional coverage was always affordable, especially compared to an event's revenue-generating potential. Being trained as an attorney helped. I was in a position to understand the very limited risks and legal consequences involved in various events and to make reasoned judgments about them. I understood that saying no to stuff that seemed risky was easier but that it was essential to our mission for me to try to figure out how to make programs happen and make informed, professional decisions about the risks entailed by potential uses.

As the volume of requests increased, we began to be able to select among the various possibilities. We also began to encourage events to take place in what we called the shoulder hours—early in the day, after work, at night, and during the winter—like the skating rink and holiday market.

We did have instances where we lost control of what was going on in the park, and we learned from those experiences. After a knock-down, drag-out battle that ended with a meeting in the deputy mayor's office, the fashion shows took over the lawn. We and the Parks Department tried to persuade city hall to keep the shows on the paved areas. We said that the lawn was the park's crown jewel and had to be protected. CFDA argued that the shows promoted one of the city's most important industries and had become a major economic engine in their own right. The president of the Nicole Miller fashion house was a friend of Mayor Giuliani's. He placed a call to the mayor, and that was that.

The shows began taking up an ever-increasing amount of time and space in the park. The producers of the shows became insensitive to their responsibility to the physical stewardship of the park and to the interests of other stakeholders. Eventually they were persuaded to leave for the greener pastures of Lincoln Center (something of a sacrifice for BPRC, as they were ultimately paying seven-figure amounts). Similarly, as a result of First Amendment issues arising out of other uses we had permitted and political pressure, we were required to permit the construction of a sukkah (a structure open to the sky, built in connection with a fall Jewish harvest festival) in the park by the Chabad movement, which has remained an annual event. Our desire to maintain the quality and availability of the public space experience had to give way to the economic and political priorities of the elected officials. Ultimately, those elected officials were responsible for the management of city-owned parks, and as nobody elected us, this was as it should be. A municipality can't and shouldn't devolve the resolving of conflicting fundamental, constitutional First Amendment demands on a public space to a private group.

I brought this philosophy of saying yes with me to Jamaica, and it proved equally valuable there. Before I was given the responsibility of managing Greater Jamaica Development Corporation's range of real estate assets, the individuals with authority over them were reluctant to allow anyone other than conventional rent payers to take advantage of those spaces. After I was put in charge, I encouraged third parties to use those facilities. I tried to come up with ways to activate those facilities and to enable their temporary use by third parties. This approach produced a tremendously successful pop-up art studio and gallery project in partnership with chashama, an organization that provides temporary space to artists. It also led to our hosting the Queens International Night Market in the downtown. Both of these activities produced wide media coverage about Jamaica's revival. In the disinvested downtown, hosting events produced huge amounts of goodwill and positive programming from community partners to whom we provided free meeting or event space and free or reduced-cost parking.

The Art of the Deal

Another of the lessons I learned about generating earned income in public spaces is to try to capture the upside potential from permitted activities. Bryant Park very much benefits from the concession activity taking place in the space because it works to capture as much of this value as it can. I first learned about how powerful this could be in trying to replace the newsstands on Forty-Second Street on the north side of the park.

When BPRC took over management of the park from the DPR, it came along with two wooden newsstands on the south side of Forty-Second Street. They were essentially large wooden shacks, operated by an individual who had acquired a license from the DPR as the highest bidder in a request-for-proposal process years before. The stands were an eyesore. They weren't operated in any way that was all that different from the other sidewalk newsstands in New York City that were licensed by the Department of Transportation outside of parks. We wanted to improve both the design and the operation of the stands so that they would comport with the standard of quality of operations we were planning for the rest of the park and as an example to the City of New York of what a quality sidewalk stand could be.

The Bryant Park stands were built against the retaining wall next to the park rather than at the curb, like most New York stands. They paid pretty good rent to BPRC at a time when every dollar of revenue counted. Not getting the income from them while new stands were being installed was going to be painful. As part of the Thompson master plan for GCP, the firm had designed a model newsstand. The model included backlit advertising panels. I took a rendering of the model to professional acquaintances I had made at TDI, which at the time was the largest outdoor advertising firm in New York City. Given that BPRC had no capital funds to demolish the existing stands and build the new ones, I proposed to the folks at TDI that they capitalize the construction of the stands in exchange for the right to the panel advertising on the two structures. They were enthusiastic about the idea, and we began to get estimates for the cost of building the stands—which came in at about $125,000 each. Astronomical, compared to the $10,000–$15,000 cost of a new shack, but worth it to transform the aesthetics of Forty-Second Street. Given the high up-front cost, TDI asked for a ten-year deal—with no obligation to pay rent during the term—in order to amortize the capital costs. There would still be rent from the operator of the stands (which we licensed to a large, national newsstand operator in order to get a first-class appearance). I didn't think I could sell a "no rent" deal for the advertising to Dan Biederman. I gave the problem some thought and asked the folks at TDI to pick a high-revenue hurdle—one that they might never expect to reach—and then to provide BPRC with a percentage of the gross advertising sales over that amount. They agreed and set the hurdle at $200,000 of annual gross income from advertising sales. They said they would give us the same amount as they paid to the city for advertising sales on the deal they had (TDI's biggest business in the city was selling the ads for subway billboards; in fact, the original name of the company was New York Subways), which was 26 percent.

Dan agreed, and we promptly forgot about the terms of the deal. We took the structures through the approval process at DPR and the Art Commission. Panel ads on newsstands were a new concept for New York, and it took some considerable salesmanship to gain city approval for the idea. Once we had the approval in hand and deals with TDI and an operator, we terminated the agreement with the existing operator and demolished the shacks—which immediately improved conditions on Forty-Second Street between Fifth Avenue and Avenue of the Americas. The Thompson-designed stands were ordered, and some months later, they arrived on flatbed trucks and were installed at the curb. Once the utilities were installed, the stands were up and running. The ad panels were sold by TDI to our friends at HBO, whose offices were across the street. I checked the project off my list and pretty much forgot about it.

A couple of years later, I got a very contrite call from someone in the accounting department of TDI. The person apologized and said that TDI had neglected to send us an accounting for the ad revenue at the news-stands for the prior year—which I hadn't remembered we were entitled to, since we all understood that the threshold was unlikely to ever be reached and that any rent to BPRC from the ads was extremely unlikely. After some quick thinking, I told the caller that it wasn't a problem but that he shouldn't let it happen again. The voice on the phone apologized and said that a messenger would be over in a couple of minutes with the statement and a check for $26,000. Shocked, I thanked him, hung up the phone, and dashed for Dan's office next door to mine to tell him about this windfall.

When we got the statement, we saw that the ad panels had been sold for more than $300,000—an amount that only increased each year thereafter. This eventually became an important revenue stream for BPRC. At the expiration of the contract with TDI, BPRC made a direct deal with HBO for hundreds of thousands of dollars.

I learned an important lesson. The income-producing potential of a well-run public space should not be underestimated. Thereafter, on simi-lar commercial arrangements, I always tried to obtain a percentage of income over a high hurdle. That strategy was also notably successful in the arrangement we made with the operator of the Pershing Square Café under the viaduct at Forty-Second Street and Park Avenue.

The codas to this story are that we fell out of love with the modern-ist bright-red Thompson design and commissioned a new design from Hardy Holzman Pfeiffer (HHP), the architects of the restaurant and the kiosks in Bryant Park. John Fontillas of HHP created a new green design, which was more in line with the early twentieth-century aesthetic of the rest of the park. That design was also eventually used in Herald and Greely Squares. John became an important part of the Bryant Park / 34th Street Partnership team and played a big part in creating the look of our projects.

Our campaign to improve the newsstands around Midtown went on for years. The law was that if you could fit a newsstand onto a sidewalk (within a six-by-twelve-foot area), you were entitled to apply for a stand and get a license. These rules were administered by my friend Frank Addeo and his staff, and they did what they could to find fault with applications as they came in. The construction of wooden shacks in front of Class A office buildings without their owners being able to do anything about it drove those property owners crazy. We did whatever we could to have the law regarding newsstands changed. The newsstand operators had excellent counsel in Robert Bookman, who was an attorney skilled at defeating the city in court every time it tried to change the rules.

During the Giuliani administration, there was a proposal to create a franchise for street furniture, which was to be driven by ad panels. The idea was to create a concession, which would be bid out by the city and would include newsstands, bus shelters, and automatic public toilets. Existing interests lobbied to kill that proposal. I served as cochair of the Streetscape Committee of the Municipal Art Society (MAS), and when Michael Bloomberg was elected mayor in 2002, I drafted a white paper for the MAS, pleading the case for an integrated street furniture franchise, which was submitted to the new mayor and his team. They eventually adopted the idea and put into place the franchise system that now exists and has led to the good-looking, well-maintained newsstands and bus shelters that now grace the city's sidewalks. The second generation of that idea is the Wi-Fi kiosks franchised by the de Blasio administration. This is another example of small projects leading to big changes in public space. It also again highlights the importance of persistent advocacy over a long period of time.

Some of the tools of placemaking take time or money to implement. Some require close cooperation with government and community stakeholders. But saying yes is something totally within the control of the public space manager and produces unanticipated and unimagined positive results. It ought to be easy to do, but for many people, it's not. It actually takes a certain discipline to say yes, and it's a discipline that is essential to creating active downtowns and public spaces.

HORTICULTURAL PROGRAMMING

Nothing gives you more positive impact from your public-space-improvement dollar than plants. When people ask me what the one thing they should do to improve public space, my response is to institute a horticulture program. Improving the perception of public space is about providing positive visual cues to users demonstrating that the space is safe and being taken care of. Colorful, well-maintained plants send that message in a number of ways. The physical material isn't very expensive, and the skills to maintain plants are widespread and easy to find. Putting plantings in places where people don't expect them sends a powerful message.

I knew absolutely nothing about gardening when I went to work for Bryant Park Restoration Corporation in 1991. My father grew some terrific tomatoes in the backyard when I was growing up (it was New Jersey, after all), and there was always mint growing outside too. That was the sum total of my agricultural experience when I arrived in the park. From that day to this, I have never had a personal garden or even a yard.

However, I had the good fortune to work at Bryant Park with Lynden B. Miller, who was a landscape painter and who had designed the restored gardens at the Conservatory Garden in Central Park at the request of her friend, the founder of the Central Park Conservancy and Central Park administrator, Betsy Barlow Rogers. Dan Biederman brought Lynden on board as the gardens' designer. Lynden taught me a tremendous amount—beginning with the difference between annuals and perennials, I'm sorry to say—and introduced me to New York's dynamic horticultural world.

Lynden brings two things to her work in horticulture: she knows plants, and she has elegant taste. As a result of her experience in the Conservatory Garden, she knew about not only what plants worked in the New York City climate zone but also what plants were hardy enough, and impressive enough, to work in an urban environment. It was Lynden who selected the Pink Impression tulip, which has become one of Bryant Park's trademarks. It was ideal for its purpose, and the first spring after we planted them, the tulips were a sensation. They have a vibrant color and a huge head and were sufficiently hardy to survive winter in the ground above the New York Public Library stack extension and the number 7 subway line. Lynden also knew that to get real visual impact, we needed to plant thousands of them.

The perennial beds were the thing we most often heard would be impossible to make work on Forty-Second Street in the New York of the early 1990s. We were told that the plants would be stolen. (We spent a small fortune on a plant security/alarm system that never worked.) The beds would be trampled and trashed. It seemed inconceivable that in the midst of the apparent urban chaos of Midtown Manhattan of 1992, two elegant, hundred-yard-long planting beds would thrive.

The large and sumptuous plantings immediately defied expectations about the social conditions in the park. They established a marker of what was possible in a public space that had previously had a seedy reputation. The perennial beds and the lush, green lawn (once we got it to work) were the most important initial elements that communicated the park's new success and safeness to the public.

Most obviously, the very presence of the flowerbeds transmitted to people that someone cared about the space—that attention was being paid. The fact that the flowers and plants were a constant presence told visitors that they weren't being stolen (more on that in a bit), and people understood that social norms were being observed and maintained in the park, with or without an enforcement presence. The maintenance of the horticultural material in Bryant Park required staff members who were always visibly working in the park. They were eyes on the street and street-corner mayors and helped people feel safe; they were obvious evidence that the space was well ordered and being actively maintained. Our first full-time gardener was an entertaining character (many of them are) who developed his own following. This individual became a great ambassador for the park. He was outgoing and knowledgeable and loved sharing what he knew about plants. Everyone loves colorful flowers and a green lawn—they just give people pleasure. Well-selected horticultural material and excellent maintenance are the essential features of any urban horticultural program and are transferable anywhere. And transfer them we did.

Once our team got good at planting and maintaining the Bryant Park gardens, we went to work figuring out how to create an urban streetscape horticulture program. We determined that the key elements of that program would be hanging baskets, sidewalk planters, and a van with a water tank and a watering wand. We bought the baskets from a catalog. Our landscaping firm, which also supplied the plants, cobbled together a watering truck from a beat-up old van. The truck carried the BIDs' logos and was highly visible on the street.

At first, the program was relatively simple, with two colors of begonias planted in the spring and watered at night during the summer to avoid traffic problems. The initiative required the cooperation and approval of the city's Department of Transportation for hanging the plants on the lamp stanchions (made easier by the fact that the stanchions were custom-installed by the BIDs) and for placing the planters on the sidewalk. The planters also required a sign-off from the Art Commission (which approves the design of street furniture in public spaces). The police department and DOT were given notice of our plans to have a truck driving around at night. The horticulture program made a huge impact and grew to include tree pits, seasonal displays (including holiday lighting in the baskets), and a much wider range of plantings. Today, some of the designs, particularly the planters in Bryant Park, done by horticulturalist Maureen Hackett (who was hired by Lynden to supervise the program day

Figure 12. A "hanging basket," bracketed to a signature Grand Central / Thirty-Fourth Street Partnership streetlamp. One of our most impactful moves.

to day and who now runs it), lean toward the showy and baroque, but they make an impression.

One tip about maintenance: there is some sleight of hand at work in a successful program. You need to buy about a third more plants than you plan to use and have a place to store and maintain them. The plants do tend to get stolen, especially when you start the program and around Mother's Day. The key to the appearance of success is replacing the missing plants every night. The thieves eventually give up. But for the program to transmit the message you are trying to send, the baskets, planters, and beds always have to appear to be full and well maintained. Missing and/or dead plants and damaged or defaced planters are much, much worse than no program at all. One of the advantages of hanging baskets is that they are hard to reach—and therefore hard to steal from or vandalize. They also have tremendous visual impact because of how they catch the eye. I'd do baskets before planters every time if I had to choose due to limited resources.

———

Active programming can transform any previously neglected public space by drawing people into it. The programming doesn't have to be fancy or expensive. What it needs, like other elements of public space revitalization I've discussed elsewhere, is critical mass. There has to be enough activity going on to establish that the space is well ordered and well maintained. Programming doesn't necessarily mean performances. It can be plants. It can be games. It can be selling food or big, splashy commercial promotions. It can be anything that is activity in the space that people find attractive. People are drawn to other people, and a regular schedule of activities in a park or plaza or on downtown sidewalks can turn a place around. The now self-sustaining programming in Bryant Park continues to be the driving force in its revitalization.

CHAPTER 7

LEARNING FROM YOUR MISTAKES

One of the principal strategies of placemaking is to take small risks and correct mistakes as they are observed. It is generally impossible to predict how people will behave in any particular physical situation. People's expectations for what they may find in a space differ, topographies differ, density of use varies from place to place. You can make your best estimate of what might work, but you can't really know. That's why it is important to carefully observe the implementation of placemaking tactics and be prepared to adjust them—depending on how people actually respond. With a minor tweak, something that might not be drawing people as you assumed it would could become a great success.

At the same time, that doesn't mean that because places are unique or different, successful public space or economic revitalization strategies that work in one place aren't transferable to another place. I have been told that the success of Bryant Park is exceptional because it is in Manhattan or because it is in Midtown, and therefore programs and strategies that worked in Bryant Park won't work in other places. In fact, before Bryant Park reopened, we were told that many of our ideas were *impossible* in the park because of its unique location. Movable chairs, outdoor movies, elaborately planted gardens—none of them would work at the corner of Sixth Avenue and Forty-Second Street, we were often told, because of the special conditions there. Now all of those strategies seem like obvious successes.

Nothing about Bryant Park's success was inevitable, and several elements of the park's redesign were failures (although none of the tactics that didn't work were among the recommendations made by Holly Whyte in his 1979 analysis of the park's problems). However, when programs didn't seem to be working, *failures were quickly identified, and new programmatic or design solutions were created to address them.* At the center of great public space management is an iterative process of observing how real people use public space and adjusting strategies to deal with issues as they arise. It is difficult to admit failure, particularly in a political environment, which comes with the territory of public space. The spotlight can be intense, and highly visible failure is certainly embarrassing. But successful public space managers have to be nimble, identify problems, and attempt new solutions until they get it right—and be willing to recognize what isn't working. I hope that by discussing a number of things that we tried in the park that didn't work, I can establish that mistakes are inevitable and that identifying them and figuring out how to fix them quickly are essential to great public space management.

The Lawn

As I discussed in chapter 5, people love broad expanses of green grass. They enjoy sitting, picnicking, playing ball, lying in the sun, or reading on them. Because of this, in many, if not most, public space developments or restorations, a well-maintained lawn area is a key ingredient. A uniform, lush, green spread of grass that is open for use communicates to the public that a space is welcoming—and draws visitors in. It also communicates to potential users that the space is under social control—that the lawn is being taking care of and, as a result, using the lawn is safe.

But in Bryant Park, the two-acre lawn was initially a failure, and it took four seasons to get it right. There was nothing preordained about the horticultural success of the Bryant Park lawn! The lawn as specified by the landscape architect was designed to support a high level of traffic—like a football field. The specified soil was mostly sand and drained quickly. We found it difficult to maintain, and in order to keep the lawn properly watered, the surface was often wet, which users found unpleasant. Because the soil was sandy and didn't hold nutrients, it also needed regular fertilization, something we didn't initially have the in-house capacity to do or regulate. As a result, if the turf wasn't wet or slimy, it often was burned out and patchy, particularly after a big event or heavy use. It was frustrating not to have one of the most visible elements of the park appearing to work properly.

It took us a couple of seasons to figure out that we didn't know how to get the lawn right and then quite a long while to find the person with the right expertise to help us. Ultimately, we developed a close relationship with Starkie Brothers, who brought in a soil expert they knew. Over a period of months, they amended the soil with rich, organic material, which held nutrients and water better, and selected a seed mix that could sustain heavy foot traffic. The combination of a denser soil that held more nutrients and water and a hardier seed mix made for a more durable turf. Because of this, we had to carefully monitor the lawn to make sure it wasn't too long or cut too short or too wet or too dry—and to know when to close it to allow it to recover after heavy use. We eventually got the hang of it, and the lawn was seen as the park's crown jewel.

Gravel Paths

The 1991 redesign included gravel paths around the lawn and gravel beds among the trees. A large, light-brown pea gravel was specified by the landscape architect for the paths and beds. This material was beautiful and looked absolutely fabulous when spread out, but it turned out to be difficult to maintain. Because of the size of the individual stones, wheelchairs and strollers couldn't move through it. Pushing wheeled vehicles across it felt like pushing them through water. The gravel moved around in the rain and needed to be moved back. This turned out to be a very big job. Kids (being kids) liked to throw the stones. Most frustratingly, as the stones started to disappear over time, we couldn't find a source for a match to replace them.

After a couple of seasons, we replaced the original crushed stone with something finer. That was an improvement, but ultimately we forgot about the gravel entirely and left the dirt paths. They aren't as elegant, but they work a whole lot better.

WIND CONCERTS

As I discussed in chapter 6, in 1992, the first season after the physical restoration, I planned a series of events so that something was going on four days a week in the park. We were concerned that after decades of being perceived as unsafe and after having been closed for construction for four years, when we took down the construction fences, the drug dealers might return and no one else. But Holly Whyte taught us that good uses drive out bad, and we programmed the park with that in mind.

My pet project was wind concerts by ensembles from the St. Luke's Chamber Ensemble featuring unamplified music written for the outdoors, like the Mozart and Brahms wind serenades for clarinets, oboes, bassoons, flutes, and horns. In my mind, these concerts would be beautiful and elegant and would set a high standard in the park for civility. The design of the park was classically proportioned, and I thought that this kind of music would evoke a kind of Versailles on Sixth Avenue. They would also be different and unique.

From the very beginning, people complained that they couldn't hear the wind concerts. And in fact, in order to hear them, you had to be sitting relatively close to the performers and have sufficient powers of concentration to enjoy these wonderful performances. Without amplification, the musicians had a hard time projecting over the ambient noise from local street traffic and just the normal hustle and bustle of the park. The folks at St. Luke's and I were the only ones who were "getting it," and because the concerts were so quiet, they had a minimal impact on the sense of activity in the park. I had to swallow hard and admit defeat, and by the end of the first season, the wind ensemble concerts were being amplified. Even with the fix of amplification, the unpopular wind concerts only lasted a couple of years and were later replaced by louder music with broader appeal, like jazz and Broadway show tunes. Lesson learned.

Inadequate Power

As initially designed by the restoration architects, the park had exactly two electrical outlets, with four plugs carrying 110 volts of current. This created a number of problems. First, the two outlets were located on either side of the stairs leading to the Bryant Monument, which turned out not to be a place where they were needed (I'll talk about why later). Initially, we bought a gasoline generator to power the small amplification system we used for public events. But as the events grew larger, so did the generators. The generators required for the fashion shows came on flatbed trailers that needed to be parked on Fortieth Street. They created so much noise that they were annoying to the folks who lived in the one residential co-op apartment building across Fortieth Street from the park. With the generators also came long snakes of cable that made the park difficult to navigate, looked terrible, and added to the expense of the shows. These work-arounds made every large event in Bryant Park more complicated, more expensive, more intrusive, and more damaging to the park.

Eventually (more than ten years after the reopening), the park's operations had generated enough income that it was able to pay for upgraded electrical service, with outlets in a park outbuilding, making the generators unnecessary. This was important to providing adequate power for the skating rink and the holiday market as well as for other large-scale events. It was an expensive proposition.

The lesson here is to think through what the electricity needs for a space will be at the design phase, place sources at a number of locations around the space in order to provide flexibility, and in a medium to large space, provide a level of service that can support the larger events you hope to host. This is an expensive item to retrofit.

No Place for a Stage

After we created the first year of four-day-a-week lunchtime programming, we then had to figure out where to hold the performances. The design seemed to provide a "natural stage" at the foot of the Bryant Monument, which is at the top of a steep set of stairs. As noted earlier, that's where the power outlets were located. But when we tried it out, we found that because the height from the lawn area to the top flight of the terrace was so great, the performers were too high and set too far back to make for a viable concert experience. As a result, we decided to move the stage to the other side of the park, on the Fountain Terrace near Avenue of the Americas.

That created its own set of problems. The Fountain Terrace wasn't high enough to enable the audience to see the performers from a short distance away. The power outlets were on the other side of the park. And the noise from Sixth Avenue traffic, which was not as much of a problem on the east side of the lawn, was a problem here. We bought a mobile stage and an acoustic shell (that we used for years) to give the presentations more presence and improve the sound projection. However, the acoustic shell created a new problem—it blocked the view of the Lowell Fountain from the lawn.

When we started the movie series in 1995, the visual problem became even more pronounced as the movie screen completely blocked the view of the fountain during the entire summer that the screen was in place (and it wasn't practical to break it down every week). Ultimately, the screen

was made up of panels that swung on an axis and were set perpendicu-
larly when the screen wasn't in use, opening up the view down Forty-First
Street and providing a less obstructed view of the fountain. Not an ideal
solution, but a workable one.

This should have been thought through at the time the space was redesigned, especially since everyone was aware that public events were a key
part of the restoration strategy. The plan should have provided a performance area that worked for performers; had adequate power; included
storage space for chairs, stands, and sound equipment (something that
we also needed to find a solution to); and visually didn't interfere with
the park's aesthetics. Obviously the compromises and work-arounds have
been effective, if suboptimal. But they took time, money, and ingenuity to
implement.

CONCRETE FOOTINGS

Perhaps the most unpredictable thing we discovered over time that the
park didn't have was concrete footings. When tents were required for park
events, which began to be a regular occurrence, the tent companies were
required to bring in concrete blocks to serve as ballasts to tie down the
ropes and wires that held up the structures. A great deal of damage was
done to the park every time tents were erected and taken down by fork-
lifts ferrying the huge concrete blocks around, breaking the historic blue-
stone pavers. We were surprised to discover how often people wanted to
put up tents for events in the park. When the fashion show tents became
behemoths, the number of concrete blocks required became equally huge.
Before and after each show, it took weeks to place the blocks at strategic
locations around the park. Eventually, plastic thirty-gallon barrels filled
with water replaced most if not all of the blocks. But moving them, filling
them, and emptying them still created some (lesser) problems.

This could have been prevented by including a grid of concrete footings set into the lawn and other park surfaces with small rings fixed to

the concrete in the redesign. These could have provided a flexible set of anchors for a range of tents. Tents and other tensile structures are tremendously useful in many ways in public spaces, and not just for events. In spaces with broad hardscape—where trees aren't possible—tensile structures can provide a relatively low-cost, temporary/seasonal means to provide shade. A footing system makes this much easier to do but is something people designing public spaces often don't think about in advance. Again, this is another very expensive feature to have to retrofit to a completed project.

PLANT ALARM SYSTEM

One final Bryant Park example of an idea that seemed good at the time we had it arises out of the many things that "they" told us we wouldn't be able to do. We were told that it would be impossible to establish high-quality planting beds a block from Times Square. "Everyone knew" that the plants would be stolen. We were advised to secure the plants, so we installed an elaborate and expensive system that ran trip wires through the root balls of the larger plants. The system would trigger a wireless transmitter that would set off an alarm in the BID's security office if plants were removed from the beds. The thing never worked, but it quickly proved itself to be unnecessary, because plant theft was never much of a problem. For all I know, the wires and transmitters are still buried in the beds. We also discovered that perennial beds in Midtown Manhattan have a huge advantage over those in most people's backyards: while we did have pigeons, we had no deer eating the plants.

Many other retoolings took place over the years in the park. These are just illustrative examples of how even at one of the most successful public space revitalization projects, management had to be constantly attentive to how the space was being used and operated and had to adapt as required. This is equally true of downtown projects.

Mistakes Downtown

Even with Bryant Park's great success, much of what we learned there goes frustratingly unlearned in other places. Cleveland recently rebuilt its most visible space, called Public Square. This $50 million project included at the time of this writing some programming tropes that have become standard in new public space designs (a food kiosk, a water feature), but when the space was launched, it was underprogrammed. Most importantly, it lacked both shade and movable chairs. The single coffee stand didn't create enough activity to animate the space—particularly during the "shoulder" periods of nights and weekends. The design, by James Corner / Field Operations, very much reminded me of Pershing Square in Los Angeles, one of the country's most glaringly unsuccessful public spaces of the last fifty years (more on Pershing Square later). Both have extensive water features and food kiosks—but are mostly hardscape with fixed seating and no shade.

Those "mistakes" aren't permanent. In my view, almost any public space can be made successful through good programming and operations. Public Square is yet another example of the importance of providing sufficient resources to program and maintain a space *after* the tens of millions of capital dollars have been expended on a renovation. Public Square has a large lawn area, which is great—but someone has to be there every day to make sure that it is adequately watered and mowed and to close it when it is too wet or stressed from use from events. Public Square needed more commercial activities—a green market, food trucks, crafts booths, and more food service. All of these activities must also take place on nights and weekends.

Cleveland has come a long way in the forty years since I went to college in Northern Ohio. Terminal Tower was near empty in the 1970s; today its interior public spaces are lively. The gigantic former Stouffer's Hotel (most recently the Renaissance) appeared empty and was waiting for redevelopment. The downtown has lots of bar and restaurant activity at night. Public Square was a forlorn, desolate space for decades, and while the renovated facility was shiny and new, because the design ignores much of what we have learned about what makes public spaces successful, it was going to need an intensive and sustained intervention to make it thrive and become an asset to Cleveland's revitalization.

PERSHING SQUARE, LOS ANGELES

At about the same time I went to work for BPRC, a similar project was underway on the West Coast. Pershing Square, the oldest public space in Los Angeles, was also the subject of a major downtown revitalization effort. In 1992, Pershing Square was closed for a $14.5 million redesign and renovation by Mexican architect Ricardo Legorreta and Philadelphia-based Hanna Olin Design. Hanna Olin was also the landscape design firm engaged for Bryant Park. The "new" Pershing Square opened in 1994. Shortly after it was completed, I visited Pershing Square and found it to be hot, dusty, and deserted. It was essentially the roof of an underground parking garage. Over the past two decades, while Bryant Park had become New York's "town square" and the stimulus to billions of dollars in redevelopment, the mostly inert Pershing Square had been the opposite for its neighborhood—a drag on efforts to revitalize Downtown LA. The square sits between the glass-and-steel office center of modern LA and the rapidly changing original LA downtown of brick, limestone, and terracotta loft buildings. It's fascinating to see how much positive activity is happening one or two blocks away from the square—without it as an anchor.

More recently, Pershing Square became the focus of redevelopment efforts, led by a nonprofit Pershing Square Renew (PSR). PSR focused its work on a design competition for a new plan for Pershing Square.[1] That competition produced a plan by Agence Ter with a price tag north of $150 million. The principal feature of the proposed design was a shade structure, which addresses one of the current park's most serious problems—the harsh effect on visitors of the otherwise delightful bright

Figure 13. A symbol of Los Angeles's inability to maintain its oldest park, Pershing Square—signaling to potential visitors that all is not well in this important public space.

southern California sun bouncing off the park's extensive open hardscape. The 1992 design featured a very large fountain and pool, which was an attractive feature and provided some cooling, but the water feature no longer operates. PSR focused its initial efforts on raising the required funds for the capital improvements, working out its relationship with LA's Department of Recreation and Parks (DRP) and creating park programming, in that order of priority. And therein lies the pressing issue of concern.

Every public space revitalization project seems to start with the commissioning of a design followed by the extensive fundraising required for the execution of that design. Even at Bryant Park, despite the central involvement of Holly Whyte from the outset, during BPRC's first twelve years, its focus was on hiring consultants and generating funds to execute their plans. Much was kept on hold until the construction was complete. But everything we have learned about placemaking practice in the last thirty years has taught us that the most successful element of public space improvement is programming and that even poorly designed public spaces can be radically upgraded by an easily implemented program of "lighter, quicker, cheaper" improvements. To its credit, thanks to the generous and enlightened support of Southwest Airlines, PSR had begun to implement a schedule of creative programming.

There is something about the bright and shiny prospect of major capital improvements that attracts community leaders and elected officials. Part of this may be that in recent decades, municipal capital dollars have been easier to secure than ongoing operating funds. Today, the DPR is relatively awash in capital dollars, with insufficient operating revenue to maintain its existing inventory of spaces. The DPR struggles valiantly to pick up the trash and cut its lawns. New public spaces in New York City like the High Line, Hudson River Park, Governor's Island, and Brooklyn Bridge Park all have yet to hit on sustainable operating models. Attention is certainly more easily focused on a great new design than on the everyday reality of trash pickup, horticultural maintenance, and park programming. In Bryant Park, the opening of the newly renovated park was the kickoff for the implementation of an extensive schedule of high-quality programming (even before the construction of the park restaurant originally thought to be essential to the project's success). But in my judgment, in retrospect, both the activities and the horticultural improvements could have brought about the park's effective revitalization—without the capital improvements. For example, we could have put out movable chairs (as we did on the New York Public Library's front terrace while the park was under construction) without the capital project. But hindsight is twenty-twenty.

Pershing Square faces some of the usual problems of public space revitalization efforts, and one interesting, difficult, and unique one. Parks departments tend to regard themselves as empires—in fact, former DPR commissioner Henry Stern referred to his realm as the "emerald empire." As empires, they are loath to cede territory. As political creatures, they also do not want to concede that they are anything other than excellent at everything within their brief. (This is something of a change from the 1970s and 1980s, when the government recognized that nonprofit organizations could assist in advancing the government's mission by providing the prospect of flexibility and lower costs. Those days appear to be gone.) It was the expectation of the DRP that PSR's sole function was to raise the money for the proposed capital improvements. Then the DRP would build out the capital project and operate and maintain the park. The problem with the DRP plan was that, to my knowledge, no successful restoration of a downtown park anywhere in the United States in the last fifty years has been done in that manner. And in fact, in 2019, PSR ceased operations, and the DRP moved ahead with a small government-funded capital project.

City parks departments, as agencies of democratic governments, are unable to expend the additional resources required to maintain and program downtown parks because of the intensity of use that results from the density around them. Parks departments must treat all parks equally, lest they be charged with favoring downtown at the expense of other neighborhoods. But because of their high level of use, downtown parks need more resources and attention, and nonprofit entities—beginning with the Central Park Conservancy—have proven to be useful vehicles for generating and/or managing the additional revenue required to run downtown parks. Parks departments also generally don't have the internal capacity to focus on the heavy programming required to create the critical mass essential to the revitalization of a single downtown park. Parks departments, by necessity, must do programs that can be implemented in multiple locations, none of which will have the crucial critical mass of activity for a downtown space.

Also, while only municipalities have the resources to perform major infrastructure improvements, for a whole range of reasons, they tend to be less-than-ideal vehicles for the execution of the aesthetic details of public improvement projects. As I explained in chapter 3, in Bryant Park, it was city dollars related to the library stack extension (a project managed by the library) that paid for the major construction work on the property.

BPRC paid for the amenities—lighting, horticulture, and concession structures. Even the well-funded Central Park Conservancy relies on city capital dollars as the backbone of its infrastructure work, for which it is difficult to raise private funds. My general rule is that municipalities should be responsible for capital improvements on the park's surface and below, and nonprofit partners can fundraise for and construct those above-the-surface features—kiosks, plants, and art, for example. There are aboveground exceptions to this general principle in larger, more complex projects. These include major buildings and lighting systems, which are also generally hard for nonprofits to find private funds for.

Getting a reliable income stream to support park programming and operations is a great challenge everywhere. BPRC first created a business improvement district to provide it with a continuing source of funding. It makes sense to have adjacent downtown property owners bear the burden of public space maintenance, as they are the principal economic beneficiaries of the park's success. The benefits are orders of magnitude greater than the cost to property owners—millions of current dollars against billions of dollars in capital appreciation.[2]

In the area surrounding Bryant Park, the value added from development around the park has been enormous. The total amount spent redeveloping Bryant Park, in terms of both capital and operations, has not been more than $50 million over the last thirty years. According to my back-of-the-envelope calculations, the increased value since 1992 of only those properties facing the park is well in excess of $5 billion (value being equated here to the capital costs of new construction). These include the Bank of American headquarters at 2 Bryant Park, developed by the Durst Organization (built for $1 billion); the adaptive reuse of the former New York Telephone Company Building at 1095 Sixth Avenue as a headquarters for Met Life and more recently Salesforce ($2.2 billion); the new construction of 7 Bryant Park for the Bank of China ($600 million); the adaptive reuse of the Raymond Hood American Radiator Building into the Bryant Park Hotel ($100 million); and the new construction of condominium

residences at the Bryant at 16 West 40th ($300 million). By anyone's stan-
dards, that initial $50 million was a very good investment. There is no
reason Pershing Square in LA or other similar projects in dense downtown
neighborhoods shouldn't produce similarly impressively leveraged results.

In Downtown LA, there are four BIDs near Pershing Square. One of
those BIDs, the Downtown Center BID, includes the four block fronts facing directly onto Pershing Square (the other three BIDS surround the park
on three sides, one block removed). None of the BIDs saw Pershing Square's
improvement as part of its mission. If the renewal of Pershing Square is
going to be a success, it is going to need its own unique stream of funds for
programming. Ultimately, as in Bryant Park, this may be generated from
commercial activity within the space, and the DRP is going to need to allow
those funds, as well as those now already being generated by the square's
underground garage, to be spent in Pershing Square rather than be spent
citywide, if that is going to happen. Initially, money will need to come from
those with the most at stake, and that is the nearby property owners. PSR or
DRP could have gone door to door with a tin cup asking for support. That
works for the Central Park Conservancy, which is bordered by Central Park
West and Fifth Avenue, among the most desirable residential addresses in
the world, but this is generally an unreliable source of operating income,
particularly in commercial districts. BID funds are more consistent and
eliminate the inevitable "free rider" problem.[3]

Pershing Square presents a fabulous opportunity for LA. Great things
are already happening all around Pershing Square. For example, the Grand
Central Market is a creatively managed, privately owned public space
that is a fantastic asset and a great success. It is just two blocks from the
square.[4] Pershing Square might have been poised on the edge of capturing
that energy and tipping Downtown LA into a uniquely Southern California vibrant, walkable, mixed-use, mixed-income district. However, as
a result of all of the resistance encountered by PSR, it ceased operations.
The Agence Terre proposal is dead. The local council member proposed
his own small capital project and occasional programming, which is now

being implemented by DRP. City hall, the BIDs, and civic leadership have all stated an unwillingness to take a leadership position in improving programing and maintenance in the park. As a result, Pershing Square is likely to remain underused and a liability to Downtown LA for another generation.

———

Public spaces are complex social ecosystems with hundreds of variables operating at the same time. The reason that top-down planning activity often fails to activate public spaces is because it is nearly impossible to predict in advance how those variables will interact in any particular place. It is only through carefully watching how people actually behave in that place with its variables that the right programming mix can be created that will make it be perceived to be safe and inviting. Mistakes will inevitably be made because of the complexity of the behavioral vectors involved. Those mistakes need to be watched and can be incrementally corrected. It is over time, through such observation and correction, that great public places are created.

CHAPTER 8

IMPROVING DOWNTOWN STREETS AND SIDEWALKS

Most of this book so far has been about revitalizing parks, and park improvement is without doubt a spur to economic development and improved quality of life for city residents, with Bryant Park as exhibit A. But the whole range of public spaces—from plazas to Main Streets—can be energized using the same set of techniques. Improving Main Streets can obviously have an even more direct impact on urban economics. Drawing more people to a Main Street not only increases foot traffic for retailers but also makes the street seem safer and induces a virtuous circle of increasing density and activity. Streets and sidewalks generally make up at least a third of a city's land area. Parks are generally only about 15 percent.[1] Streets and sidewalks are a huge and underutilized resource for cities everywhere. They deserve serious thought and attention from placemakers.

Cutting-edge thinking among urbanists and the progressive development community is that American consumers are tired of covered shopping malls and are seeking a return to the walkable downtown retail experience. That's what one hears at the Urban Land Institute and the International Downtown Association, and David Milder's blog analyzing retail trends on medium- and small-sized city downtowns is required reading on this subject (http://www.ndavidmilder.com/blog). But what makes the experience of being on Main Street great? What would make it better? What do we enjoy about being there? What opportunities does this create for aging downtowns across the country?

Improvements to retail facades and merchandizing can have many economic impacts. It is certainly true that people differ in their aesthetic preferences and that aesthetic preferences are often driven by culture and class. These are difficult and serious questions, deserving of more public discussion. They have become more difficult in recent years with the large changes taking place in the retail industry as a result of changes in consumer preferences and the internet. There is a growing realization that much retail space cannot generate the amount of gross sales per square foot that were possible in the late twentieth century.

But there are measurable economic impacts from such improvements.[2] They include increases in first-time customers, increased sales, and higher rents to landlords. There also is a "viral" effect to visual improvements—other retailers tend to improve their properties in response to a critical mass of upgrades along retail corridors. These upgrades include both physical enhancements and better uses. Better-designed and -merchandised retailers, in my experience, also attract sellers of more diverse and higher-quality merchandise. A depressed retail corridor often has many stores selling similar, low-quality goods, as I saw in Jamaica, Queens.

I Speak for the Trees

Jamaica Avenue in southeast Queens, New York, is a one-mile retail subdistrict in a city of more than eight million people and a region of more than sixteen million. For almost its entire length, there is a span of exactly one hundred feet from building line to building line, although the width of the adjacent sidewalks and street varies by block. The street has heavy

Figure 14. The first sidewalk bench we put out. "Everyone" told us that it would become a detriment. Instead, sidewalk benches have become an important feature of the New York City streetscape.

vehicle traffic, with on-street parking on some blocks, more than forty bus lines serving the downtown, and front-door deliveries with double-parked trucks clogging traffic, and the avenue serves as an important (if congested) east/west through-corridor for cars and trucks. Pedestrian counts at its three main intersections are similar to those at Manhattan's most highly trafficked corners. Even after the recession of 2008, retail vacancies remained low. Retail rents at the time this book was written ranged from $60 per square foot in midblock locations to $150 per square foot at prime corners. There were few retail spaces larger than five thousand square feet. The retail mix was heavily oriented toward regional apparel chains catering to a discount customer, with fast food restaurants, local banks, a multiplex movie theater, and a few national retailers mixed in. The primary trade area was generally defined to be a population of about 600,000. While the downtown once boasted three department stores, it more recently had none.

By some measures, particularly the vacancy rate, this was an economically healthy retail corridor. But many people in the community with whom I spoke during my decade working there felt that there was something wrong. They found that the quality and variety of retail offerings did not reflect the preferences of local consumers. They stated that retailers and developers mischaracterized the neighborhood as being lower income. Four blocks north of Jamaica lies one of the most affluent neighborhoods in Queens (Jamaica Estates, birthplace of President Donald J. Trump). The area south and east of the avenue is entirely a community of color, long a neighborhood of African American homeowners and more recently a destination for Caribbean, South Asian, and Central American families. While there are nearby census tracts that do qualify as low income, Queens, surprisingly, is the only county in the United States where African American median household income exceeds that of white families.[3] The principal complaint of local residents about the downtown is that the retailers there do not serve their needs. Middle-class families of color told me that they do their shopping in other places, such as the Roosevelt Field and Green Acres Mall on Long Island and Rego Center and Skyview Mall in other neighborhoods in Queens.

To me, the pedestrian experience on Jamaica Avenue for its entire length is mostly unpleasant. I have spent a great deal of time thinking about why that is. With hundreds of millions of private dollars being invested in housing, hotels, and large-format retail spaces in the neighborhood, there is a need to make sure that area's Main Street is an asset rather than a detriment to the area's economic revitalization.

I've concluded that the one hundred feet between buildings lines along Jamaica Avenue needs to be rethought and reallocated in order to make the street a great place. Those one hundred feet are the equivalent of eight to ten lanes of traffic, if the space were given over entirely to cars. At present, for most of the length of Jamaica Avenue in the downtown, there are two parking lanes and two travel lanes in each direction, along with a moderately wide sidewalk. I would recommend that a new balance should be struck among the claimants to the space, where now the private car (both moving and parked) is essentially privileged over buses and pedestrians. The distribution of space between the sidewalk and street needs to be reevaluated, with buses (perhaps assigned to a dedicated one-way center lane) and pedestrians given preference over private cars.

However, most importantly, the street needs trees. After looking at thousands of images of the best retail streets in the world and in looking carefully at retail streets around the United States and Europe during my travels, I've noticed one relatively inexpensive and easy-to-implement thing that could make Jamaica Avenue (and any other similar retail corridor) better: more and larger trees. Trees seem to make great retail streets. We in the public space management business have embraced seating as a key move in park improvement (and more seating on the sidewalks of a Main Street is definitely a good thing), but we talk less about what an important element shade is.

Once you've given people shade, then you need to provide places for them to sit. Sidewalk benches are a relatively inexpensive way to improve the pedestrian experience. Perhaps the best way to enliven Main Street sidewalks, once you've planted trees, is to allow restaurants and cafés to provide movable outdoor seating—even on narrow sidewalks. Parklets in parking spaces, pioneered in San Francisco, can provide even more space for tables and chairs, again requiring prioritizing the needs of people over the requirements of automobile speed and volume. People sitting and socializing on the sidewalk create highly visible downtown activity. I have noticed that in Spain, municipalities permit restaurants and bars to put tables on just about every available sidewalk and median, even if they aren't immediately in front of the restaurant. Restaurants and bars charge a one-euro premium per dish or drink for outdoor service. As a result, Seville, for example, has one of the liveliest retail zones I have seen.

A good illustration of the importance of shade is the failed Pershing Square in Los Angeles. The essential problem with Pershing Square isn't that it is poorly designed, doesn't have enough seating, has too much

Figure 15. A restaurant in Granada, Spain, with outdoor movable seating. Nothing does more to enliven a public space than food and movable chairs.

hardscape, or is poorly maintained and programmed. While all those things are true, the reason that people avoid the most important public space in Downtown LA is that it is too darn hot. The winning team in the design competition, led by Agence Ter, understood this, and the centerpiece of their proposal for the redesign of Pershing Square was a large shade structure.

Look at the Cours Mirabeau in Aix-en-Provence, France, perhaps the most beautiful "high street" in the world. It is characterized by magnificent chestnut trees, broad sidewalks, and outdoor café seating. The Cours invites everyone to linger. It is both lively and comfortable to be in. Now, most modern retailers will tell landlords that they don't want trees blocking their shop windows and that ideally they want their frontage to be an unobstructed tall glass box. Why do they want this? I suspect it is unverified conventional wisdom. My guess is that they don't really know whether

unobstructed glass storefronts produce higher profits. My experience is
that local and regional retailers seldom have a systematic view of what
drives sales. They know what they think has worked for them over time,
and they do that. They are concerned that doing something else will reduce
their sales. Given that most regional and local retailers complain that their
operations are marginal, this may be a serious concern for them. But my
general observations are that large trees are the things that are distinctive
about most great shopping streets.

ANIMATING RETAIL CORRIDORS

Jamaica retailers know that whatever they are doing now enables them to
at least break even, and they don't want to mess with that formula. Retailers block their windows with paper signs. They crowd their selling floors
with as much merchandise as they can jam in. They hawk incomprehen-
sibly through loudspeakers. Paco Underhill, author of *Why We Buy*[4] and a
student of Holly Whyte, would tell them they are just plain wrong in their
approach to merchandising and are reducing their gross sales through
their conventional but dysfunctional practices.

In order for public and retail spaces to be successful, they have to
be in areas that people want to visit. I'm convinced that great streets
make for great sales, and there are data to back this up. The transformation of State Street in Chicago from a deserted transit way to one of the
most active midmarket retail corridors in the country was driven by a
brilliantly redesigned streetscape with broad sidewalks and ubiquitous
horticultural displays. Great retail streets not only have trees and seating
but are also characterized by continuous retail frontage and a regular
rhythm of doors. All those elements are essential. In Jamaica, for example, the sidewalks need shade and seating, but they also need sidewalk
restaurants, bars, and cafés. Jamaica Avenue is not unique. These kinds
of improvements are of benefit to Main Streets in downtowns across the
country.

Figure 16. In my view, the most beautiful downtown street in the world, the Cours Mirabeau in Aix-en-Provence, France. The historic trees are the defining element.

A reimagined Main Street will be essential to sustaining Jamaica's burgeoning renaissance. Jamaica Avenue has the potential for a distinctive future, serving as a unique, high-quality retail corridor supporting and reflecting a relatively affluent community of color. A formula combining shade, seating, great plants and flowers, a continuous retail street wall, and sidewalk dining and drinking can be a winning one anywhere. Thoughtfully programmed Main Streets are coming back, and transforming them into great places is essential to their renewed success.

Improving the Downtown Streetscape: Look Up

Downtown Jamaica had two of the first business improvement districts in all of New York State—one on 165th Street and one on Jamaica Avenue. The principal motivation for the creation of the BIDs in the late 1970s was the maintenance of streetscape improvements paid for by federal transportation dollars. These two corridors got near-identical treatment to the failed State Street transit mall in Chicago: metro-modular lamp and signal stanchions integrated with traffic directional signs, redbrick pavers, and Belgian-block crosswalks. The crosswalks became eyesores, dotted with black asphalt patches, and in many places have been nearly completely destroyed. The brick pavers may not have been properly set and created substantial trip-and-fall liability for the BIDs. The BIDs no longer had the resources to keep the pavers in a good state of repair and to pay for the required insurance. Those expensive surface treatments became a liability rather than an asset. They generally looked crummy.

I often counsel public space managers not to design in anticipation of poor quality maintenance. High-quality maintenance puts eyes on the street and communicates that a public space is under social control. Good maintenance is essential for successful public-space-improvement projects—so when designing for improvements, it is best to assume that the resources will be put in place for proper upkeep.

But just about the least effective, most expensive thing you can spend your public-space-improvement / downtown revitalization money on is distinctive sidewalks, signature corners, curb cuts, crosswalks, and inset plaques. Very few people actually notice them. Pedestrians tend not to look down. While a broken sidewalk definitely contributes to a sense of disorder in public spaces, the only upgrade they really require is a simple repair. Except in rare and specialized instances (like historic districts), high-design sidewalks and other surface treatments don't generally set the stage for an improved public space experience the way trees or retail presentation do. Nor do they create a higher-quality aesthetic environment, because people using public spaces just don't perceive them. Sidewalk treatments don't have visual impact. It's not what you'd expect, and it seems counterintuitive, but actual experience leads to the conclusion that this is the case.

This was true even before people's eyeballs became glued to their phones. Fancy capital improvements create unnecessary maintenance issues. For some reason, a lot of groups think they haven't done anything unless they've spent tons of money on hardscape. But that's not what makes space users perceive public places as great. This is another example of how programming and maintenance are more important than design and construction. Generally money is better spent on a full-blown horticulture program—which people *will* notice and which *does* improve the perception of public space—than on surface improvements.

To improve Main Street corridors, I recommend an even, well-maintained tinted, poured concrete, perhaps with an interesting pattern, rather than investing a great deal of money in fancy surface treatments. If your organization has unlimited resources and wants to spend tens of millions of dollars on sidewalks, go ahead and make my (and your contractor's) day!

Green Spent on Pink

This conclusion comes from my experience at Grand Central and 34th Street Partnerships, where we floated tax-exempt bonds to pay for streetscape improvements. That money went to new lamp and signal stanchions, new metal halide luminaires, trash baskets, planters, benches, and pink granite signature corners. The corner treatments gobbled up what I recall to be about half of the capital budget. Because of underground infrastructure issues, they were difficult to install. But what I really noticed about them was that nobody else did. Even today, after twenty years, few people know they are there. Yes, they are nice looking, and yes, they demarcate the boundaries of the BID—or they would if anyone noticed them.

They are also difficult/impossible to maintain. All the various agencies and enterprises that need to get at the infrastructure in and around the roadbed jackhammer away at them. It is not the highest priority of the contractors for the local utilities to maintain the integrity of these high-design corners. The BIDs need to monitor this work to make sure that the corners are properly replaced after the infrastructure work is complete. The BIDs have a continuing obligation to pay for the higher-quality surface treatment as well as to replace broken pavers due to ordinary wear and tear.

The "Walk" That No One Can Find

Another example of any expensive physical project that had limited impact: At Grand Central Partnership, we also used bond money to commission artist Greg LeFavre to do bronze sculptural panels to be installed on the sidewalk on East Forty-First Street between Madison and Fifth Avenues in order to create Library Way leading up to the front entrance of the New York Public Library. The panels included one hundred quotations from great literature selected by the library's staff and edited by James Keller, then of the *New Yorker* magazine. My colleague Val Dent and I spent hours reviewing the images proposed by Greg to match the quotes and then proofreading the plans for the panels—maybe a hundred times. When you are casting in bronze, whiteout doesn't quite do the job for fixing typos.

The panels turned out quite beautifully—if anyone sees them, which they definitely don't. I suspect that Val and I are the only ones who remember that they are there. It's likely that no one reading this has ever noticed them. Go look. They are quite nice. But the process of creating them took two years and millions of dollars for fabricating and installing the panels. All for not very much impact. The concept of Library Way added little value since hardly anyone notices it.

Dealing with Visual Chaos on Main Street

Sidewalk Vending

When I went to work for Grand Central Partnership, among my first assignments from Dan Biederman was to figure out how to deal with sidewalk issues that created a sense of disorder for pedestrians and degraded their experience. Those issues were bringing order to street vending, controlling the proliferation of newsracks, improving the appearance of newsstands and payphones, and making public toilets more available. In dense urban centers, sidewalks are not only public spaces but also highly contested real estate, and in New York City, the regulation of activity on them by a range of competing users is arcane and labyrinthine. Not only pedestrians care about sidewalks. Adjacent property owners have a responsibility for cleaning and maintaining their sidewalks, and they care about the activity in front of their multimillion-dollar investments, especially given its impact on ground-floor retail. In Midtown Manhattan, many buildings have vaults under the sidewalks that expand their basement space—and so property owners are concerned about how much weight is put on them and whether anyone is punching holes in them.

A range of commercial activity takes place on New York City sidewalks, and these uses are heavily, if often ineffectually, regulated. There are actually separate governing schemes for *four kinds of sidewalk vendors*: general merchandise, food, veteran, and First Amendment.[5] The DPR has its own scheme for concessioning vendors within city parks as well as on adjacent sidewalks and even sidewalks across the street from a park! The city permits individuals to erect newsstands at any sidewalk location that meets certain siting criteria—with no discretion by the city with respect to the location. If the proposed structure fits, the applicant is entitled to a permit. This is still the case, even with the decline of print media—and newsstands have become part of the city's advertising-driven integrated street furniture program (which also includes bus shelters). The Department of Transportation manages the enforcement of some (but not all) of these rules and is ultimately responsible for the physical condition of the sidewalks and with seeing to it that sidewalk uses don't interfere with transportation (bus stops) or public safety (fire hydrants).

Sidewalks are also the classic "public forum," and under the First Amendment of the United States Constitution, speech activity on sidewalks is provided a high degree of deference. Regulation of First Amendment activity on sidewalks, which includes not only individuals handing out flyers or making speeches but also newsstands and newsracks, is subject to "strict scrutiny" by the federal courts. As a general rule, First

Amendment activity on sidewalks may not be more highly regulated than any other sidewalk activity. In New York City, a wide range of groups and individuals, particularly including the newspapers, have been highly protective of their sidewalk rights.

Vending presents an interesting set of issues, particularly given that many of us in the business of placemaking have changed our views about commercial activity in public spaces over the past twenty-five years. When I first got involved in this kind of work, we all came to it with the assumption that part of our job was to protect public spaces from "commercialization" and from their being hijacked for private use and private profit. This was the basis for widely held community objections to the building of restaurants in Bryant Park. In the eighties, the leading New York City parks advocacy group, the Parks Council (now called New Yorkers for Parks), was categorically opposed to commercial activity in parks. But since then, in part due to the success of the Bryant Park Grill and Café in contributing to the animation of that formerly neglected space, many of us have come around on this issue. We realize that appropriately sited, curated, and regulated commercial activity is a positive generator of activity in public spaces. The extent of commercial activity is a question of the careful balancing of demands by prospective users and activities.

However, sidewalk vending in New York City, as it is currently regulated, is a heavy contributor to the sense of public spaces being chaotic in many places where communities are working to improve the quality of life, including outside of the central business districts of Lower and Midtown Manhattan. In the late 1990s, we at the major Manhattan BIDs felt that the sidewalk-vending environment had improved and had become more orderly and better located. Working with city government, we had put in place rules and resources for the enforcement of them that produced results that made sidewalks and public spaces seem less chaotic. But in recent years, the situation appears to have deteriorated, with carts getting larger and the rules less rigorously enforced.

This is also an issue outside the Midtown core. On Jamaica Avenue, there were many days when vendors seem to be everywhere, selling from tables, out of large trailers parked on the sidewalks, and directly off the ground. They crowded the sidewalks and left trash and grease in their wake. When people came to Jamaica Avenue and said they didn't feel comfortable shopping there, the uncontrolled atmosphere created by vending was a big part of what these first-time visitors were responding to (as were the chaotic retail signs, which we will come back to shortly).

Local elected officials are generally unsympathetic to pleas from merchants, property owners, and community board members to do something about this problem. First, some advocates see this as a "big guy" versus "little guy" issue: the folks with stores are trying to eliminate competition from people with carts and tables. These advocates see street vending as a means of entry-level entrepreneurship for recent immigrants and others with limited ability to raise capital. They cite the long history of sidewalk vending in New York City, conjuring up a vision of sidewalk peddlers on the Lower East Side one hundred years ago. Also, the complexity of the current regulatory scheme leads most policy makers who look closely at sidewalk vending to throw up their hands. The lack of a legislative response drives brick-and-mortar retailers (who pay rent for the space they occupy) crazy.

This regulatory complexity is a major problem. It makes the job of the police department, which ends up having to enforce the rules, extremely difficult and frustrating. The police officer on the beat certainly has many other issues with which to be concerned. NYPD had a sidewalk peddler unit, with a number of officers well versed in the arcana of vending regulation, but they have always been a small group focused on Midtown and Downtown Manhattan. There are few enforcement resources available for other commercial areas of the city. In addition, the sanctions available to enforcement agents are generally not terribly useful. Vendors regard tickets written for violations as a cost of doing business. Without sustained, everyday enforcement, vending in most places is essentially unregulated.

Recently, food vending became a problem even on the sidewalks around Bryant Park, where it is clearly prohibited.

The regulation of food vending is made even more complicated by the rise of the food truck, which has become the vanguard of gentrification and a symbol of urban food culture. Essentially, there is no regulation of food trucks in New York—beyond parking regulations. And what's the recognizable legal difference between a truck parked at the curb selling lobster rolls and a sidewalk cart purveying dirty-water dogs? Here we get into the potential problem of legislating in favor of hipster aesthetic preferences for bahn mi over knishes.

One thing we do know is that in New York City, mobile vending carts have metastasized in size in the last decade. At one time, they were all around the same size, about four feet by twelve feet. Their size is regulated by DOT rules requiring sidewalk clearances for pedestrians and the space between the carts and objects of street furniture. But around 2000, some clever cart builder figured out that you could fit much larger carts on many wide sidewalks outside of Midtown and even in some Midtown and Downtown Manhattan locations. As a result, mobile food carts have become long and tall, and most of them have garish displays of flashing lights.

The number of mobile food vending carts is limited by a cap on the number of permits issues by the city (in this case, the Department of Health—adding another layer of complexity).[6] The places where food carts can go are limited not only by where they can fit but also by a list of streets and blocks on which food carts are prohibited: The list is so detailed and lengthy that no one tasked with enforcing the rules could possibly memorize it. Some of these prohibitions are the results of hearings held by the city in the late 1990s as an attempt to bring some order to the chaos.

With the rise of the larger mobile carts and the restriction of more Manhattan streets, many vendors have chosen to leave Manhattan and locate in commercial districts in the other boroughs. At the same time, vendors of nonfood items are subject to a separate set of locational rules with an entirely different set of prohibited streets. Vendors of First Amendment material (which includes calendars, CDs, and children's board books) are permitted to sell wherever other vendors are permitted to sell.

The First Amendment vendor regulatory scheme is complicated by the fact that under a post–Civil War state law, disabled veterans were exempted from almost all regulation.[7] Given that First Amendment vendors could be wherever other vendors were permitted and that disabled veteran vendors could sell almost anywhere, First Amendment vendors too can sell almost anywhere. Got it? An attempt to impose some level of regulation on disabled veteran peddlers in the late 1990s in the state legislature resulted from a colossal lobbying effort by the city, opposed by state veteran groups. A scheme was enacted by the legislature that prohibited disabled veterans from selling on most streets downtown and in Midtown Manhattan.[8] Legislators said that the battle between proponents and opponents of the bill was the "bloodiest" they had seen (with major backroom arm-twisting from both sides), and the experience, they said, was one they would not choose to repeat. As a result, when the legislation expired as a result of a sunset provision in the early 2000s, no rational person was prepared to attempt to revive it—and vending chaos again ensued.[9]

There is certainly a positive place for well-located, well-designed vending in urban spaces—particularly for food. Street food is solidly established as part of the urban fabric. But street vending in New York City today is a major inhibitor to an improved perception of public space and remains a serious obstacle to enhanced quality of life in downtowns and increased levels of economic activity around the city.

The possibility of improving the regulation of vending does exist. In the late 1990s, a number of us, including Liz Lusskin, then of the Downtown Alliance, and Ray Levin of the Fischbein Badillo law firm, worked together to craft a scheme that would attempt to comprehensively improve the location and regulation of all types of vending (food, general, printed material, disabled veterans). The bill was introduced by then city council member Ken Fisher as Intro. 110-1998.[10] In drafting our bill, we tried to be particularly sensitive to the constitutional protection of First Amendment activity. Hopeless romantic that I am, I still believe that the proposal has merit.

Intro. 110 was based on what we called a "warrant" system, whereby vendors would be assigned specific spots from which to vend, and those spots would be limited to one on a block front, with a list of blocks from which all vending would be excluded. The idea was both to limit congestion and to associate particular vendors with particular spots, which we thought might provide a greater incentive for vendors to raise the level of capital investment in their carts and thereby improve their physical presentation and product offerings. We thought that if vendors knew that they had a claim on a particular spot, they would believe that an investment in their cart would be relatively long term and safe. We were particularly interested in promoting the ability of business improvement districts to partner with vendors within their districts in making such upgrades. Our proposal was assigned to the council's Transportation Committee, where it languished.

I spent a good deal of time thinking about how to improve the character and quality of vending in Downtown Jamaica when I was working there. Mostly we played "whack-a-mole" with illegal vending—when the police occasionally devoted staff to vending enforcement. Greater Jamaica Development Corporation had resources available that could potentially help vendors improve their businesses and quality of life. GJDC had long operated a revolving small business loan fund, which made loans of up to $300,000 to what we called "nearly bankable" small businesses on favorable terms. It seemed to me that these funds could be used to enable vendors to upgrade their carts—if we could be sure that those carts would remain in Downtown Jamaica. My thought was that perhaps we could develop an attractive, high-quality prototype cart or carts on which we would be willing to make loans—secured by the carts. The carts might also provide a level of uniformity that might help in "branding" the downtown.

Building a relationship with vendors through the loan program might also have provided an opportunity for GJDC's business services team to work with the vendors to improve the quality and diversity of their offerings in order both to better serve workers, shoppers, and visitors to Jamaica and to improve vendors' bottom-line results.

GJDC operated five parking facilities in the downtown, including three garages. It was my thought that we could make space available in our facilities for the overnight storage of mobile food carts, making it easier for vendors to operate in Downtown Jamaica. The storage areas might be outfitted with restroom and commissary facilities for their use. Under current practice, vendors have no such facilities available to them—presumably having a significant impact on the quality of the hygiene they are able to practice in plying their wares. Providing running water and perhaps even refrigeration might also improve the quality and diversity of offerings vendors could provide. You don't want to spend too much time thinking about the fact that those amenities are not currently available to New York City food cart vendors.

The quid pro quo for providing such facilities to vendors for no or low cost would have been to work out a locational arrangement that would move the vendors off Jamaica Avenue and the main north-south streets and onto side streets and perhaps limit their number at any single location, thus improving pedestrian circulation and the appearance of the downtown. The ideal ultimate result of such an initiative would be allowing better-located (with respect to sidewalk traffic), better-looking, cleaner, more hygienic vending; providing a more varied and interesting range of food and other offerings; and making them a distinctive and attractive feature of Downtown Jamaica. My idea was for all of this to happen cooperatively as a voluntary arrangement worked out between the vendors, GJDC, and the local BIDs—much like the agreement that created the multivend newsrack regime that we set up at Grand Central Partnership in Midtown in order to eliminate the blight of hundreds of individual newsracks. I was never able to persuade various stakeholders to meet to discuss the proposal, and it made no progress.

The other big idea regarding food vending that I thought might benefit the downtown was to close off traffic at a central block (which ended in T-intersections at both ends) from 11 a.m. to 8 p.m. to create an outdoor food market, perhaps featuring both food trucks and carts as well as movable tables and seating. Despite some considerable efforts and our very high level of pedestrian activity, we were unable to attract quality food trucks to the downtown. My thought was by creating a unique outdoor food venue, we might be able to draw a higher quality of vendor—and thus new visitors—to Jamaica. Again, a best-case scenario would include being in a position to curate the food offerings—rotating vendors and selecting the most imaginative and the highest quality offerings as the market's economic viability proved itself.

These projects would have required cooperation not only among the many vendors and the local nonprofits but also with the police department and the Departments of Transportation, Health, and Consumer Affairs—which all have jurisdiction over vending. A project like this would also have required buy-ins from local merchants (most of whom are generally hostile to vending) and the affected community board (which is usually at the forefront of trying to control underregulated commercial activity in public spaces). A scheme like this, if successful in Jamaica, could have provided a template for other New York City commercial corridors, like Flushing, Downtown Brooklyn, and the Hub in the Bronx.

None of this is very likely to happen, given the amount of work that would be involved in coordinating it and particularly given the difficulty of persuading a critical mass of vendors to participate (which is what ultimately led me to give up on the project). But given the major contribution to a sense of disorder made by underregulated and poorly merchandized vending, I think it remains an important initiative. Creating such a program is certainly no more difficult than the replacement of scattered newsracks with a voluntary, organized system of well-maintained multivend racks that we were able to implement in Manhattan that I described earlier in this book.

In recent years, the political landscape has become more supportive of unregulated street vending. A bill to expand vending was introduced in the city council in 2017 as Intro. 130-2016,[11] a report was issued, and a hearing was held. The council's press release summarized the bill's provisions and the council's objectives in proposing it.[12] The upshot of the legislation was to double the number of food vendor permits. The descriptive language of the bill and the language of the press release reflect the substantial interest on the part of council members in promoting vending and the limited recognition of or interest in the negative impact vending has on downtown revitalization efforts. The mayor's expressed objection to the bill killed it.[13] Even more recently, a state senator has proposed removing much of the regulation of street vending.[14]

Bad Retail Signs

I once gave a tour of Downtown Jamaica to a major retail developer. It was his initial close look at the downtown. We met in a restaurant, and when we walked out on the sidewalk, the first words out of his mouth were, "The streets look awful. The signs are terrible." Nothing is more of an obstacle to downtown revitalization than poor storefront presentation—and nothing is more difficult to fix. Not even regulating street vending is as hard as trying to improve retail signs, storefronts, and the merchandising visible from the street. Unfortunately, many Main Street improvement projects begin with retail sign improvement because they are clearly such a problem. But the low probability of success in improving retail presentation dictates that working on this issue should actually be a low-order priority.

Malls are able to have high-quality signs and retail presentation because of their unitary ownership. Leases give mall owners review rights for retail presentation and have a long list of rules regarding their signs, storefronts, and displays—and mall owners tend to enforce those rules. Downtowns have multiple owners and even more individual retail tenants. There is little incentive for any one landlord to enforce the sign provisions in the lease, since the woman next door isn't enforcing hers and all the landlord really want is his monthly rent check. Why alienate a high-rent tenant who pays every month over a trivial issue like how his or her store looks?

Of course, there is an argument for funky signs and an interesting urban cacophony. I haven't been to Hong Kong, but photos show a frenetic quantity and quality of retail signage. There is also the "grit" school of urban design—designers who advocate for a hip industrial or vaguely threatening old Forty-Second Street aesthetic. Similarly, there is something to be said for charming but disorderly brick or cobblestone pavers like those in the historic neighborhoods of Philadelphia. But I would argue that when dealing with downtown revitalization and improving the perception of public space, creating a sense of order and control is the most practical path to drawing people back to the center. Certainly there are neighborhoods that thrive on difference, and they can provide tremendously exciting urban experiences. These places have tended to develop organically over time and have acquired their unique character over decades—Williamsburg and Dumbo in Brooklyn, for example. But my point is that if a downtown finds itself disinvested and depopulated, improving the perception of safety and order will draw people back to them. Williamsburg is an incredible place—but its current vitality would be nearly impossible to reproduce somewhere else!

For downtown management organizations and local development corporations, working to improve how the street presents itself seems nearly impossible. First, your landlord stakeholders really don't want you annoying their tenants with demands for better graphics that they don't understand. The tenants know their businesses, and small retailers regard their businesses as fragile. They don't want to mess with what works. Their garish neon signs, paper ads in the windows, and racks on the sidewalks are what they have always done, and their business has always produced a profit—"So please, leave me alone and let me do my business." And who are BID managers, with their fancy city planning degrees, to criticize successful local merchants? Maybe they once worked a cash register when they were in high school, but really, what do they know about retailing? At the same time, in speaking with most local or regional retailers, they will also generally tell you that their business is marginal and that they are just getting by. They say that their fear is that if they change any element of their business, it will fail.

This is the classic case of the Tragedy of the Commons—a race to the bottom where each store owner does what he or she thinks is in the store's interest, resulting in an aggregate effect that hurts all stores—and the community at large. Not only might store owners not be making as much money as if they engaged in higher-quality merchandising, but the entire downtown may not be reaching its either quantitative or qualitative potential. Because the downtown seems chaotic, fewer people may be coming to it than might potentially do so. Because their merchandising is haphazard, they might not be generating the sales per square foot that local demographics indicate are possible. These things are nearly impossible to measure. But most of us involved in downtown revitalization believe them to be true based on our firsthand experiences.

An argument is often advanced by "progressives" and "community activists" that "retail improvement" and "gentrification" lead to a loss of local character, homogenization, and a decrease in quality local retailers. They criticize the proliferation of banks, drug stores, and national clothing store brands in some neighborhoods. In my experience, regional and local retailer chains often sell inferior goods at higher prices in lower-income neighborhoods. One regional retailer with stores in Jamaica told me that when a Target or Walmart opened near one of his stores, he closed it—because he couldn't compete with the quality of merchandise at the price those national retailers could offer. Unlike most so-called mom-and-pop stores, national retail chains generally are required to pay minimum wage and overtime and offer at least a modicum of benefits. They are successful because they offer products that people want at attractive prices and provide a retail experience that consumers enjoy. Retail is a very tough business, especially today with the impact of the internet and consumers wanting to spend less time window-shopping or shopping at all. Many communities, including Manhattan, now struggle with a large number of empty storefronts. The successful local retailer selling a unique, high-quality product is a very rare thing—and exists more in the imagination of those neighborhood activists than in actual neighborhoods. In Jamaica, local residents most frequently asked why Target, Victoria's Secret, Macy's, and Red Lobster didn't have stores on Jamaica Avenue.

One of the initiatives we pioneered at Grand Central and 34th Street Partnerships was a retail improvement program, the brainchild of the talented Norman Mintz, the industrial designer, who had been the successful downtown manager in Corning, New York. The program at 34th Street Partnership was, and continues to be, led by my good friend Dan Pisark, who knows more about this stuff than anybody. The initial program model was to provide free storefront design services to Midtown retailers. Very few showed interest. We then enriched the program by offering in addition to pay half the cost of storefront renovations. That also found few takers. Such programs have proliferated and continue to not show terribly good results. Even those programs that offer to provide free design and pay 100 percent of the upgrade cost have difficulty finding interested storeowners. It is a great challenge to persuade retailers to improve their presentation.

Government regulation isn't much help. Zoning rules dictate where flashing neon signs can and can't be. Buildings department regulations often govern letter size and projection limits. But materials, typeface selection, and color go to the heart of design quality and can't be constrained by government. Interior paper and other signs, solid roll-down gates, and piled-up merchandise inside the store visible through the windows are nearly impossible to control. They contribute to visual chaos in many downtowns. Buildings departments, which generally have insufficient resources to do their important work of protecting building safety, don't really want to get involved in matters of aesthetics.

But working with local government can prove valuable. One of the most effective things we did at the 34th Street Partnership was to work with the Department of Transportation, which had jurisdiction over the sidewalk, to ban the projecting canopies affixed to it. In 1992, the street was overwhelmed with projecting structures that retailers saw as advertising for their businesses. Some were gigantic. Most were garish. None was for protection from the weather for customers. Many blocked great-looking historic facades. Because DOT had authority over streets and sidewalks, those canopies were subject to the agency's rule-making authority. We persuaded DOT officials that the canopies served no useful public purpose, were often obstacles to pedestrian flow, and were generally eyesores. DOT published a rule in the *City Record* banning poles holding up the ends of the canopies from being affixed to the sidewalk and limiting the distance awnings could project from buildings (some of which, at the time, cantilevered several yards over the sidewalk). They waited the requisite period. They held the required public hearing (at which only we, the retailers we had enlisted to support the change, and a few medical practitioners trying to defend their signs appeared). Thirty days later, the ban became effective, and the streetscape was transformed. The impact was amazing. The opening up of the view along Thirty-Fourth Street vastly improved the visual experience of shopping there. Since all of the canopies came down at the same time, no business suffered from a competitive disadvantage. It was one of the most dramatic downtown improvements I have experienced and was a major step toward attracting new retailers and offering higher-quality and more varied merchandise to the district.

New York State has an excellent Main Street program that subsidizes downtown retail facade improvement across the state, but the program's resources are limited, and the state imposes no minimum design standard, so the outcomes vary. New York City has (incorrectly, in my legal view) determined that BID revenues cannot be spent on private property, hamstringing the ability of New York City BIDs to work on this issue with their own dollars.

Downtown managers need to be sure that the design professionals with whom they contract to assist them in this work are familiar with best practices in Main Street improvement—which unfortunately is not always the case.[15] Those Main Street program dollars are precious, and it is important to make sure that they are effectively spent. What we have seen is that when a relatively small critical mass of landlords or retailers upgrade their signs and retail presentations, other property owners and merchants feel obliged to upgrade as well. This creates a virtuous circle. If a downtown management organization wants to improve the retail signs on its Main Street, it needs to create a program that focuses on establishing such a critical mass by whatever means are necessary. Those means are always going to be expensive and require the expenditure of public or quasi-public funds on private property, and the process of finding cooperative retailers is going to be hugely time consuming.

There was a lovely art deco structure in Jamaica with a terrific first-floor banking room, the facade of which was blanketed with unsightly signs. Almost all of those signs were compliant with New York City's building code. The landlord told me at the time that in order to secure leases with his tenants, allowing them to post the signs was essential. There wasn't much I could do to help improve the look of this handsome building scarred by poor signs. It was frustrating. Nonetheless, this work is important to attracting high-quality retailers and improving the downtown experience for pedestrians. National retailers care about how their brand is presented and don't want to have it tarnished by association with a retail strip they regard as substandard—whatever the economics and demographics of the surrounding community. Innovative small retailers and start-ups selling unique or unusual items want to be associated with a quality environment. Only by getting a handle on how existing merchants present themselves to consumers can these new companies and developers interested in making large capital investments in bigger format spaces be attracted to downtowns.

VISUAL MONOTONY, BLANK WALLS,
AND THE IMPORTANCE OF DOORS

At the opposite end of the aesthetic spectrum is the problem of *blank* walls and large buildings with only one ground-level door. Inactive first floors of large buildings are even more of a placemaking problem than chaotic signs. Varied building signs at least signal a certain level of downtown activity. Dead blocks created as a result of bad design decisions prevent street activity and as a result promote a sense of a lack of safety.

The issues around architecture and placemaking are among the most interesting and controversial in the field. I have argued here that in the creation of public spaces, programming and maintenance are more important than design. One of my themes in this book has been that just about any public space, no matter how "badly" designed, can be made active through programming and maintenance. With respect to buildings, though, there are ground-level design features that can eliminate human scale and a sense of place.

Over the last thirty years, the city, state, and federal governments all built major new structures in Downtown Jamaica in order to stimulate economic activity. These included an extensive campus for York College, a one-million-square-foot building for the Social Security Administration (SSA), a home for the family court, and a lab and office development for the Food and Drug Administration (FDA). All of these structures drew on a similar design vocabulary that influenced many large urban buildings of the 1960s and 1970s. The York campus in particular has a fortress-like presence on the street with cement walls and is surrounded by a high fence. The campus was designed with a fairly large number of entrances that were set in severe hardscaped plazas. But ultimately, all but two of those entrances were kept locked, leaving only those two doors for security staff to police.

I suppose the idea at the time was to protect the people and activities inside these buildings from the imagined ravages of the contemporary

urban environment. The goal was to create islands of solid, concrete calm
in seas of municipal unrest. The family court building was built with only
two entrances (front and back) and no first-floor windows. The FDA was
built on the York campus off the main traffic street, with only one public entrance leading to a parking lot surrounded by a fence. The massive
SSA building was set in the center of the downtown on one of the busiest
corners. While it was designed with multiple doors and street-level retail
space, only one door was used and the retail space was never rented. These
are not positive attributes.

A lot of the discussion of design and placemaking is about the problems created by "starchitects." No architect that I know of says that he or
she intends to ignore a building's context. When I was working at Barnard
College, the designer we engaged to create a new campus building made
a great point in her competition presentation about how her firm was
all about contextual design. She then designed a structure with one door
(on the interior of the campus); the back of the building, which faced the
street, was made up of mostly opaque panels. By context, she meant that
her building made reference to other nearby structures in terms of form
and color, and she succeeded in that. But the building was a solo composi-
tion set apart from the city, the sidewalk, and pedestrians.

From a pedestrian and a placemaking perspective, the number of doors
on the sidewalk and the materials and ability of light to enter (and exit)
the first three floors are crucial. What happens to the design above the first
three floors isn't all that important to how the public spaces around the
building are experienced by a pedestrian. The folks at STIPO have given
as much thought to this as anyone I know.[16] The more doors you have
leading to the sidewalk, the more activity the building creates. Large structures with only one or two entrances limit street life beyond anything else
I can point to. Similarly, the more glazing there is at eye level and just
above, the more the building contributes to the liveliness of the pedestrian experience—although long stretches of glass curtain wall, with no
doors and limited activity behind them, also read as blank. Blank walls

are antithetical to the public space experience. This is particularly true of many big-box store buildings that have one door in the front, blank walls on the two sides, and a loading dock in the rear.

I'm not arguing here that there is no place for high design structures that are entirely expressions of an architect's artistry. What I am saying is that city streets and downtowns are generally not good places for such structures. I'm also saying that high design structures that are next to streets and sidewalks need to observe some basic principles as described by STIPO (and others) about contributing to the pedestrian experience. That's not to say that there aren't brilliant exceptions. The plaza in front of the Centre Beaubourg in Paris certainly hops. But an architect ignores the basic principles of doors, windows, and the amount of window coverage of the first three floors at his or her peril of deadening the public spaces adjacent to his or her structure.

In Vancouver, for example, city planners and designers are paying attention to the pedestrian experience in just this way. New, large high-rise residential structures without ground-floor retail are required to have maisonettes or professional offices on the street level with their own doors to the sidewalk. That animates the street—much like the beloved town-house blocks of New York City.

Going back to Jamaica, Queens, improving the public spaces in the downtown around these large government buildings continues to be a challenge. The government agencies that run these buildings haven't really gotten with the program of placemaking (despite the Federal General Services Administration's "good neighbor" initiative[17]). At the SSA building, contractors showed up one day without notice and started building hulking bollards around the building, presumably for security purposes. In one place, they built out the sidewalk into a city-designated bus lane in order to create space for the bollards—and made the bus lane nonfunctional. Supposed security concerns (that may not be based on actual research and facts regarding effective strategies for increasing security) are a great threat to placemaking (which may increase the security of public spaces, with good uses driving out bad). Of course, all of this requires balancing the various interests affected.

Another example from Jamaica: taking down the fences around York College and opening more of its doors would make the spaces around the campus more active and inviting. Creating sidewalk uses around public buildings, like chairs and tables, might activate those spaces. The leaders of the Queens Public Library showed some sensitivity to these issues in renovations of the central library branch (which itself is of a merely functional design) in Downtown Jamaica.

Architects working in an urban context need to pay attention to the way their designs relate to the street. The lower floors of their structures need to be active and open to light. They need to push back (politely) against security concerns that are not evidence based. Architects have the power to do a lot of good in enabling activation of the public spaces around their buildings (and a good deal of harm if they ignore the pedestrian experience).

Dull, deserted Main Streets are fixable. Shoppers, visitors, and even residents can be brought back to them. It requires providing those Main Streets with a sense of place and making people want to be there. As with so much of the rest of placemaking practices, many of the effective tactics seem counterintuitive or at least contrary to conventional wisdom. But by favoring pedestrians over cars and trucks and properly maintaining and programming downtowns, they can be made lively and vital. Fixes can be as simple and inexpensive as planting trees and flowers and providing people with places to sit. It also requires regulating the commercial activity that occurs between the buildings to avoid the chaos of vending and poor retail presentation.

CHAPTER 9

SUBURBAN MAIN STREETS

WHAT WORKS

A good deal of the focus in the field of urban revitalization has been on the largest cities. In *The Creative Class* in 2002, Richard Florida highlighted a return of college-educated young people and retirees to center cities. Big cities across the country celebrated their revitalized, twenty-four-hour downtowns and competed to attract young creatives as the latest economic-development strategy. While that movement was certainly real and visible, Joel Kotkin pointed out in *The Next Hundred Million*[1] that the number of individuals moving downtown was relatively small and that most Americans like their cars and backyards and continue to prefer the suburbs.

According to Kotkin, while 26 percent of Americans characterized where they live as "urban," more than twice as many people—53 percent—say they live in the suburbs.[2] What does placemaking have to offer the majority of Americans who live in the suburbs? Can their quality of life be improved by improving public spaces outside of dense urban environments? These are important questions because they affect a majority or near majority of Americans. Dealing with suburbs is more complicated for placemaking, which focuses on walkability, when those suburbs are designed around the car. But there are certainly ways in which suburban quality of life can be enhanced by giving priority to pedestrians over cars in planning for suburban Main Streets and by improving the maintenance and programming of suburban parks and public spaces. Thinking about creating spaces for social engagement in the suburbs requires thinking about expanding the definition of public spaces to include places like libraries, schools, and even shopping malls. Libraries in particular, in the technological transition away from print, can be reimagined as public spaces and programmed for social engagement. Almost every community has a library, and those libraries can serve a unique role in less dense communities in drawing residents together.

Placemaking has a great deal to offer suburban communities. Those of us interested in community building and economic development need to spend more time working in the suburbs (as well as in smaller cities and rural communities—more about that in chapter 14). Take, for example, two communities in Westchester County, New York: Larchmont and Sleepy Hollow. They are very different communities, with contrasting demographics and with very different Main Streets and public spaces. In both towns, the public spaces had too many empty stores and virtually no street life. It's interesting to note as well that a number of places farther north along the Hudson have experienced revitalization. The city of Hudson has a Main Street jammed with restaurants and stores selling art and home furnishings. Beacon is the home to a contemporary art museum. Even farther north, Saratoga is a model of downtown revitalization done right.

LARCHMONT

The village of Larchmont has two downtowns. One is focused around the commuter train station and the other is along a six-lane state road. Larchmont is a commuter suburb twenty miles from Manhattan, with

Figure 17. The empty movie theater in the center of Larchmont, New York. Empty theaters are challenging to repurpose and program.

a population of about six thousand and a median household income of about \$165,000.[3] Notwithstanding the relative prosperousness of the community and the fact that it actually has a town center served by transit, which many suburbs do not, in recent years, those commercial corridors have had many empty spaces. Residents of Larchmont and its neighboring towns tend not to shop in the village's downtown.

In 2017, I went for a look. The commercial center at the transportation hub has excellent "bones." It has interesting vernacular architecture and a critical mass of colocated retail spaces. But on any given Saturday, the main commercial corridors of Larchmont had many cars and oddly few people. The downtown had a number of municipal lots and quite a bit of curbside parking. Both were unmetered and had a two-hour limit. While most of the spaces were full, there are enough empty ones to indicate that anyone coming to the downtown could reasonably find a space on a prime shopping day.

Palmer Avenue, the main street near the train station, is a four-lane (with two lanes of parking), low-capacity street. Most of the retail is one story, with only a small number of national chains. The architecture is of high quality, and the retail signs are for the most part understated and attractive. There were a few restaurants, but the activity in those eating and drinking establishments was not visible to pedestrians because they had small windows and curtains and blinds obscuring them. A thoughtful sidewalk improvement program had recently been implemented with quality surface treatments (expensive but noticeable and positive), benches, and trees (which, being newly planted, are quite small).

The other retail center is the Boston Post Road. The Post Road is a main thoroughfare, with heavy, fast-moving traffic; narrow sidewalks; and a good many blank walls. Just beyond the downtown, on either approach to Larchmont, the Post Road was lined with strip malls, midbox retailers, and other pedestrian-unfriendly uses. The civic center, the library, and village hall are just off the Post Road. Occupancy rates and rents were higher on the Post Road than on Palmer—no doubt due to the traffic counts.

To increase pedestrian traffic, the fundamental change that needed to be implemented in Larchmont's downtown was rebalancing the allocation of public space in favor of pedestrians over cars. That's a pretty radical notion for communities designed around cars, but that was what needed to happen in order to animate central public spaces, increase economic activity, and improve the quality of life for village residents. Given the conventional wisdom about the relationship between parking and retail in suburban retail centers, it would take a lot of persuading to get this right and to implement pedestrian-friendly design.

Consumer spending patterns are in flux, something that retail guru David Milder has called "the new normal."[4] Milder concludes that consumer retail habits are in the process of radical change as a result of the internet and generally lower levels of customer spending. Downtowns and retailers need to adapt to those changes by providing an enhanced social experience for consumers and by exploiting multiple distribution channels. Thought and energy has to be expended on generating more activity among the stores in suburban downtowns; methods include putting out movable tables and chairs, creating parklets in the street bed, encouraging food and beverage purveyors to put tables and chairs out on the sidewalk for as much of the year as possible, and creating a regular schedule of public events. Empty stores can be animated through temporary uses like art studios and galleries. People today don't window-shop as a leisure activity. Rather, they are looking for positive social interaction with their neighbors, even in forms as simple as people watching! That's what will get them away from their screens and monitors and into the downtown.

The Larchmont downtown had a highly successful seasonal green market in a train station parking lot on the other side of the tracks from Palmer Avenue. Its location away from the center of the downtown diminished the positive impact it had on activity in the center of the village. The green market should have been moved to a more central location on the other side of the tracks—perhaps even to a street closed for the purpose.

The pedestrian experience in crossing the commuter railroad tracks had to be improved. The quarter-mile bridge over the tracks serves as a barrier between residential neighborhoods and the downtown. The wide and long bridge is overdesigned for the car traffic it carries, had no shade, and felt deserted and exposed.

Downtown zoning needed to be revised to increase residential density. More people living in the downtown area create more pedestrian customers for retail. Larchmont's rail station, with access to commercial centers in both Manhattan and Fairfield County, presents an attractive opportunity for mixed-use, mixed-income, transit-oriented development. Village-owned flat parking lots present a valuable opportunity for development (with the developed lots being replaced with well-designed parking structures on other lots in order to maintain the number of available spaces).

Also particularly problematic for Larchmont was the presence of an empty single-screen movie theater in the downtown—something characteristic of first-ring/streetcar suburbs around the country. With an empty movie theatre, the challenge is to find a use that activates the theater on a daily basis. Movie theaters that have been taken over by communities for use as local arts centers have generally presented too few events and an insufficient level of activity to generate the critical mass that would allow them once again to become an asset to the downtown.[5]

Larchmont has the benefit of being the home to many high-net-worth families, and the capacity likely exists within the community for acquiring underutilized property assets and repositioning them—with progressive community leadership and the right legal/financial structures in place. Many downtowns find that the owners of underutilized property are from outside the community, uninterested and difficult to reach. In my experience, the best way to deal with passive ownership that is creating negative external effects in a downtown is either to bring to the owner a potential tenant who is so attractive (paying a high proposed rent, or of sufficient size to be a secure credit risk, or both) that it is difficult/impossible to turn the opportunity down or to buy the current owner out at a handsome price and reposition the property through adaptive reuse to enhance its value to an active investor. Both of these are certainly challenging to organize—but worth the effort for key properties.

Who can/should take a leadership role in effectuating these kinds of changes in policy? In Larchmont, there was certainly interest in city hall for change, but this is not the kind of work that small-city mayors normally take on, since their role is seen as primarily helping existing businesses (as opposed to the traditional economic-development work of attracting *new* business). In larger places, business improvement districts have in the past been advocates for placemaking, but as I argued earlier, small BIDs (and BIDs in smaller towns and cities have limited resources almost by definition) tend not to have the money to be very effective. In Gloversville, New York, discussed in chapter 14, the county economic-development entity actually hired a person to lead the downtown revitalization effort as the result of the advocacy of an unusually thoughtful local elected official. In most places, I suspect it will take private-sector leadership of both volunteer residents and business people to inaugurate people-oriented downtown redefinition.

Sleepy Hollow

Sleepy Hollow is on the Hudson River on the other side of Westchester County from Larchmont. While it is a commuter town, thirty miles from Manhattan, served by the Metro-North Railroad, it has an entirely different character from Larchmont. It is larger, with a population of about ten thousand people, and it is significantly more diverse. A majority of the population of the village is Hispanic, principally Central American, who primarily live in the dense downtown area. The non-Hispanic village residents live mostly in areas that are more typical of the familiar leafy Westchester suburbs. Two Metro-North commuter stations are easily accessible to the village. The median household income (MHI) for the village is around $54,000, but the MHI for those who are Hispanic and live downtown is considerably lower.[6]

Sleepy Hollow has a significant place in American literary history as the setting of Washington Irving's (1783–1859) "The Legend of Sleepy Hollow." Irving was the Stephen King of nineteenth-century America as well as America's Homer—the bard of our national myths. His book *The Life of George Washington* cemented in public memory the iconic image of "the founder of our country," and his *Tales of the Alhambra* was an international best seller. Irving wrote the ridiculously silly but culturally influential *A History of New York* under the nom de plume of Diedrich Knickerbocker. His short story set in Sleepy Hollow is still widely read and anthologized and has created a Halloween-focused cottage industry in the river towns of Westchester County, New York, including its namesake.

Sleepy Hollow was known for a very long time as North Tarrytown but changed its name in 1996 to take advantage of its association with Irving's story about the infamous Headless Horseman. The most important economic fact about Sleepy Hollow's modern history is that it was home to a ninety-acre General Motors automobile assembly plant. In its heyday, the plant employed 2,100 people. As a result, North Tarrytown was more of a working-class community than the other Westchester County Hudson River towns, and the village's retail businesses were geared to serving the plant's employees. When the plant closed in 1996, it left an empty, environmentally degraded site.

In 2006, Diversified Realty Advisors of Summit, New Jersey, and SunCal of Irvine, California, partnered to purchase the property from GM, which adjoins the Hudson River and presents the potential for waterfront exposure, and proposed to build 1,177 residences, 35,000 square feet of office space, 135,000 square feet of retail, and a 140-room hotel. The project, called Edge on Hudson, was, at the time of this writing, the subject of a nearly completed two-year zoning special permit application to the village, and site remediation was nearly complete. As part of the special permit, the developers agreed to turn over to the village an adjacent seventy-acre site for its use as a public space and a facility for its public works department along with some cash to pay for capital improvements to the property.

Figure 18. Chestnut Street, Valley Street, and Washington Street come together just over Beekman Street—Sleepy Hollow, New York's main street. The downtown sidewalks need animation.

The legacy of the Rockefeller family also has a big footprint in Sleepy Hollow and adjacent communities. The village is the home of Historic Hudson Valley (HHV) and its Philipsburg Manor property, which draws about one hundred thousand visitors a year. Kykuit, a Rockefeller estate, last used by Governor Nelson Rockefeller, is nearby. Visitors to Kykuit must purchase their tickets at Philipsburg Manor. Nearby is the Michelin three-star restaurant Blue Hill at Stone Barns, one of the country's most important farm-to-table restaurants (where the prix fixe was $258).

While Irving himself lived in the village of Sunnyside in Irvington just to the south, he is buried in the Sleepy Hollow Cemetery, along with Brooke and Vincent Astor, Walter Chrysler, Andrew Carnegie, Samuel Gompers, and a host of other notables. The cemetery is part of the Headless Horseman / Halloween mystique of the area and draws an international clientele of tourists in the fall.

The village prizes its distinctive identity as an economically and ethnically diverse community with a dense downtown. The village faced the
significant danger that once construction of the huge Edge on Hudson
project is complete, Beekman Street, the village's main thoroughfare con-
necting the Route 9A / Broadway north-south artery with the Edge on
Hudson and the waterfront, could become merely a driveway for the project. Beekman had a few bars and restaurants as well as many bodegas and
other businesses serving the local Hispanic community. The architecture
along Beekman, while not particularly distinctive, is a fairly uniform rep-
resentation of early twentieth-century vernacular commercial design.

The village needed to concentrate its economic-development energy in
a small, defined geographic area—in its case, on Beekman Street between
Kendall and Lawrence Avenues. The goal should have been to create
a critical mass of activity in that corridor in an attempt to attract business from existing residents, new homeowners at the Edge on Hudson,
and visitors to the HHV properties. Creating critical mass is an essential placemaking tactic. I have found that when economic-development
projects are clustered—generally no more than one or two blocks from
each other—they have significantly greater secondary impact. Synergies
are created. Their proximity amplifies their power and creates secondary
effects. Private investment tends to be drawn to a critical mass of development. The whole is much more than the sum of the parts.

However, when such projects are spread out all over town, as unfortunately they often are, no matter how well designed or thoughtful those
projects may be, they tend to have limited secondary effects. They become
"one-offs" and don't draw other development activity near them. A good
example of this is Newark, New Jersey, which for decades has had a number of high-quality economic-development projects, including a performing arts center and a new office building for the Prudential Insurance
Company. But those projects aren't grouped within short walking distances of each other and as a result have not generated much in the way

of synergistic results. The issue of critical mass in downtown revitalization projects cannot be overemphasized.

There were already three or four bars and restaurants in or near Beekman in Sleepy Hollow, and the village needed to raise their profile—particularly in a partnership with HHV—and add to their number. Village residents of the neighborhoods outside of the downtown tended to go to other nearby communities for their entertainment and dining. This, no doubt, arose out of Sleepy Hollow's long reputation as a working-class town that is a little rough around the edges. That perception needed to be changed without materially altering the village's appealing existing character.

The public space along Beekman, from building line to building line, probably reflecting the village's early nineteenth-century history, is only sixty-five feet, presenting a challenge for public space animation. Notwithstanding, I believe that existing restaurants could have been encouraged to place movable tables and chairs on the sidewalks as well as on parklets built in parking spaces in front of those storefronts. I learned from my travels in southern Spain that almost no sidewalk is too narrow for café tables and chairs because the objective isn't pedestrian throughput but public space animation. The critical mass effect is just as important for bars and restaurants. Clusters of bars and restaurants create a destination and tend to be more successful. To facilitate this, a municipality can assist in the creation of new eating and drinking establishments by reducing the economic risk to developers and operators by reducing the capital investment required. For example, a local development entity can do the build-out of the kitchens and mechanical systems of empty retail spaces and perhaps take control of those spaces and lease them out at submarket initial rent in order to attract restaurant operators to the downtown by decreasing their initial operating risk. This is essentially what we did in creating the Bryant Park Grill and Café and the Pershing Square Café, both of which were catalytic developments for their neighborhoods. The food and drink establishments of Sleepy Hollow also needed to have a higher

visible presence on the websites of the major local attractions: HHV
and the cemetery.

The village might aggressively have attempted to have owners make
their vacant retail property along Beekman available to artists as work
spaces at low cost on a month-to-month basis in order to activate those
areas—particularly at night. The downtown already had a high density
of residents who appeared to spend a lot of time outdoors in the warmer
months. Some of that activity was regarded by village leadership as antisocial, including the sale of hard drugs, so those places needed to be repro-
grammed with positive social uses, following the maxim that "good uses
drive out bad." One possible idea for a key empty parcel in downtown
Sleep Hollow was the creation of a market: perhaps a night market, featuring the food of the countries of origin of local residents, including
Ecuador, Columbia, Chile, Puerto Rico, and the Dominican Republic. A
Latin American food market would have enabled entrepreneurial activity
by local low-income residents, been unique in Westchester County, leveraged the unique Latino character of Sleepy Hollow, and drawn visitors
from around the region. Such a market could have begun with booths
under canvas, and if it had become sufficiently successful, it could have
been moved to a food hall built specifically for the market.

As in Larchmont, the existing very successful farmers' market, which
was well run by a village group, needed to be moved from a park that is
not particularly close to Beekman, the main street, either into the roadbed
or to a nearby parking lot to maximize the potential synergies with other
village businesses. Its park presence did not create the powerful critical
mass adjacencies and as a result failed to maximize its potential to assist in
village revitalization.

On one block along Beekman, in front of an elementary school, planters and benches had been put out, but they were not well maintained.
Plantings and hanging baskets along the main street were also not well
maintained. The practical purpose of streetscape improvements is to convey a message of social control of public space. Not maintaining them

sends exactly the opposite message—that nobody cares or is watching out. That sidewalk was in a key location for animation. The planters needed to be replanted and taken care of, and the block needed more intensive programming. Its location in front of a school made it a good location for the selling of food (and, of course, ice cream) out of stands or maybe trucks. Perhaps a regular crafts fair (featuring Latin American goods sold by local residents) could have been successful here. Between the sidewalk and the school was a large parking lot, which ordinarily produces a dead spot. But programming this block could have turned a liability into an asset.

Sleepy Hollow was invisible to drivers who are passing through town. The main street is perpendicular to the secondary road through the village. The gateways into the downtown needed to be more clearly marked. You can drive by Beekman (as I have many times) on Route 9 and not even know that there is a commercial district there. The best solution would have been a sculpture or mural highlighting the village's history and perhaps listing its businesses. But even a banner (which I generally view as lame) would have been better than the attractive but uninformative historic clock.

The village was very focused on what is called the "East Parcel," which is across the Metro-North tracks from the Edge on Hudson and was deeded to the village by the developers along with some money to design and build out new public space. While additional public space is always welcome, especially in a community as dense as the center of Sleepy Hollow, the East Parcel was too far from the activity of Beekman Street (or Sleepy Hollow's other two commercial corridors) to contribute to its revitalization. In addition, it is essential to note again that maintenance and programming are more important to the success of public space than design and capital investment. In the short term, the village needed to focus on inexpensive, flexible solutions to activating the parcel to see what kind of uses residents would actually take advantage of. Putting out chairs and tables, erecting temporary shade structures, and making available chess boards and bocce balls all would have been low-cost ways to activate public space. But such programming has to be tailored to the preferences of local residents, and extensive outreach needs to take place to engage those likely to make use of the new space in a discussion of what activities they might like to see there. King Park in Jamaica was in the center of a Central American community, and soccer players frequently took over nearly every open inch of the space in numerous simultaneous matches, even where there was no grass, goals, or marked lines! So soccer would definitely be a likely successful activity in Sleepy Hollow. Once programming began, trial and error would be essential to determine the right mix of activities that serves local park users.

Most importantly, in developing the parcel, the village needed to make sure substantial resources for maintenance and programming were identified in its operating budget before committing to tens of millions of dollars of capital funds.

The issue of parking tends to dominate discussions of revitalization of Main Street corridors. The only local transportation in the village was a county-run bus that ran hourly at most. While Sleepy Hollow owned only one off-street lot, there were a number of privately owned lots that could have become available to the public in the evening. There was also additional surface parking planned for the Edge on Hudson and the East Parcel. The village might have thought about running a tram from Route 9 (where the existing village-owned lot is located) along Beekman to the Edge on Hudson (which was to have its own parking) as well as to the two Metro-North stations used by the community. The tram might have been paid for out of receipts from a repriced parking system. Rates at the curb should have been raised in order to increase turnover and to encourage parkers to use off-street lots. The entire system should have been priced in such a way as to pay for its management, enforcement, and the tram. Such a tram should have reduced vehicle traffic on Beekman and increased the village's walkability.

———

Suburban downtowns have great potential to become vital public places. The stereotype of suburbs as vast cultural wastelands is snobbish and overstated. As Kotkin explains, most Americans live in suburbs—and will continue to do so for decades to come, notwithstanding the preference of urban elites for large cities. The tools that have been developed over the last two decades to improve the urban core can be used outside that core. The possibility of improving the quality of life in and the level of economic activity of suburban public spaces (and perhaps even reduce automobile use there) is real—and important.

CHAPTER 10

HOMELESSNESS AND EQUITY IN PUBLIC SPACES

For people of goodwill working to revitalize public spaces in this country, the issues of homelessness and equity are unavoidable, difficult, and politically hazardous. I described in chapter 4 the political and legal challenges faced by Grand Central Partnership arising out of its decision to directly provide services to the homeless. I'm certainly not an expert on the issue of homelessness, but addressing the problems created by the presence of people effectively living in public spaces has been a constant in my work. As a result, I have had the privilege of working with dedicated and knowledgeable individuals like Robert Hayes, the founder of the Coalition for the Homeless, and MacArthur "Genius" Grant winner Rosanne Haggerty, the founder of Common Ground (today called Breaking Ground) and now the leader of Community Solutions. Bob and Rosanne have dedicated their lives to thinking about how to address the needs of the severely disadvantaged. I have learned a great deal from each of them.

There are (at least) two major populations of individuals without shelter. The much larger group is composed of homeless families. Families, however, are rarely present in public spaces. The people generally found to be living in public spaces or engaged in antisocial behavior in them are single adults. Homeless families have a complex array of needs—but those needs are different from those of the much smaller group of single adult homeless individuals. Homeless families—often single mothers with children—aren't frequently found on the street. Their issues often have more to do with accessing government benefits or the direct loss of housing than those arising out of mental illness or substance abuse. By contrast, single homeless adults are often resistant to receiving service and are on the street in no small part because of their defiance of authority. Their unwillingness to be told what to do prevents them from accessing money, health care, and other services and results in a preference for living on the street.

It is single adult homeless people with whom public space managers need to be concerned, and it is they who I will be discussing in the rest of this chapter. The data show that a significant majority of single adult homeless clients have mental health and substance abuse issues, and sometimes both.

The question of why people living in public spaces is deemed to be a bad thing is at the heart of the philosophical issues around approaches to addressing homelessness. I have talked with people who believe that individuals without shelter have a right to occupy public space because they have no place else to go and/or because their visible presence reminds the public of the ruthlessness and heartlessness of capitalism and American society. There are others who believe that improving public space is inherently elitist, motivated by a desire to displace the most disadvantaged. Still others argue that public space revitalization is a forerunner of "gentrification," the leading edge of changes in community character and the removal of poor people from a neighborhood. These are serious challenges that no thoughtful person can reject out of hand.

But as I discussed in chapter 2, rightly or wrongly, most other visitors regard the presence of apparently homeless people in public spaces as an indication of a threat to their physical safety. Allowing homeless people to sleep in or engage in antisocial activity in public spaces is effectively to remove those spaces from being available to be used by others. One need only walk around Market Street and the Civic Center in San Francisco to understand the obvious problems created by people living and engaging in antisocial behavior in public spaces. It is often difficult or even impossible to walk up or down the stairs to the Muni on Market Street in San Francisco without having to walk over someone. There is no *good* way (either morally or physically) to walk over someone.

Few rational people choose to live in the urban outdoors. Again, the San Francisco Civic Center is a good place to find evidence of this. It is not a tolerable "lifestyle choice" for individuals to occupy public space full time, without access to sanitary facilities and protection from rain, snow, and cold weather. In my admittedly nonprofessional judgment, anyone "choosing" to live that way is engaged in an antisocial activity.

Given those assumptions / first principles, the question then becomes, How do you humanely and compassionately provide appropriate services to unsheltered people in public spaces? Dealing with homelessness by enforcement likely implicates constitutional issues, is not compassionate or humane, and, perhaps ironically, is not effective. With enforcement, the people doing the enforcing have to keep coming back. Once the enforcement agents are no longer present, the situation tends to revert, and the unhoused tend to return.

The key to assisting people without shelter who are occupying public spaces is to evaluate their needs and to secure for them the services they require. Since many, if not most, single adult homeless people are on the street because they are resistant to service, effective outreach to them requires persistent offers of service and highly trained outreach workers who can both gain their trust and evaluate their needs. This is not simply about offering the unsheltered housing but requires evaluating clients' needs and providing appropriate services, whether they be health care or mental health or addiction services. Housing options for service-resistant clients are a necessary but insufficient precondition to meeting their needs and addressing the cause of their antisocial behaviors.

Improving public space is inclusive. It makes those spaces accessible to more people from the community. Further, when public spaces are improved, there are enormous positive secondary effects on the surrounding neighborhood. New residents and businesses are attracted to the area. Those residents generally tend to be higher income and whiter than existing residents—bringing what is often derisively called "gentrification." But I will make the unconventional argument here that gentrification also brings economic and racial integration to communities as well as improved retail options and a higher quality of life in public spaces.

THE PARABLE OF HENNEPIN: HOMELESSNESS IN MINNEAPOLIS

Hennepin Avenue in downtown Minneapolis has a lot going for it. Its anchor institution is the Hennepin Theatre Trust, which runs three of the historic theaters on the street. It also has a number of dining and hospitality options. There are some wonderful facades of early twentieth-century structures. It is also a block from the Nicollet Mall, one of the first urban revitalization/pedestrianization projects of which I am aware. In the spring of 2017, I was asked to visit Minneapolis, at the invitation of the Hennepin Theatre Trust, to evaluate the situation there and make suggestions.

The perception of safety in downtown Minneapolis as of this writing, and specifically on Hennepin, was poor. A good deal of this negative perception seemed to be driven by a sense that the street was "overwhelmed" by homeless individuals, clients of local social service providers, occupying the public spaces of the street. In fact, an attendant at a parking lot in the neighborhood told me that working there was "bad" and that he was often required to break up fights that take place on the sidewalk adjacent to the lot.

Minneapolis is undergoing economic changes that are different from those of other major cities. Big businesses have relocated, some of them recently, outside of the downtown. Major arts institutions, like the Walker Art Museum and the Guthrie Theater, are not located in the downtown.

The winters in the Twin Cities are cold and snowy—and both Minneapolis and St. Paul have extensive systems of skyways between buildings and parking decks. As a result, the number of pedestrians at peak hours in good weather during colder (and even warmer) months is far less than one would expect given the density of office workers.

But there are strategies that have proved effective in other places to address these issues—particularly with respect to assisting the homeless. It seems ironic that Minneapolis, with its strong cultural institutions, leading philanthropies, and progressive business community, once a leader in the downtown revival (with projects like Nicollet Mall), has not taken advantage of what has been successful in other places.

It has often proven to be true that the perception of the number of people engaged in antisocial behavior in public spaces is greater than the actual number. Irregular and antisocial behavior delivers cues that people pick up on, making them feel as if their physical safety is being threatened. The seeming unpredictability of the people who appear to be free from social norms in public spaces creates this fear—some of which is based on experience and some of which, unfortunately, is not. Most people overread both the probability and the extent of this threat. If you see two or three homeless people during a three- or four-block walk, you feel that the public space is being "dominated" by the homeless. If you see the same person sleeping on the sidewalk two or three times in a week, you read that as half a dozen different people. We all do this. Overreading means that the "problem" is actually less prevalent and therefore less difficult to address than it appears.

In Minneapolis, there were about a dozen people—no more than that—who appeared to be in need of service or hanging out on the street along Hennepin at any one time. They were not engaged in aggressive panhandling; in fact, most were reticent to make contact with other people. The social service needs of these individuals were unlikely to be overwhelming. They might have been assisted and found places that were better *for them* than the sidewalks of Hennepin Avenue.

In Downtown Jamaica, Queens, more than a dozen facilities provide services for homeless individuals and families—the densest concentration in the borough. At Greater Jamaica Development Corporation, we were able to virtually eliminate street homelessness from around 2010 to 2015 by identifying people in need when they appeared on the sidewalks and in public spaces and then providing them with high-quality outreach services.

In Queens, we had the benefit of a citywide program to provide outreach services to the homeless. The city contracted with providers by borough, and in Queens, we were fortunate that the agency with the outreach contract was Breaking Ground. Breaking Ground is the city's largest provider of supportive housing for the formerly homeless. In founding the organization, Rosanne Haggerty created some of the earliest and highest quality supportive housing programs in New York. The first, in 1991, was the highly successful Times Square Hotel. Rosanne's current endeavor, Community Solutions (https://communitysolutions.org), is a national resource deploying the best problem-solving tools from multiple sectors to help communities end homelessness and the conditions that create it.

In Jamaica, Breaking Ground's outreach workers were well trained, highly skilled, compassionate, persistent, and effective. In our experience in Queens at the beginning of the decade, they were able to persuade all the people living in public spaces in our community to accept service within a week of our identifying them as being in need. Our strategy was relatively simple. We had on staff a community member, Thomas Crater Jr., whose job it was to ride around the downtown on a bike and identify issues needing to be addressed—streetlights that were out, dumping of commercial trash, street trees needing replacement, and individuals on the sidewalks in need of services. Tom got to know these people and their situations, and while not a social service professional, he was generally able to make relationships with them. After some interaction, they almost always told him all about their lives and the challenges that they faced. Tom let our Jamaica Alliance Ambassador staff know about these individuals and their locations, information that we then communicated to Common Ground. Common Ground would dispatch an outreach worker, generally the same day, who would talk with Tom, contact the individual, evaluate his or her needs, and offer him or her service. This is the strategy that places like downtown Minneapolis need.

Two elements of Breaking Ground's approach appeared to me to be essential to their success. First, they were persistent. If an individual was resistant to service, the outreach workers would return every day to offer them service and to attempt to persuade them to come indoors. The second is that, with Tom's vital assistance, they identified the services required by that particular individual and then contacted an agency with the capacity to meet that need on the client's behalf. Working with Tom, they encouraged the client to take advantage of the services on offer.

This practice is less obvious than it sounds, because most agencies specialize in what they do, and they try to fit clients into their programs rather than try to find an appropriate provider of the services the client requires. The reverse, client-centered approach has proven to be more effective. We are fortunate in New York City to have a wide range of available services among social service agencies addressing the entire spectrum of client needs. Given the number of social service facilities near Hennepin Avenue, if this wasn't true in downtown Minneapolis, it ought to be.

In Jamaica, we also worked with the programs in the community to limit their external effects. Those external effects of social service providers are a significant problem on Hennepin Avenue. By sitting down with the management of the various facilities, we were able to communicate to them the negative impacts (when they occurred) that their facilities imposed on the neighborhood and work with them to devise solutions. New York City's homeless services agency, the funder of these programs, was helpful in persuading the service providers to change their practices where they had unintended negative effects and in identifying appropriate resources that could be used to address them. For example, a facility housing formerly homeless families had a curfew policy that locked out male clients who returned after 10 p.m. This resulted in the curfew violators sleeping in a nearby park. We were able to persuade the agency to provide a space inside their building for their late-returning clients.

The basic effective tactics in providing services to unsheltered individuals in public spaces are to identify or create a high-quality outreach program, to work with agencies already receiving resources to address the needs of the homeless, and to engage local government, thereby making sure that the full range of requirements of clients is being met. I believe that this approach has the capacity to be helpful in many communities, including Minneapolis.

EQUITY AND PUBLIC SPACE

Homelessness raises a raft of crosscutting concerns about individual rights, the causes of economic disadvantage in our country today, and our society's stubborn unwillingness to assist those suffering from serious mental health issues, including substance abuse. Conflicting interests and ideologies play out in policy discussions about how public spaces are governed and managed.

As I've stated, successful restoration of a sense of order to public spaces is not principally about enforcement. The apparent decline in the quality of the public space experience in the second half of the twentieth century was driven almost entirely by how safe people felt they were on sidewalks and in parks. Many sensed that the public realm of shared space was chaotic, and as a result, they feared for their physical safety. Some of this fear may have been exaggerated or perhaps incorrect, driven by race- and class-bound assumptions and stereotypes. But even if the threat was not real, the perception of it kept people from visiting, working in, shopping in, or investing in neighborhoods, downtowns, and other public places perceived to be unsafe. Much of the success of improved public spaces over the last two decades has been based on improving those perceptions—making public spaces *feel* safer by employing broken-windows management (discouraging low-level disorder and providing high-quality, detail-oriented maintenance) and placemaking practices.

Public spaces—sidewalks and parks—belong to everyone, and individuals who dominate those spaces by using them for the everyday activities of their private lives or to engage in informal commercial activity are excluding others from sharing in their use. As an attorney, I recognize what a sensitive area concerning the exercise of individual rights this is. Enforcement based on an individual's status is a violation of his or her legal rights and of the norms of a just society. That is the most important reason service is preferable to enforcement as an approach to low-level antisocial behavior.

Where negative social ecologies have been created, "breaking the circuit" may be a way to take back the space for the public. Bryant Park had long been a haven for drug dealers and their clients, and some sections of the park were "owned" by them for years. Greeley Square, at Thirty-Second Street and Sixth Avenue, had even more long-standing networks of threatening behavior going back decades. Greeley reportedly had individuals dealing in hard drugs, publicly drinking, and interacting with pedestrians aggressively. Both Bryant Park and Greeley Square were substantially physically restored and during the capital construction had fences around them. After both of those spaces were reopened and reoccupied by the public, I realized that the building of the fences and the exclusion of the public for some period of time had disrupted the patterns of antisocial behavior that had established themselves in those spaces. During the restoration work, people went elsewhere. In neither case were the criminal social systems displaced only to reappear somewhere else. They were broken up and eliminated. If you were to go to Bryant Park or Greeley Square and their surrounding blocks, you would not find the drug dealing and public alcohol consumption that were evident in those places in the earlier 1990s.[1]

In both cases, we did notice at the time the of the parks' reopening that some of the former park denizens returned to sidewalks across the street

Figure 19. The reprogramming of Greeley Square in Manhattan near Thirty-Fourth Street was, perhaps, an even more remarkable turnaround than Bryant Park.

from them. This is where one of Holly Whyte's most important principles comes into play: good uses driving out bad. Active programming of the parks drew the general public in, and the bad actors found they could not retake and dominate the space. They didn't try to reestablish themselves. Bad actors don't want to be around positive social behavior. They want to be sheltered from sight and activity. Opening spaces up to more people and activities defeats the pattern—the social ecology—of antisocial behavior.

Both Bryant Park and Greeley Square had full-time security and maintenance staff providing "eyes on the street" after they were reopened to the public. The initial successful programming in Bryant Park was the daily schedule of concerts discussed in chapter 6. In Greeley, movable tables and chairs and high-quality horticulture, along with occasional events, were enough to draw crowds and keep the drug dealers looking out the window of the greasy spoon across the street from returning to the park.

When they gave up hope of taking back the park, they disappeared from the neighborhood.

Using enforcement as the sole means of reestablishing order in public space takes enormous resources to be effective and does not create a long-term solution. Those resources are usually withdrawn after the passage of time and the antisocial behavior returns. It has been proven to be far more effective to work with social service professionals to deal with the mental health and substance abuse issues of individuals occupying and engaged in antisocial behavior in public and to make spaces unwelcoming to illegal activity and antisocial behavior by breaking up long-standing social ecologies and replacing them with positive activity. Well-run, well-programmed public spaces are a benefit to everyone, regardless of race or class. They are the great social equalizer, where people of diverse backgrounds and economic situations can come together in a democratic society. Half an hour sitting in Greeley Square drives this point home.

GENTRIFICATION IS GOOD

The claim that successful urban revitalization results in "gentrification" and is therefore a bad thing is a widely held view of observers of public space. In my experience, the situation is much more nuanced, and the data suggest that this "conventional wisdom" is not completely accurate.

When most people talk about gentrification, they are referring to two different things. What folks mean when they talk about gentrification, I think, is the displacement of neighborhood residents. They believe that rising rents and landlord greed drive longtime residents from the neighborhood. However, people also use the term *gentrification* to mean *cultural* changes to communities. This ranges from new (and often more expensive) retail options to changes in demographics—generally higher income and ethnically different residents moving into a neighborhood and changing its character. One often hears this complaint about the changes that have taken place in Harlem.[2]

I would like to suggest that the social and economic integration that are the hallmarks of gentrification may actually bring economic benefit and political power to previously dispossessed people. What I regard as neighborhood "improvement," I would argue, promotes a just and more equitable society where everyone, regardless of background, is treated with equal concern and respect. In my opinion, social integration is a good in and of itself, creating communities that honor difference. In addition, housing and educating low-income people in the same communities as higher-income people may well provide those lower-income people with tools for economic advancement. We know that geographically segregating and concentrating low-income people has proven to lead to higher levels of social dysfunction. The Far Rockaways in Queens, where dense housing for low-income residents was created in the 1970s, resulting in one of the poorest and most distressed neighborhoods in New York City, is illustrative of this.

The Furman Center's *State of New York Housing and Neighborhoods in 2015*[3] explains that in New York City, displacement through gentrification is not a significant effect, but it also tells us some interesting things about the dynamics of improving neighborhoods. The study found that in New York City over the last forty years, the neighborhoods that have experienced the greatest increase in the creation of new housing units are those that were the most depopulated during the urban decline of the 1960s and 1970s. This likely means that the new arrivals in "gentrifying" neighborhoods like Harlem, Bushwick, and Williamsburg are moving into newly constructed housing and are *not*, for the most part, displacing existing residents. Their data also tend to show that median rents rise in gentrifying neighborhoods because the new units, rented to new residents, charge more—*not because rents in preexisting units go up*. The data seem to show that rents for preexisting units in gentrifying neighborhoods increase no more than those generally across the city. So the results of gentrification may not necessarily mean only that poor folks are forced out of gentrifying neighborhoods but also that higher-income folks may be moving in—that is, that as a result of market forces, previously depopulated neighborhoods may becoming more racially and economically integrated. This would be a kind of market-driven, voluntary (as opposed to government-mandated) integration.

This study was to this date the only one of which I was aware regarding the displacement effect of neighborhood improvement that was nonanecdotal and that was data driven. While the possible conclusions I have drawn from it are contrary to the conventional wisdom regarding the effects of "gentrification," the academic and popular literature on gentrification tends to draw their conclusions from small samples or ethnography rather than from longitudinal studies over extended periods of time against a valid constant base. This is because these effects are so difficult to measure. The same problems of measurement affect attempts to accurately measure the impact of public space improvements over time. It is difficult to establish a valid comparative constant.[4] But the Furman Center study is solidly constructed and based on a broad, established data set. Unfortunately, the widely held views about "gentrification" are based on sets of unchallenged assumptions. They are unchallenged in part likely because of the furor and calumny that contrary information would invoke. The Furman Center study tends to confirm the conclusions I have drawn from close personal observation that I hope are divorced from any particular ideological agenda.

The second objection to gentrification is essentially a nostalgic resistance to change. One hears advocates say that "they are taking away *our* neighborhood." The argument is made that something valuable and essential about a place is being lost by new, higher-income residents who aren't black or Hispanic moving in.[5]

Cities are dynamic places and are constantly subject to changing demographics and economics. That is simply the nature of urban life. New York in particular has long welcomed newcomers from many nations and backgrounds. Are the advocates opposed to cultural gentrification suggesting that we stop all neighborhood changes? Is that even possible? Are they against social, economic, and racial integration—and the improvement of the economic situation of the disadvantaged? If so, what is their model?

The most socially successful new residential projects in New York are mixed-income (and generally mixed-use) developments. New York City has potent programs to support the development of affordable units for lower-income residents. The city's agenda to increase the availability of affordable housing units has proved to be a remarkable success. Putting people of different incomes and backgrounds in the same multifamily building seems to benefit all the residents. The Moda project on Parsons Boulevard in Jamaica, developed by the Dermot Company in conjunction with the New York City Economic Development Corporation, the Department of Housing Preservation and Development, and the Housing Development Corporation, is a great example of this. It is a 50/30/20 project (50 percent subsidized moderate income, 30 percent market rate, and 20 percent low income). Sitting in the lobby, it is impossible to tell who is who. By contrast, we have had a disastrous history in New York of concentrating low-income people in certain neighborhoods and projects at a high density. Again, Far Rockaway, for example, remains a low-income, segregated, high-crime neighborhood.

Mixed-income development may produce far better social results. While there is a great deal of federal subsidy and substantial political force behind the creation of apartments for the lowest-income New Yorkers, it may well be that it is better for those residents and better for the city as a whole to create more mixed-income projects—integrating low-income people in developments with higher-income families.

Gentrification can bring positive social outcomes to a community that benefits residents of all backgrounds and income levels. It brings about social, economic, and racial integration without the political upheaval and unintended effects of integration through court mandate or other forms of legal compulsion. It brings higher-income families into the local schools and improves those schools' performances (which has also become controversial).[6] It provides a market for higher-quality and more diverse local retailers. We need more solid research on this, but it may well be that gentrification improves the economic situation for lower-income people and actually enables families to advance themselves out of poverty.

PROGRAMMING FOR EQUITY

Princeton sociology professor Patrick Sharkey has documented the impact of voluntary organizations on the revitalization of public space.[7] Sharkey attempts to demonstrate that perhaps the most effective path toward community revitalization involves improved perceptions of public spaces leading to "voluntary" (as opposed to government-mandated) ethnic and economic integration. Sharkey observes that this may be the most positive change that has occurred in cities—and particularly low-income neighborhoods—in the last two decades. His most striking finding is that improved conditions in cities across the country in the 1990s have saved the lives of thousands of young black men. Sharkey's book suggests that perhaps the best way to address the shocking economic inequality that successful cities now face (well documented in Richard Florida's latest book[8]) is to nudge social institutions toward racial and economic integration.

I once received a call from a highly respected community leader in southeast Queens. He called to express his concern that all the new development activity in Downtown Jamaica, Queens, was going to produce traffic congestion, parking problems, and "new people." He complained that the community was losing control of its situation. I was taken aback! I said to him, "But isn't this the economic development you worked to bring to the community for your entire political career?" I suggested that these kinds of social and economic forces are not susceptible to fine-tuning.

One theory of urban chaos holds that it has "root causes": the commonsense idea is that urban crime is the result of poverty and lack of opportunity, and therefore, the best way to reduce violence is to improve those social and economic conditions. But I would like to suggest something else. By making better places of low-income communities and attracting a more ethnically and economically diverse population to them, the communities themselves and the life circumstances of the worst off in those communities may be improved. Providing appropriate services for the homeless occupying public spaces is often an early step toward improving those public spaces, making them accessible to more people and generally improving the neighborhood's quality of life—and improving conditions for homeless individuals themselves. Neighborhood revitalization that improves the quality of life and sense of safety in a community and as a result attracts new, higher-income residents could possibly lead to positive local changes that benefit all community residents of every economic and ethnic background. Social integration through the improvement of neighborhoods and public spaces could be a major force in reducing social and economic inequity.

CHAPTER 11

ARTISTS, DOWNTOWNS, AND CREATIVE PLACEMAKING

In chapter 6, I discussed the creation of the Bryant Park performing arts series and its importance to the park's revitalization. From its earliest days, Greater Jamaica Development Corporation recognized that supporting artists and artistic activity was an important tool for economic development. In its very early years, the founders of GJDC essentially squatted in an abandoned city building and led its conversion into a community school of the arts. It also attempted to develop artists' live/work space in an abandoned city firehouse in the eighties, long before that became a "thing." Real estate developer Tony Goldman, a commercial placemaking practitioner of the highest caliber, discovered the positive economic impact of visual artists and profited by attracting them to SoHo in Manhattan and Wynwood in Miami.

Music and dance can animate otherwise neglected public spaces. Artists need inexpensive space for making their art. They are often the first college-educated people to move to "pioneering" neighborhoods, leading to their revitalization. Presenting the visual arts in public spaces can draw people into them and demonstrate that there are people who are taking care of the space.

As a result, "creative placemaking" seems to be all the rage with institutional funders. Numerous organizations have entered the fray: Artplace America, Artspace, the Mayor's Initiative for Creative Design, the Kresge Foundation Arts & Culture Creative Placemaking program, the Local Initiatives Support Corporation, the National Endowment for the Arts, the Knight Foundation, the Levitt Foundation, Southwest Airlines, and the Surdna Foundation are all supporting creative placemaking. It's a lovely idea for policy makers and institutional funders to be able to support artists, promote economic equity, and engage in economic development, all with the same grant funds.

But do we all mean the same thing when we employ the phrase "creative placemaking"? How can we define it? Funders are using "metrics" to analyze the "impact" of their "investments" in creative placemaking during their grant cycles. But what possible metrics could determine the efficacy of such a thing as creative placemaking, and is the normal grant period an appropriate period of time for measurement? The whole area is pretty murky about how the arts and artists foster public space revitalization and what approaches actually work. Doing this effectively requires more than simply encouraging artistic activity in otherwise disinvested or underutilized public spaces.

I've been involved in quite a few attempts to employ arts programming to restore and improve public spaces as well as to stimulate economic activity. Some have been hugely successful—in fact essential—to the projects where they have been used; in other cases, not so much. The one quality that I can put my finger on that has distinguished the impactful projects from the lame ones is "critical mass." There needs to be sufficient artistic activity within a defined place and time in a creative placemaking project for it to have an impact. The artistic activities induced by creative placemaking, like other revitalization projects, need to be physically close to each other and need to take place regularly and often in order for them to have an effect on a neighborhood's quality of life. Also, arts-led initiatives always take more than one year to have any meaningful result and in some cases take as long as five years for secondary effects to occur. Solid placemaking practice, as I've pointed out repeatedly in this book, requires patience and consistency. Creative placemaking is no exception.

In Bryant Park, given the park's longtime unsavory reputation, we weren't sure whether people would return to the park in large numbers after the end of the four-year construction period in 1992. We planned to "prime the pump" for activity in the park by creating a program of *regular* lunchtime performing events four days a week from early June to late September. The idea was to draw people into the space by providing positive activity. What made this work as an exercise in creative placemaking was that the programs were presented on a rotation of events that were on the same day and time every week—that is, every Thursday at 12:30. It was that consistency that created the essential critical mass.

I know that many BIDs and downtown management organizations organize a few days of concerts over a summer or an annual festival to bring people into a public space. Funders also like them because you can count how many events their money has bought and how many people have turned up at the events. While these may be nice events and people may enjoy them, in my experience, they aren't all that helpful in revitalizing public space if visitors can't count on events taking place there when they randomly turn up. Not many people say, "Oh, I think I'll go eat lunch on the courthouse steps on Wednesday." One-off events don't have enough presence to change people's minds about the character of an inactive space.

JAZZ OVERKILL

Consistency, unfortunately, isn't enough. With support from the Rockefeller Brothers Fund and Deutsche Bank Americas Foundation at Greater Jamaica, we programmed daily weekday jazz concerts with trios and quartets in Downtown Jamaica for fourteen weeks. A jazz professor at a local college did the programming, and as a result, the quality of the concerts, if you were a jazz fan, met a very high standard. But we found that the series didn't have much impact in terms of drawing crowds or changing percep-tions. Part of the problem was that the small ensembles didn't make much of an impression in the large public spaces where we presented them, par-ticularly outdoors. Also, what the professor wanted to program and what the musicians wanted to play weren't necessarily what audiences wanted to hear. We were able to experiment a bit over the three-year life of the grant. We found that Caribbean music drew larger crowds than jazz and that larger ensembles made more of an impression. We also added dancers from a community dance school to the mix, which drew the parents and friends of the kids. Those larger concerts proved to be more expensive, so we were able to program fewer of them, and as a result, they didn't have much impact either. The concerts failed to generate any "buzz," they didn't seem to have much in the way of secondary effects, they didn't attract much publicity, and we received little in the way of positive community comment about them. All of this, again, goes to the difficulty of actually measuring the impact of such events. One measure was for certain: we had no demand for them to continue.

New Year's Eve Madness

For five or six years in the mid-1990s, I was responsible for producing First Night, New York, a family-oriented, alcohol-free New Year's Eve festival of the arts for Grand Central and 34th Street Partnerships.[1] It was conceived of as rational counterprogramming to the disorder of Times Square on New Year's Eve. There were dozens of events at half a dozen venues around Midtown. It took months to put together and cost hundreds of thousands of dollars. It had little to no presale and was a show that opened and closed on the same night. The economics of First Night took nerves of steel that I, for one, didn't have. While in most years, it got considerable media cover-age promoting the safety and fun of Midtown Manhattan, in retrospect, as an annual, one-night affair, it lost a ton of money and wasn't worth the effort in terms of improving the perception of Midtown on New Year's

Eve or in general. It had difficulty breaking through the tremendous attention paid to the ball drop in Times Square. For several of the years, the
event included waltzing on the main concourse of Grand Central Terminal with the Orchestra of St. Luke's, which was a great event that I loved
being involved with, but it also didn't have a sufficient positive impact to
be worth the expense. On the ground, it was overwhelmed by the chaos
in the terminal on New Year's Eve. Our goal for First Night was to change
the perception of Midtown and Grand Central on New Year's Eve—and it
obviously didn't do that.

THE BIG CRINKLY

Working with dealer André Emmerich, who I had cold-called through a
personal connection, I created a public sculpture program in Bryant Park.
We placed a massive Alexander Calder stabile called *Big Crinkly* on the
lawn over a winter season. It looked spectacular and created a sense of
activity during an otherwise dormant time. This project had the requisite
critical mass. André's gallery paid for the installation and insurance—and
by the end of the installation, the gallery had sold the piece to a collector as
a result of the publicity that was attendant to the installation. *Big Crinkly*
is now in the collection of the De Young Museum in San Francisco. This is
an excellent example of a win/win deal between the nonprofit and a for-
profit business. Working with André, the Public Art Fund, and other dealers, we arranged a number of other winter large-scale art installations. All
were a great addition to the park. André was a cultured and gracious man,
and partnering with him was one of my great personal and professional
experiences.

THE GENIUS OF POP-UP GALLERIES

Working with the artists' organization chashama, we took an empty building owned by GJDC that had once been a dentist's office and turned it into

studio spaces and an art gallery, with the former treatment rooms being turned into artists' work spaces. Chashama paid for utilities and no rent to GJDC and charged no rent to the artists. The artists and chashama fixed up the building to make it usable, and chashama did a terrific job recruiting among artists in southeast Queens, all of whom were people of color. One of the artists worked in the medium of roadkill and taxidermy—really![2] The artists made that building hum from the afternoon until late into the night for months. We had an open house every Thursday night that drew large crowds, and folks regularly hung out outside the gallery chatting until after midnight. The artists seemed to be nocturnal—in the studio spaces, the lights tended to be on late at night. Jamaica was otherwise generally empty at night, especially late, and the chashama project created nighttime activity both in a storefront and on the street, which greatly contributed to the perception of safety in the downtown. One of the artists even developed a following among disengaged, twentysomething young men from the local community. He taught them drawing and took them on trips to museums in Manhattan.

I regard this project as the signal turning point in the downtown's revitalization. The studio/gallery was in place for about two years. It had critical mass because it was open and lit most of the time, and the space was in a prominent location in the downtown. This use of the previously underutilized retail space ultimately attracted a buyer for the building—a local architecture practice previously located elsewhere in Queens. The move of that firm to storefront space in Jamaica was a major step forward in the downtown's economic revitalization.

Later, the fantastic group No Longer Empty (NLE) occupied an empty retail space on the pedestrianized 165th Street Mall. NLE's model is to create activities that are heavily programmed and carefully curated. Critical mass is in their institutional DNA. They do a great deal of research and work to integrate their projects into the local community. They study the history and sociology of a community and develop their program to highlight the neighborhood's unique character. This serves to both draw local

Figure 20. The little building in Jamaica, Queens, we turned over to cha-shama, an organization that populates empty storefronts with artistic activity. It became a lively center of action.

people into the project and to amplify its impact.[3] What was previously an empty storefront became a vibrant space, with constant programming and a large number of visitors. Again, all this took was the provision of free space for about six months. And again, during NLE's residency, the landlord received a market-rate offer from a tenant wishing to occupy this long-vacant space. NLE remains a presence in Jamaica in partnership with other community-based organizations, including York College.

As demonstrated by these projects, animating vacant retail space not only increases downtown activity but also has the added benefit of making the particular space easier to rent—demonstrating the store's ability to attract pedestrians and shoppers. Pop-up artist spaces are one of the most powerful tools I know to attract new tenants and investment to a disinvested downtown.

The Value of Free Space

Like many disinvested downtowns, Jamaica had a good deal of empty and underutilized space. This included not just empty stores but underused institutional space as well. We provided the renowned, pathbreaking theater company Mabou Mines with the key to a small nineteenth-century cemetery chapel that we had restored and that was not being used. Mabou Mines operated it for its theater artists' residency and fellowship program while a new facility was under construction in Manhattan. The building was occupied round the clock, seven days a week for rehearsals and teaching. Mabou Mines offered to provide internship and training opportunities for the students of the adjacent York College. Word also got around to other performers about the availability of this lovely space.

We provided free rehearsal space to the pioneering Beth Morrison Projects to prepare for a national tour of Missy Mazzoli's opera *Songs from the Uproar* at the underused, city-owned Jamaica Performing Arts Center (JPAC), a former church that has been adaptively reused into a theater space. The artists found that they loved the accessibility of Jamaica and provided a free performance to the community at the end of the rehearsal period. Again, word got around among performers of the availability of high-quality free/inexpensive rehearsal space in a community that was eager to host them. And again, a lot of this activity was at night—helping animate the downtown at a time when it was generally quiet and as a result perceived to be unsafe.

The Good and Bad of Murals

One of the truly great creative placemaking success stories is Wynwood in Miami, where the Goldman family has presented fifty artists, many of them household names in the art world, covering more than eighty thousand square feet of walls. Tony Goldman was one of the geniuses of placemaking, and the Wynwood Walls project put this formerly neglected neighborhood on the map. Murals have also been successful in creating a sense of place in the Mission District in San Francisco, where the wall paintings are reflective of neighborhood culture and are of high quality. In Cincinnati, where the scale of the wall paintings is tremendous, murals have a real impact. But mural projects are often difficult to distinguish from the graffiti that marks social disorder, and if they are too small or too spread out, they don't develop sufficient critical mass to help change neighborhood perception. Mural projects (like public sculpture) are essentially inert. They require either serious professional curation or an authentic neighborhood visual culture as well as constant vigilance to preserve their integrity. Again, free space is what makes them tick.

ARTISTS' HOUSING

At first glance, the development of artists' housing seems like a surefire way to attract artists and activity to disinvested neighborhoods. Tony Goldman was hugely successful in renting abandoned loft space in SoHo in Manhattan to artists as live/work spaces (even when living in those spaces was actually illegal!). He effectively created SoHo as an artists' community by starting a restaurant and renting out the space above it to artists. Artspace of Minneapolis is the nationally recognized leader in developing artist housing, having begun in 1979. But financing and populating artist housing is much more difficult than it looks, unless you are prepared to use private dollars to construct and subsidize the operation of the project. The regulations around government housing subsidy programs make it difficult to single out artists as potential tenants (as the subsidies are generally keyed to income rather than by profession). The rents required to attract artists to new neighborhoods are generally insufficient to cover debt service for construction and the cost of operations of residential space, so subsidy from somewhere is essential to making the project go.

PS 109 in East Harlem in New York is a cautionary tale. It is the adaptive reuse by Artspace and local community groups of an abandoned school building as artist space. The project was eventually completed and is now occupied by artists and art organizations. It cost $52 million to produce eighty-nine units of artists' housing.[4] It took more than ten years to develop the building—the sponsors had particular difficulty piecing together the required financing from six different sources.[5] It obviously took a great deal of patience and creativity to get to a completed and occupied development. Almost $11 million of the project's costs were provided as government grants (as opposed to loans, which are easier to secure) in addition to $25 million in subsidized tax credit financing. This kind of financing structure simply isn't easily replicable or scalable because of its complexity.

I do think artists' housing projects may be transformative for neighborhood revitalization, but the most efficient way to develop such a project is with privately raised subsidy dollars, with philanthropy providing equity/grant funds and a nonprofit development partner with sufficient capacity providing operating subsidy. This would get around the regulatory issues and makes the execution of the project less complex. It also takes visionary private-sector supporters with substantial capacity.

THE BOTTOM LINE

The key elements of successful creative placemaking are consistency, quality curation, and free space—all of which contribute to creating the required critical mass. In order for public events to have an impact, they have to be presented on a reliable regular schedule so that they have enough of a presence to contribute to the public perception of the space. They also have to be of sufficiently high quality to reflect well on the space—but also populist in appeal in order to draw a crowd. You just can't put any old thing out there—but you also don't have to fuss too much. To have an impact, public space programming takes time—as long as five years of sustained activity. That's certainly how long it took Bryant Park to establish itself. Free and/or low-cost space provided over an extended period of time to artists is

an easily used tool to promote creative placemaking. Both visual and performing artists find space essential to create their work. Making such space
accessible to them is a magnet. It creates activity downtown, particularly
in the "shoulder" periods of nights and weekends, and produces a "buzz"
about the neighborhood among a new group of people who were previously unaware of what it has to offer.

CHAPTER 12

REAL ECONOMIC DEVELOPMENT

Over the last fifty years, a wide range of economic-development agencies, departments, and entities have been created around the country. Their goals primarily have something to do with retaining and attracting businesses to a particular place in order to have more jobs in that place. While ideally those would be net new jobs, created out of new ventures and entrepreneurship, for the most part, most economic-development strategies are actually about moving existing jobs from one jurisdiction to another. The most powerful tools economic developers have are government subsidies: reduced taxes, government-owned property offered at a discount, cash grants, and tax-exempt borrowing rates. But it is actually quite difficult to pinpoint what truly stimulates *new* business and job creation—real economic expansion, value added, and new wealth. Even in the best cases, economic development is usually a zero-sum game. When a business in one place expands, it is because it is, at best, taking customers from another firm in another city, another state, or another country. We don't have a solid understanding of where entirely new jobs and economic value come from. The entire Amazon HQ2 project, in which jurisdictions all over the country were trying to outdo each other in attracting Amazon, put these issues in high relief.

The government also attempts to improve a local economy by moving one of its functions, and therefore its employees, to a particular place. On the biggest scale, this could be a military base. In an urban setting, it could be a large government office. In Jamaica, I was able to observe the impact on the community of the results of effective lobbying efforts to attract a college, a one-million-square-foot government office building, a court, and a laboratory and office space to the community. I noticed that government office workers rarely left their offices to eat or shop. Most employees came from outside the community. When electronic record keeping was introduced, the largest governmental office employer in Jamaica halved its workforce, leaving a massive structure mostly filled with empty file cabinets. The multiplier effect from such a tremendously expensive project didn't seem very powerful. When the jobs left, there was a vacuum. There was no real expansion to local economic activity. Only the college seemed economically connected to the community.

These two approaches—subsidy (as with Amazon in Long Island City, New York) and government office moves—are effectively bribing people to bring their businesses to a place (incentives) and forcing people to work in a place (government installations). Neither has demonstrated the capacity to create net new jobs or to increase economic activity and wealth creation in the medium to long term (hence Amazon's quick retreat from Long Island City as a result of opposition from local elected officials). Conventional economic-development activity is certainly better than nothing, but maybe not that much better. In my experience, over the long term, its impact is generally negligible.[1] With incentives, besides the problem of only moving existing pieces around on the board, when the benefits go away, the jobs usually depart as well. With the mobility of capital, inducements don't seem to organically root businesses in a certain place. In addition, for the most part, the more effective incentives are, the more government money they require.[2] The media regularly reports, at least in New York State, on the high amount spent by the government per job "created." The more targeted and carefully crafted a benefits program is, the harder it is for businesses to qualify and the fewer jobs it is able to attract. For example, in Jamaica, we worked to promote New York State's Start-Up New York program, which provided handsome tax exemptions attached to the creation of new tech jobs in New York State. The program was carefully targeted—both geographically and programmatically. We found it to be so narrowly constructed that we were unable to find any businesses to qualify, despite substantial efforts to identify and pursue them.

When government offices are forced to move to a place, that place often lacks amenities for employees, and in Jamaica, few high-quality amenities came to the community as a result of such moves. Frankly, many government employees aren't very highly compensated and don't seem to spend much money in places in which they are forced to work. When government priorities change and the function moves elsewhere, the community is left, for example, with an abandoned military base that it can't figure out what to do with. In Jamaica, when the Social Security Administration downsized its workforce, its facility became a white elephant. It is difficult (for security and logistical reasons) for the government to share space with the private sector, so the empty space couldn't be rented to businesses.

Placemaking for Economic Development

But this book is about an economic-development strategy that *does work*—that is, *creating places where people and businesses want to be. If you make a downtown or a community interesting and desirable to people, they move their businesses there because their employees want to be there and the employees they are attempting to attract want to be there.* This is place-based economic-development activity. In is exemplified in the difference between Google and Amazon's real estate decisions in New York City. Google has expanded to become a major factor in the New York City

economy without subsidy or incentives because it made a business decision that it needed to be in New York City due to the fact that the talent
it needed to recruit wanted to live here. A full-court press was put on to
attract Amazon to Queens, centered on tax incentives and access to government property. However, Amazon seemed to be less sold on New York
as a place and quickly retreated once it was subjected to negative press and
political attention. My guess is that given the same need to attract talent
that faces Google, Amazon will now begin the process of quietly creating
an expanding presence in New York City, perhaps even in Long Island City,
using only as-of-right subsidies (as opposed to discretionary incentives
negotiated with public officials). These companies want to be in New York
because their employees and potential employees are drawn to New York as
a place.

In addition, the people attracted to places because they want to be
there seem to come up with actual new business ideas, a rare few of which,
rather than poach jobs from other places, actually create value and add
completely new economic activity. I'm not sure why and how this works.
The business of consciously making places more inviting actually requires
fewer resources than paying benefits to a business to move or building
a government facility for them to move to. Placemaking does, however,
take time and patience. But because place-based economic-development
strategies develop organically over time, they stick. The results of making
places more desirable and improving the quality of life for residents and
workers get deeply embedded in the social and economic environment
of a community, and the people and organizations that are attracted as a
result stay and grow in the place they have chosen.

In the 1980s, the commercial area around Bryant Park was a dead zone.
Almost no one wanted to work there. Today, developers put a Bryant Park
address on their billion-dollar office (and most recently residential) buildings in order to market them. My back-of-the-envelope estimate of the
total increased value of property around the park since 1992 is an amount
in excess of $5 billion. The total cost of the Bryant Park capital restoration

was less than $20 million. The annual budget for programming and oper-
ating Bryant Park in the year of its reopening in 1992 was just over $1 mil-
lion (which initially came from the business improvement district and
private funders and today mostly comes from park concessions, making it
a self-sustaining operation). I would call that some pretty serious leverage.

Perhaps the most visible recent example of the efficacy of placemaking for economic development is Detroit. For decades, Detroit was what
I call a museum of bad urban revitalization ideas. Private-sector leaders
were drawn to big concepts and major capital projects, like the useless
and rather gloomy People Mover and the soul-deadening and space-age
fortress-like Renaissance Center. That is not to mention that last resort of
economic developers: the casino that was developed in Downtown Detroit
some years ago.

This was all revolutionized by the revitalization of Campus Martius
Park right at the heart of the downtown. A formerly abandoned space
at the center of a traffic circle, Campus Martius Park was, following the
Bryant Park model, heavily programmed to attract visitors. The program
included movable chairs, food service, and seasonal ice-skating. More
recently, an urban beach has been a huge success. That success stimulated
the imagination of local entrepreneur Dan Gilbert, who moved his business from the suburbs to be adjacent to the campus. When that proved to
be great for his company, he began to extend its spirit gradually outward
around the downtown as his businesses acquired more property.

Why is Silicon Valley where it is? Was Hewlett-Packard provided with
incentives to be there? Of course not. Tech businesses were drawn to the
area most obviously to be near Stanford, both out of nostalgia for the owners' alma mater and for access to the university's talent pool. I think equally
importantly, the area was within commuting distance of San Francisco,
which many highly educated people regard as the most livable city in the
world. (That has created its own slew of problems.)

If this formulation is true, why aren't more economic-development
organizations involved in trying to stimulate economic activity by

working toward improvements to public spaces? The principal answers are, because this kind of work can be risky and because it takes time and discipline. Placemaking is not a quick fix. It doesn't deliver instant results. But the five-year period that I believe most place-based development projects need to succeed is shorter than the time period involved in producing serial unsuccessful projects, like the myriad failed projects attempted in Detroit from the 1960s through the 1990s. The period from the day Bryant Park Restoration Corporation opened its doors to the day the revitalized and programmed space opened was about twelve years. It was another four years before the project hit its stride. Some projects are successful more quickly—like Campus Martius Park.

For economic-development agencies, this suggests that refocusing their resources and expertise to support placemaking activities would likely be transformative to their missions. For starters, this is because making places where people want to be is additive and doesn't merely move economic activity from one place to another. It isn't as much a zero-sum game as the deployment of incentives or government installations are. For example, many state agencies already have "Main Street" programs. But those programs have limited resources, particularly when compared with capital improvement and tax incentive programs. As a result, Main Street programs have had limited effectiveness. But fully funding these programs and staffing them with well-trained programmers and designers would likely reap significant rewards. States should provide meaningful economic-development dollars for retail presentation improvement. State funding should support the establishment of clean and safe programs where density is insufficient to support a business improvement district. It should provide seed capital for adaptive reuse of disinvested properties and for projects that promote pedestrianization of Main Streets. State governments need to encourage designing and planning for people rather than for increasing the speed of cars. I would argue that with these kinds of programs properly funded on a state-wide basis, neighborhoods in big cities and smaller cities and towns that have not yet caught the wave of economic revitalization produced by renewed urbanism can experience those same improvements.

Chaotic signs and poor retail presentation are a serious detriment to downtown revitalization. Most Main Street programs give small grants to support retail improvement. But retail improvement is the most difficult problem faced by Main Street placemakers because they are dealing with many private property owners who don't see the benefit of improving the retail presentation as beneficial to their asset. This is a classic case of the "paradox of the commons," where individual users acting independently according to their own self-interest behave contrary to the common good of all neighborhood property owners.

If a state economic-development agency came in with sufficient resources to redesign and replace all the signs in a downtown in compliance with thoughtful design guidelines, it might help kick-start the revitalization of downtowns across that state. If they also provided resources that enabled local organizations to make empty retail space available at low or no cost on a month-to-month basis to artists and makers, this too could be a powerful tool for downtown revitalization. Statewide programs like these would cost a fraction of the expense of a single capital project or most incentive programs used to attempt to attract a large new corporate venture.

Other government agencies could also stimulate improved desirability and quality of life of downtowns and public spaces. Departments of Transportation in some places already promote traffic calming, streetscape improvements, and greening. They should be provided with the resources to expand and staff those efforts. Parks Departments might fund and train staff for the creation of downtown and local horticultural programs. Commerce Departments could provide resources for activating empty retail space and encouraging food trucks and other downtown eating and drinking activity. New York State is already deeply invested in assisting brewers and distillers.

There are certainly some instances where incentives or the relocation of government operations do provide a considerable boost to local economic activity. Amazon's HQ2 competition was on its face an attempt to maximize the benefits the company can obtain where it develops a new headquarters facility. But the benefits from tax and grant programs are occasional and need to be carefully targeted. The proposed move of Amazon to Queens is a cautionary tale. Objections were raised by elected officials and community members to the incentives that were proposed to be provided to attract the company to Long Island City. Amazon wanted to be in New York City, wanted to be provided with government benefits that were negotiated in secret without the involvement of local elected officials, and then killed the project in order to extricate itself from the neighborhood politics. The fact is that Amazon probably really wanted to be in New York because its employees and the workforce that it wants to attract prefers to be in New York City, and specifically in western Queens. By contrast, clearly making centers of economic activity more desirable places for people to be through thoughtful programming is a proven but undervalued and powerful tool that needs to be more broadly employed and funded. Amazon will be back.

ADAPTIVE REUSE

An important and underutilized tool in the economic-development kit is for a local nonprofit to be the buyer of last resort for distressed property and the assembler of key development parcels. This strategy isn't frequently used because it requires equity capital (which many/most NGOs don't have), takes time, and carries the risks inherent in incurring debt and managing property. But it can be quite powerful. By purchasing (or long-term leasing), improving, and repositioning an abandoned or derelict real estate asset, not only are the negative externalities associated with that parcel removed from the neighborhood and the market, but the purchaser now has an ownership investment in the community it is working to improve. That investment has the potential to generate economic benefit from the success of the nonprofit's efforts to improve the neighborhood.

Also, ownership of key sites gives the local development entity the power to influence what gets developed on those sites. This is one of the more potent forms of "nudge" to the local market that a nonprofit can exercise in advocating for neighborhood improvement.

Community development organizations tend to shy away from the risks associated with property ownership. I'm not aware of any business improvement districts, for example, that actually own property. But I would argue that this is a form of downtown revitalization that ought to be seriously considered by more of the professionals who are working on downtown improvement. This kind of program requires the involvement of a nonprofit because the time and risk involved are more than for-profit developers can tolerate—especially in disinvested communities.

Under the leadership of its longtime president Carlisle Towery, Greater Jamaica employed this strategy extensively, and as a result, it has played an important role in the revitalization of Downtown Jamaica. GJDC's executive vice president Helen Levine and its financial advisor Susan Deutsch led the efforts to obtain and structure the financing required for the execution of this program. Both worked for GJDC for decades. The Midtown Manhattan BIDs also worked this way by leasing and developing the Bryant Park Grill and Café and the Pershing Square Café. These organizations employed a range of financing and operating structures to improve these key sites. The Cincinnati Center City Development Corporation (known as 3CDC) has been successful in deploying its real estate assets to transform Over-the-Rhine, which was, as recently as five years prior, disinvested and violent, into that city's most vibrant neighborhood.

GJDC's office is in a building donated by the Trump family, who lived near the downtown in Jamaica Estates. This eighty-thousand-square-foot art deco structure was in poor physical condition and was nearly empty when the Trumps transferred the title to GJDC. GJDC obtained a mortgage loan on the building from a major insurance company (which is much more difficult to do today, as financial services companies are rarely willing to make loans on vacant or nonperforming assets), the proceeds of which it used to make repairs to the building and make it marketable to tenants. GJDC then sought out government and nonprofit renters. GJDC tried to lead the market by providing a quality of space not otherwise available in this disinvested downtown. It sought landmark designation for the building. It restored the building's attractive art deco features created by Rene Paul Chambellan, one of the period's most noted architectural artists (whose work is featured at Rockefeller Center and the American Radiator Building). It upgraded the elevator system and installed air-conditioning in the office suites. The structure is now fully leased, one floor is occupied by GJDC, and it produces net revenue that supports GJDC's operations.

This also demonstrates an important benefit of nonprofit adaptive reuse—which is the preservation of historic and architecturally significant structures. Many times development projects result in the demolition of the very buildings that give a downtown character, as dictated by the economics of the venture. When a nonprofit becomes the property owner, profit maximization is not the only metric by which a project can be evaluated. The positive externalities created by buildings that incorporate high-quality vernacular architecture are something that a nonprofit development corporation can figure into its evaluation of an undertaking. A community-based organization also has the ability to spend what otherwise might be seen as "noneconomic" amounts of money on restoring and preserving architectural features that contribute to a neighborhood's sense of place. Sometimes such adaptive reuse efforts have development rights that can be transferred to an adjacent property in order to generate additional cash.

Such local development projects by a nonprofit need only to break even or produce a manageable negative cash flow during the initial years of a development if the community impact of a venture will be positive and/ or catalytic. This kind of calculus is impossible for almost any private, for-profit developer. At Greater Jamaica, all such undertakings became cash-flow positive over time and experienced significant capital appreciation over decades.

GJDC also purchased distressed properties for use by other organizations. As a New York State Local Development Corporation, it was legally empowered to accept property without a bid from the City of New York.[3] The city turned over a number of parcels at low or no cost to GJDC. In a number of cases, it took title to derelict property (which, generally, the city had taken in tax lien proceedings), borrowed money secured by a mortgage lien on the building, improved the building to working order, and transferred title to another neighborhood nonprofit along with the mortgage lien. In that way, the nonprofit acquired a building for its use and occupancy—with occupancy costs limited to the costs of operation and the servicing of the mortgage. As the local market improved, the nonprofit then had the benefit of the increased value of its equity in the building. The neighborhood lost an eyesore and gained an active use of a previously abandoned property. Both Community Mediation Service and Neighborhood Housing Services of Jamaica were the beneficiaries of this strategy. GJDC has owned many other properties in the downtown at one time or another. All have been successfully redeveloped or adaptively reused.

As in many downtowns, parking was a major issue for Jamaica. Competing suburban retail centers provided free parking to their customers. The City of New York owned several flat lots and parking structures in Jamaica. Through the 1990s, the city's parking facilities in Jamaica were seen as dark, poorly maintained, and dangerous. From early in its history, GJDC was involved in working with the city to provide high-quality, low-cost parking to shoppers, office workers, residents, and other visitors to the downtown in an attempt to retain and attract shoppers. In the early 2000s, it bought two structures and two lots from the city, using tax-exempt industrial development authority bonds (of about $15 million) to pay half the appraised value of the property to the city and provide working capital for the upgrading of the facilities. GJDC created Jamaica First Parking (JFP), a separate entity, to operate the parking and contracted with Edison Parking to operate them.

JFP improved the lighting of the lots and garages, upgraded the eleva-
tors, and provided high-quality security services. It shoveled the walks
and plowed the lots. In time, it also added a horticulture program. Using
the cash flow from the parking system, it built an additional garage. For
years, it worked to keep rates low in order to encourage economic activity. Ultimately, the parking operation became a reliable source of income
for GJDC, just as the Bryant Park Grill and Café now provides substantial
financial support for the programming in Bryant Park. In fact, as a result
of its real estate operations (including periodic transactions), GJDC is
largely self-supporting—which has some irony attached to it.

Around 2010, the city revoked the property tax exemption that had earlier been granted to the parking facilities. GJDC challenged the revoca-
tion, winning relief in the Appellate Division of the Supreme Court. The
city appealed that ruling to the state's highest court and won a reversal.[4]
Now the system supports GJDC to a lesser degree but also provides almost
$1 million a year to the city's general fund. GJDC's revenue-generating
capacity is a victim of its own success! But because of the increasing interest in development in Jamaica, due in no small part to GJDC's work,
GJDC now controls these key development sites, which have substantial
economic value and a very low amount of financial leverage.

GJDC also used property ownership as a tool to take control of key
development sites around the transit hub on Sutphin Boulevard. This was
a risky and expensive project that ultimately paid substantial rewards to
GJDC. Site acquisition began with the sale by Chemical Bank of a branch
office building to GJDC when, through merger activity, the branch became
redundant. Over a period of almost fifteen years, using Port Authority
funds, New Market Tax Credits, and mortgage loans from banks (using
the property's value and cash flows for security), GJDC assembled two
important sites. There were years of high interest rates when the parcels
had negative cash flows. One of the two assemblages was ultimately sold at
a loss but to a high-quality developer for an important hotel project. The
other site was sold at a substantial gain. Both projects will ultimately be of

great benefit to the economic health of the downtown. There was nothing particularly unique about Jamaica or GJDC in taking on these projects and making them successful. It took a willingness to incur risk that many similar places and organizations unfortunately aren't willing to take on.

Buying and selling property requires skill and patience. It carries significant financial risks—particularly from interest rate fluctuations and tenant defaults. But ultimately, its success is tied to a development organization's attainment of its central mission of neighborhood improvement. Economic-development entities in Buffalo and Cincinnati appear to have employed similar strategies with great success. The recent inability of banks and other lenders to loan on undeveloped and nonperforming properties makes this a more difficult strategy for nonprofits just starting out. It might present an opportunity for large philanthropies and government economic-development agencies that wish to engage in program-related investments. In its forty-plus-year history, GJDC has never missed a loan payment (although it did on more than one occasion violate the technical terms of loan covenants and need to seek forbearance from cooperative and understanding lenders). GJDC has been an excellent client to a number of financial service organizations and law firms—who have made handsome profits from its work. GJDC's program of property ownership and management has perhaps been its most significant tool in the revitalization of Downtown Jamaica, and I would suggest it is one that might well be emulated by other organizations engaged in similar work.

Government support for downtown placemaking and programming activity has not been a central part of government's economic-development agenda. Neither has been the adaptive reuse of disinvested or underutilized property. But given time, these are the most powerful tools for downtown revitalization. They are the programs that have the capacity to produce new jobs, create wealth, and expand economic opportunity.

THE CHANGED ENVIRONMENT FOR NONPROFITS

When GJDC was formed in the late 1970s, government and major foundations saw nonprofit entities as their most important tools in working toward urban revitalization. Government and foundations established community development corporations (CDCs) to work in low-income neighborhoods all over the country. CDCs were seen as closely tied through their governance structures to the communities that they served—more so than a city government that was located downtown and that had a broad range of concerns. As private nonprofit entities, CDCs were not subjected to most of the constraints that made local government seem so sclerotic. They were free from municipal procurement, personnel, and contracting requirements, enabling CDCs to work more flexibly, more quickly, and less expensively. At GJDC, in its early years, the government provided most of its annual operating funds, with very few strings attached. The source of much of this money was the CDBG program administered by the Department of Housing and Urban Development.

I watched this situation begin to change in the mid-1990s. CDBG funds began to decrease. Government officials became less interested in partnering with community-development nonprofits (even as they dramatically expanded their reliance on social service nonprofits). The government became greatly concerned about the risks being taken by CDCs. They felt that CDCs were engaged in programs and projects that had the potential for creating problems, programs and projects over which local government exercised little direct control. The government was concerned about potential policy and financial issues that might be caused by entities it didn't control, issues for which the government might ultimately be responsible and for which it might be blamed in the media.

When highly trained professionals began to be employed by New York City agencies beginning just after 2000, replacing lifetime political employees who had long experience but narrow training and often few technical skills, these new employees—planning school graduates, for example—were just as knowledgeable about cutting-edge economic-development program initiatives as their CDC colleagues. Those highly professional government workers believed that they knew as much about the right economic-development policies as folks in nonprofits—and they were the ones in control of the money. They and their private foundation counterparts now often seek to have CDCs execute *their* programs with government and foundation dollars—not the CDCs' own.

Another aspect of this situation is the resentment that some government officials felt about the compensation many CDCs and other economic-development nonprofits pay their senior executives, which grew tremendously during the 1990s. When I went to work for GCP, government officials seemed obsessed with Dan Biederman's compensation from the three BIDs (which was about $400,000 in 1993). There was constant jockeying by various public officials to make the BIDs reveal Dan's salary, which was not required to be public information at the time. At one point, the city's business services commissioner demanded to know Dan's salary before releasing BID funds. He asked Dan to provide him with the information verbally and promised that he would share the information only with the mayor. Of course, the next day, Dan's pay appeared in the newspaper. In my view, much of the distrust the government has for CDCs and BIDs, at least in New York, may have been generated by the nonprofits paying so much more than similar government jobs to their top employees.

At the same time that the Federal Department of Housing and Urban Development has shrunk CDBG funding to the local government, the New York City government has diverted what remains of those funds for its own use rather than passing them through to community-based organizations. The amount of CDBG money now available to local groups is negligible and is distributed in small competitive grants that come with detailed restrictions on use. The CDBG funds that paid for the general operations of GJDC in the 1980s are no longer generally available.

The drying up of CDBG money, the government's distrust of the independence of CDCs, and the government's desire to impose detailed controls on them seriously limit the effectiveness of these organizations. At the same time, many have become politicized and risk averse and are no longer as creative or entrepreneurial as some once were. In recent years, I have observed occasions where government was actually *more* flexible and creative than the local community organization in an attempt to address a local problem—and the nonprofit was resistant to change. In the 1990s, the Midtown Manhattan BIDs were laboratories for new ideas, like place-making and broken-windows management. Now BIDs mostly stick to the "clean and safe" activities of street cleaning and providing "ambassadors." Under its new management, for example, GJDC has become much more sensitive to the concerns of local elected officials and city agencies—after decades of fierce independence, even when most of GJDC's funding came through city government. It has few programs of its own not initiated by the government. At the same time, with the new cadre of highly trained professionals now working in New York City government, local government has become more interested in issues of design and small-scale policy experimentation. This creates a tremendous opportunity for a renewed partnership between nonprofits and local government.

Independent nonprofits proved to be important partners to the government in executing economic-development strategy. They have demonstrated the capacity to engage in place-improving work that the government can't execute because of risk aversion, issues of scale, and inflexibility in contracting. The government doesn't have the resources or the capacity to sweat the details of place management required in heavily used downtown parks (as is the case with Pershing Square in Los Angeles). Government agencies, while responsive to ultimate control by elected officials (which nonprofits are not) are incentivized to be risk averse, and elected officials operate on short timelines that are dictated by their terms of office. CDCs have the ability to take greater risks and to patiently execute projects over extended periods of time. They can participate in the real estate market in ways that are impossible for the government because of its regulatory framework. The principal government tools for economic development of incentives and facility location have not proven themselves to be effective vehicles for creating sustainable, value-adding, improved commercial conditions.

Creating desirable places will attract, retain, and create new businesses and produce local economic vitality, as many government officials now recognize. Conditions are ripe for unusually productive relationships between nonprofits and the government. Locally elected government officials can further change course to employ nonprofits to engage in placemaking to foster community improvement rather than maintaining a dubious and, thanks to Amazon, now politically unpopular policy of government subsidy of economic development. It can delegate innovation, experimentation, and risk taking to nonprofits and support that delegation with funds and regulatory backing. BIDs and local development entities should be in the business of attempting creative solutions to improving and managing public space.

CHAPTER 13

DOWNTOWN JAMAICA

Jamaica, Queens, is now experiencing dramatic change. It has been a part of New York City since 1898, and for centuries, it was the civic, transportation, and commercial center of Long Island. In the late 1950s and early 1960s, that began to change, as businesses and white families began to move out of the downtown to settle farther east on the island, in the same pattern that economically decimated so many American downtowns in an arc that runs from St. Louis to Boston. Within a decade, Downtown Jamaica, home to the first supermarket in the country (King Kullen) and the first Macy's store outside Manhattan, lost its three department stores, its daily newspaper, and its three local banks.[1]

What was left was a rich physical and social infrastructure. Jamaica was an early rail center and remains the home of Long Island Rail Road's main transfer station and headquarters. As a result, it was the center of the Queens County bus network, with scores of lines passing through or terminating there. The downtown was also served by three subway lines, two of which were elevated as they arrived in Jamaica. The John F. Kennedy International Airport was nearby. Jamaica was the home of the

Queens supreme and family courts as well as the central library for the huge Queens Library system. Demographically, southeast Queens was also one of the largest communities of African American (largely middle-class) homeowners in the country.

But for decades, despite hundreds of millions of dollars of government investment in moving the elevated subway line underground, streetscape improvements, the construction of York College (a senior college of the city university system), new family and civil court facilities, and hundreds thousands of square feet of federal offices for the Social Security Administration and the Food and Drug Administration, Downtown Jamaica maintained a reputation for a lack of public safety and resisted new private investment. Those public investments seemed to have very limited secondary economic effects.

The mile-long retail corridor of Jamaica Avenue in recent years reflected a retailing environment similar to those that have long existed on the Fulton Mall in Brooklyn; the Hub in the Bronx; and 14th, 34th, and 125th Streets in Manhattan—with many of the same retailers and property owners—featuring discount stores and mostly regional chains. Downtown Jamaica has few sit-down restaurants, only one operating movie theater (with multiple screens), no department store, and only a few high-quality national retailers.

What Is Happening in Jamaica Now

But by 2018, there were a number of major projects around the Long Island Rail Road station. The first to go into construction was a three-hundred-room Courtyard by Marriott / Fairfield Inn and Suites, being built by a private developer who became a major player in Downtown Jamaica, investing in a number of key sites. This project is unsubsidized and reportedly used offshore capital for its equity. About fifteen years ago, GJDC tried to buy the site for $2.5 million. The current developer bought it for what was that time an astonishing $6 million and held onto it for almost a decade before beginning construction.

Adjacent to the Marriott project is a sixty-thousand-square-foot parcel, assembled by GJDC and sold in mid-2015 to BRP Companies, a private, minority-owned affordable housing developer, for a seven-hundred-thousand-square-foot mixed-use project. Equity financing for that project came from Goldman Urban Investments. New York City Housing Development Corporation and Department of Housing Preservation and Development provided loans and subsidies for affordable housing. The land sale closed at the end of 2016. The project's seven hundred units are both mixed income and entirely affordable/subsidized. As a result of the requirements of the Low-Income Housing Tax Credit program, all of the units in one of the two towers are for low-income residents.

The third major station area project is three hundred units of affordable housing on Ninety-Fifth Avenue, the tallest tower in Jamaica, built by Artimus Construction. That project also took advantage of the city's affordable housing subsidy programs. The site is made up of two parcels that we at GJDC regarded as "holdouts" from a much larger, adjacent, sixty-thousand-square-foot site owned by the Stark family, longtime, major area property owners.

GJDC put significant effort into a one-million-square-foot megaproject for the Stark site—a proposal to build a Korean-developed Merchandise Mart. The developer Washington Square Partners, the builder Jeffrey Brown, the design firm of Greenberg Farrow, and consultant Jonathan Rose were all involved in that venture. The New York City Economic Development Corporation granted $4 million to the project for demolition and remediation of the distressed former meat-packing plant on the property—which at the time was a big step forward for Jamaica. That sixty-thousand-square-foot lot and a ten-thousand-square-foot lot across 148th Street from the larger parcel, also owned by the Stark family, remain empty.

Artimus has also secured a ground lease for a site on the other side of Ninety-Fourth Avenue from its other project, a building formerly occupied by a seafood wholesale operation, where they again plan affordable housing. Artimus is an outstanding organization that does high-quality projects. They have a real commitment to the communities in which they work.

The former GJDC marketing center on Ninety-Fourth Avenue and Sutphin Boulevard was sold to Able Development in the fall of 2015. Able is developing a 250-room Hilton Garden Inn on that property directly across Sutphin Boulevard from the AirTrain terminal. That project is receiving no government subsidy or other support, although it was sold to the developer by GJDC at a favorable price.

The biggest development in Jamaica is not near the transit hub but is on the site of the closed Mary Immaculate Hospital across from King Park, Downtown Jamaica's only open space. When the St. Vincent's health care system, then called Caritas, went into bankruptcy, the Dormitory Authority of the State of New York had a $45 million lien on the property. We at GJDC attempted to intervene in the proceedings to hold off the sale in order to find a high-quality use for the site. GJDC's leadership was deeply concerned about the potential for conversion of the hospital into a gigantic facility for the homeless and the negative effect of such a social service–related use on the community. We were unsuccessful in preventing the sale, and the property and another Caritas parcel were sold for less than $10 million to a speculator. The speculator flipped the site to major real estate owners, the Chetrit family, also reportedly for less than $10 million. The Chetrits at one time had a major interest in what was once the Sears Tower in Chicago (renamed the Willis Tower), which they sold for what was reported to be a ten-figure gain. Nothing happened on the Mary Immaculate site for a number of years, but active development began taking place after 2015. On the main hospital site facing the park, hundreds of market-rate units have been created within the shell of the former hospital structure. It is planned to be entirely "market rate" and completely without subsidy. The presence of hundreds of market-rate apartments on King Park is going to have a major positive impact on Jamaica.

United American Land has a 150,000-square-foot midbox retail project at 160-08 Jamaica Avenue. This is another company with an outstanding track record of building attractive, contextual projects and signing up high-quality tenants. Among the tenants are Burlington Coat Factory and H&M—quality national retailers new to Jamaica. The project includes a Chipotle, and across the street is a new Starbucks. This should also make a major difference in the downtown.[2]

One interesting point is that while some neighborhoods across the city complain about the generic quality of national chains, the proliferation of banks and drug stores, and the loss of unique local retailers, in Jamaica, the attitude is different. Members of the community most frequently requested that GJDC bring Red Lobster, Victoria's Secret, and Starbucks to the downtown. Community members felt that national retailers had "redlined" Jamaica and were unwilling to locate in a community of color, depriving them of the opportunity to access those perceived-to-be higher-quality products and services.

The Impact of Placemaking on Jamaica

All of this development began after 2015, driven by the changed perception of the downtown that is the result of the placemaking activities of GJDC and the Jamaica Avenue BID. This dramatic improvement in a disinvested neighborhood that had languished for decades, which came about largely because of the improvement of the perception of its public spaces, hasn't received the attention it deserves, even in the placemaking world. This is principally because the board and president of GJDC had heavily invested in the vision of Jamaica as a satellite office center contained in *The Second Regional Plan*. As a result, much of the placemaking work in Jamaica, which was not geared to attracting office tenants, was done without drawing much public attention. In addition, as the economic situation in Jamaica started to gain momentum, a number of local elected officials created programs to demonstrate support for improved conditions in the downtown, creating their own narratives to explain the neighborhood's progress.

I am convinced that it was the work we did in improving the perception of public space in Jamaica that pushed it past the "tipping point" for economic revitalization. Decades were spent on conventional economic-development tactics—particularly in obtaining public sector funds for new government facilities in Jamaica. Tens of millions of dollars and thousands of hours were expended on site assemblage for potential office buildings. The advantages of Jamaica's transportation infrastructure were endlessly touted. Two attempts were made to persuade JetBlue, the borough's largest employer, to relocate its headquarters to Downtown Jamaica without success. Tens of millions of dollars in earmarked federal transportation funds were secured for infrastructure improvements to address concerns raised by JetBlue about suggested sites. Those efforts were ultimately unsuccessful, and JetBlue is now headquartered in Long Island City. A senior JetBlue executive reportedly said that the company didn't want to be a "pioneer."[3]

Investments began to be made in Jamaica only when developers became convinced that the public spaces of Jamaica were safe and that positive social activities were taking place in its parks and on its sidewalks. I believe that the continuing transformation of Jamaica is every bit as important a story as the revitalization of Bryant Park. But unlike Bryant Park, it isn't a block from the offices of the country's most important newspaper—it is fifteen miles away. The transformation of an aging Main Street serving a community of color into a vibrant, desirable place, due in large part to public-space-improvement activities, is just as significant and remarkable a story and just as much of a model for other downtowns as the changes the BIDs brought to Midtown Manhattan.

THE ROLE OF NONPROFIT ORGANIZATIONS IN REVITALIZATION

The essential elements leading to this dramatic change in the late 2000s were concerted efforts to improve the perception of the downtown, led by

Figure 21. Marriott Hotel under construction on Archer Avenue in Jamaica, Queens. Billions of dollars in new investment was catalyzed by placemaking.

GJDC and the local BIDs through placemaking strategies, as were GJDC's own site assembly and development work. Zoning changes enacted by the city in 2007 to increase density in the station area enabled development that would not previously have been possible, but the most powerful instrument in New York City's usual development promotion toolbox—city-owned property—was almost nonexistent in this community.

When GJDC was founded forty years ago, as discussed earlier, non-profits were seen as an essential partner to the government in improving local commercial conditions. I've noticed in recent trips to Buffalo and Cincinnati that nonprofit Local Development Corporations (LDCs), in partnership with cooperative, progressive local governments, have been the principal drivers of successful, sustainable downtown economic revitalization in those places. However, over my twenty-five years of involvement in downtown revitalization and public space improvement, I have seen a change in this view in New York City: a profound skepticism about the role of private nonprofit entities in economic development. This results from both increased sophistication and capacity among government economic-development professionals and a concern among public officials about potential problems that might be created by initiatives not controlled by the government.

There continues to be, however, a vital role for private, nongovernmental entities to play in local economic development—and risk is at the center of this function. Risks of all kinds are of great concern to both elected and appointed public officials. A failed project can be career ending for either—particularly in the take-no-prisoners "gotcha" world of tabloid journalism in which the public sector operates in New York. LDCs and BIDs are well positioned to take such risks, to take the blame if projects don't work out, and to provide distance for the government from the failure. Of course, such risks must be carefully calibrated by the nonprofits, and good management can minimize the negative impact of projects that don't work out. Where risks have been properly assessed, any damage caused by failure can be fully and quickly remediated. Without taking on risk, it is *impossible* to make real social and economic change in distressed downtowns and public spaces. In my experience, every failure I have encountered has been able to be quickly addressed through remediation—and in a few cases with a superior outcome as a result of the fix.

PERMISSION/FORGIVENESS

Sometimes in dealing with the government, it is better for nonprofits to ask forgiveness than permission! When GJDC approached the city's Department of Transportation for a permit to place hanging baskets on lampposts around Downtown Jamaica, DOT demanded that we perform complex, expensive wind tests on the baskets—even though they were firmly attached to the poles and did not actually "hang." We withdrew our application. Then we put them up anyway. There were advantages to being way out in Queens, fifteen miles from city hall. The program is a huge success and has made a major contribution to the sense of social control on the streets of Jamaica.

In order to deal with a severe problem of taxi hustling and chaos among livery cabs around the LIRR station, we worked with the city's Taxi and Limousine Commission (TLC) to create a taxi line outside the station. The commissioner of the TLC exercised a certain amount of flexibility in the establishment of the "pilot" program. A local livery cab company agreed to provide the cars on the line in exchange for the exclusive right to provide service to the line. We bought a prefabricated booth for the cab company dispatcher to occupy. We required that the company provide twenty-four-hour coverage for the booth. Since the booth was lit and occupied twenty-four hours a day, seven days a week, we had full-time "eyes on the street" and a source of light and activity, all paid for by the cab company. The program was a great success and tremendously improved the sense of social control at one of the most visible places in the downtown that had previously seemed dark and threatening. This location was the first exposure that many visitors had as they arrived in Jamaica. As a result of the taxi stand, the taxi hustlers aggressively soliciting rides from travelers leaving the station (something to which I was regularly subjected) were gone, as were the frequent fistfights among drivers for fares.

What we didn't do was apply for the required license from DOT to put a structure on the sidewalk, which would have required reviews by DOT of the site but also by the city's Public Design Commission of the structure, which was ordered from a catalog and was not a terribly "high design." We had the capacity to take on the risks of noncompliance—of which we were well aware.

Several years after the installation of the booth, I got an irate call from a longtime colleague at DOT demanding that we remove the booth and seek a permit. She had me when she said that I, of all people, knew the rules for "revocable consents," the kind of permit required for such a structure.

I politely suggested to her that if DOT wanted the booth removed, they could come and take it away and it would be OK with us. Of course, I knew that would never happen. DOT was not going to go to the trouble and didn't have the resources. Because the booth was on a sidewalk adjacent to state property, there was no one to cite for a violation of DOT rules.

The dispatch program became obsolete with the advent of the city's Green Cab Program, which provided an increased level of licensed service to areas outside of Manhattan.[4] When Uber and other ride-sharing apps came along, the dispatch service became even less necessary, and it disappeared (as has the booth, apparently). But with the advent of the new, legal services, the previously existing chaos among taxi hustlers went away.

Both of these programs presented risks to GJDC, particularly of annoying important public officials. But success can be a great healer, and annoyed public officials are more likely to look the other way for a program that has proved itself.

One further point is that the government is often willing to be flexible in applying rules to projects that it deems to be temporary or to demonstrate the feasibility of a novel approach to solving a problem. In many cases, administrative rules explicitly make exceptions for temporary uses and "pilot" programs. Building a program on a temporary basis can be an excellent vehicle for gaining government authorization of an otherwise difficult-to-approve project. Again, the nonprofit is taking the risk that at the end of the permitted period, the relevant agency can demand the termination of the pilot program. There must be a sincere willingness on the part of the nonprofit to pay the cost of taking down the physical aspects of the project. The more it demonstrates its credibility in doing so, the more the agencies involved come to trust the nonprofit as a partner in experimentation. Generally, though, an experimental program that proves to be successful will ultimately gain the requisite government approvals.

Nonprofits have other process-related benefits in driving urban revitalization. They can make decisions quickly, with minimal levels of approval required and without cumbersome restrictions on contracting and personnel hiring. They can borrow money from banks (as well as using conventional public finance vehicles). They can reinvest operating surpluses back into new mission-related projects. Also, the decision-making is closer to the ground—a properly governed nonprofit has a board of local stakeholders who are more in touch with community needs than centralized government officials, particularly in a place as large as New York City. But high-quality governance, including complete financial transparency, is the price private nonprofits must pay in order to responsibly exercise this kind of flexibility.

WHAT WE DID

GJDC's role in catalyzing improved conditions in Jamaica was essential. Over twenty years, it purchased and improved disinvested properties (including parking facilities) as well as assembled key sites for development. It worked to improve the perception of outsiders of the neighborhood through placemaking strategies. These included establishing three BIDs (two of them among the first in the city) and creating its own security and horticultural improvement programs (which the BIDs themselves did not have the capacity to provide). GJDC created and maintained a robust and effective retail attraction and retention program. From its very early days, GJDC saw the arts and artists as an important part of downtown renewal. It not only programmed arts events for the downtown but adaptively reused an abandoned city structure into a community arts center and an abandoned church into a performing arts facility. As described in chapter 11, GJDC provided low-cost gallery and studio space for artists as well as low-cost space for artists for rehearsing and creating theater and music works. It pushed to ensure that programming in public space was a regular part of the pulse of the downtown rather than an occasional event.

There is much more for local nonprofits to do in order to "nudge" downtown redevelopment in a positive direction. GJDC became more effective as it de-emphasized a top-down master-planned approach to securing government facilities and attracting office towers and tenants that the market was clearly resisting. It instead stimulated the nascent market forces for housing, larger-format retail spaces, and hotel rooms.

By contrast, the decades-long attempt to foster office building development was a bust. The 2007 rezoning of the downtown, while essential in removing the manufacturing restrictions from key sites, probably over-zoned some of the lots around the transit hub, making them more difficult to develop, as property owners sought to be paid more for development rights on their property than the sites could economically justify. Today, powerful market forces are at work inducing development in Jamaica. Markets can be nudged, but they can't be controlled, and it is nearly impossible to do a fine-grained plan for them. I continue to believe that concerns about gentrification and displacement may be misplaced. Alan Erenhalt wrote clearly about this in an excellent book review in the *New York Times*.[5] As he so wisely says in his review, "Gentrification has winners and losers. Urban decline makes losers out of everyone."[6]

THE FOURTH REGIONAL PLAN: THE LIMITS OF PLANNING AND PLACEMAKING

The release of the Regional Plan Association's (RPA) *The Fourth Regional Plan* in 2017 got me to thinking about the relationship between placemaking and area planning.[7] Places and pedestrians are well integrated into the plan: its recommendation number 23 (of sixty-one states): "On city streets, prioritize people over cars."[8] Arguably recommendations number 57 ("Remake underutilized auto-dependent landscapes") and 61 ("Expand and improve public space in the urban core") also have placemaking casts to them. There is even a page on the plan's website for "Places."[9] This is a signal of how much placemaking practice has worked its way into planning culture, and this is a very good thing. But the nature of regional planning is decidedly top down and large scale—particularly when it comes to talking about expanding and/or upgrading transportation infrastructure—and it puzzled me as to how people-oriented thinking about urban revitalization fits into creating a large-scale, long-term vision for an area.[10] *The Fourth Regional Plan* again puts a focus on Jamaica—as a potential regional office center.

As I have noted, the efforts that went toward creating a regional office center in Jamaica, in retrospect, were probably misplaced and likely slowed its development. It certainly was logical to conclude that because of Jamaica's unique density of transit infrastructure and its general underdevelopment, it would be an efficient and desirable site for office towers—but the private sector remained unpersuaded. The best example of this is the unsuccessful campaign, with multiple initiatives over the years, to attract JetBlue to Jamaica.

The major rezoning in 2007, designed to encourage office development around Jamaica Station, failed to catalyze any office development. In fact, what private investors did turn out to be interested in for that area was the development of housing, retail space, and hotel rooms. Once the perception of the downtown was improved though successful placemaking activity, more than a billion dollars were set loose in redevelopment activity after 2015 for these types of uses. (The same scenario has played out in Downtown Brooklyn, which was rezoned as an office center and instead has become an archipelago of unanticipated, tall residential towers because of the great demand for both affordable and market-rate residential space. There has turned out to be a very limited market for new office space in Downtown Brooklyn.)

The failure of the plan to change course about Jamaica's future reflects the challenges faced by regional planners. Principally, what appears to planners to be logical and best isn't necessarily what actual people spending/investing actual dollars (residents, business owners, developers) prefer in real time. Projects shoehorned into an abstract plan unsupported by market forces generally fail. As Yogi Berra probably didn't say, it's difficult to make predictions, especially about the future.

The RPA made every effort to make the formation of the Fourth Plan as inclusive as practically possible. They engaged a wide range of stakeholder groups in an exhaustive number of events geared toward civic engagement. But when a plan like this is written, in order for it to be taken seriously by elected officials and other thought leaders, it has to take into account the political forces that are likely to constrain policy outcomes. The RPA itself has a lot invested in its history of involvement in southeast Queens. Longtime leaders in Jamaica, with decades of engagement with the RPA, continue to be committed to the vision of Jamaica as a satellite-office city. In the making of the plan, there was no serious countervailing force for an alternative vision of Jamaica Center—and hence the continued featuring of Jamaica as a commercial center in the plan.

I had a conversation about Jamaica with a longtime civic and commercial leader, one of the regional thinkers whom I most respect. He told me that in his view, the development of the Jamaica station area for housing and hotels is a missed opportunity. I disagreed and explained to him my view that that the development of the downtown as a center for affordable housing, retail space, and hotel rooms will produce excellent results for the region, the city, and the neighborhood. Jamaica is developing into a vibrant, unique mixed-use, mixed-income community of color. It will provide a wide range of lively living, shopping, dining, and entertainment options. As it continues to develop, it won't be like any other community we now know—and that is likely to be a good thing, including for the people who have lived in the neighborhood for decades. It will become a new and exceptional kind of urban center.

From a place-based perspective, the plan got a good deal right. Emphasizing transit and thinking seriously about the pedestrian experience (as opposed to using automobile throughput as the only planning metric), as the plan does, are basic placemaking concepts. Also, the plan's focus on enhancing and enlarging public space is obviously important to improving places. But with respect to the future of Jamaica, the plan probably has it wrong.

At the same time, I'm not sure that placemaking has much to contribute to thinking about how major future infrastructural investments ought to be made or where they should go. What can placemaking tell us about where to put new transit lines, how to finance transit improvements, or how the governance structure of transit agencies might be changed to lower the costs of transit infrastructure? I don't think very much. These are difficult, complex policy and political questions—and the RPA has proven over the decades to be a serious, thoughtful analyst of such questions as well as a source of creative ideas for answers. Importantly, the RPA, as both independent of government and free from the restrictions created by the borders of political jurisdictions, is in a unique position to provide this kind of evaluation—with some autonomy from the interest groups that ordinarily affect government decision-making. There are both large-scale problems out there and competing interests to be reconciled in setting regional priorities and creating a regional vision. Placemaking, while it has an important role to play in informing and creating context for the conversation, is limited in what it has to contribute to that discussion.

THE FUTURE OF JAMAICA

There is still more to be done in terms of placemaking in Jamaica. The pedestrian experience on Jamaica Avenue needs dramatic improvement (more space for pedestrians, shade, and seating), traffic at key intersections has become impossible, and bus speeds are snail-like. The allocation of space among pedestrians, cars (both moving and parked), and buses needs to be rethought, and the nonprofits can play an important role thinking this through and executing a new vision for the street.

GJDC, the BIDs, and other community-based organizations need to continue to create opportunities to take advantage of the low-cost space in the community for artists and "makers" in order to encourage a lively, attractive scene in the downtown (tech, by contrast, doesn't seem to have much of an interest in southeast Queens). The nonprofits have a role in encouraging high-quality design as development picks up its pace. Importantly, they can be an advocate for ensuring that the social and cultural elements that make this community distinctive aren't lost as development proceeds. Jamaica has the potential to become an attractive, vibrant, affordable, unique community of African American, Caribbean, Central American, South Asian, and other residents—and a national model. There is no doubt in my mind, though, that it was our placemaking activity in Jamaica that was the key catalyst in making this possible.

CHAPTER 14

REVITALIZING SMALLER
TOWNS AND SPACES

Placemaking practice should become at least as important in smaller cities and towns as it is in big city public spaces and downtowns. Over the last thirty years, the focus of community revitalization efforts has been almost exclusively urban, with the most attention paid to its impact on the biggest cities. We've learned that making great downtowns and public spaces can be catalytic in improving the quality of life for city residents, and the evidence for this can be seen in large cities across the country. This focus on the biggest urban centers made sense, given the significant economic and social decline of American cities beginning in the 1950s and the 1960s, when cars and suburbs were in and cities were out. Cities were abandoned, and many downtown commercial buildings emptied. Today, these cities have a new problem: because of their economic success and desirability, many neighborhoods in these coastal gateway cities have become unaffordable for young and creative people—Richard Florida's "creative class." Much has been written about the deep economic divide in New York, San Francisco, and Los Angeles. Florida has most recently observed that the "middle class" has been priced out of the most dynamic urban centers.[1]

At the same time, in the regions between the coasts, outside of the cities that participate in the world economy, people seem to feel left behind. There is much talk about "coastal elites" versus "flyover country." In his best-selling book *Hillbilly Elegy*, J. D. Vance opens a window on the sociocultural world of the Scotch-Irish of southwestern Ohio.[2] Vance, a former marine and Ohio State and Yale Law School graduate who once worked for venture capitalist Peter Thiel, has returned to live in his native Ohio. He is clear eyed about the folks among whom he grew up. While Vance lovingly describes the tight bonds that hold Appalachian families together and their devotion to a shared if often self-destructive southern rural culture, he also describes their suspicion and disengagement from community institutions, even religious ones. Vance writes about a deep cynicism about politics and a profound alienation from cities, education, and national cultural trends among his family and former neighbors. As described by Vance, these people have little shared social experience outside of their families. They are profoundly suspicious of outsiders.

A similar worldview is portrayed in Lynn Nottage's play *Sweat*, winner of the Pulitzer Prize in 2017.[3] *Sweat* is about industrial workers in a small city in Pennsylvania; the characters are both white and black; and Nottage, the playwright, is African American. Nottage's characters have great depth, and she writes with genuine understanding. The play is about the fallout from the closing of a local factory that is the community's largest employer. Most striking to me about the play was less the economic impact of the plant closure on its former employees (which, of course, is substantial) and more the closure's political and social impact. The workers become helpless, angry, and defeated when the factory closed—and they set upon each other. The loss of work led to the loss of community and identity. Both of these works vividly illustrate the social disengagement being experienced by so many people between the coasts. I would argue that such disengagement is a likely source of much of the political anger now dividing the country.

Going forward in order to maximize their social impact, placemakers will need to shift at least some of their focus from big cities to smaller cities and nonurban communities. Reengaging those who feel cut off from the social life of the places in which they live should become a major focus of placemakers.

The largest cities are generally doing pretty well—with a few notable exceptions. But to my knowledge, not much attention is being given to rebuilding the social ties in the less dense parts of the country through the creation of quality public spaces. I use the term *public space* here in the broadest possible sense to include parks, downtowns, schools, libraries, or even coffee shops. The large swath of people who feel disengaged from their wider communities and as a result fall back on tribal impulses to fear the "other" needs to be socially reengaged. One thing we might be doing right now in order to renew the national civic culture is to focus on working with the citizens of smaller and rural communities to reclaim their public spaces and create opportunities in them for social interaction and engagement.

Project for Public Spaces (PPS) is already working on a Department of Agriculture initiative dealing with design in rural spaces—so there is a precedent for this kind of work.[4] The community-building programs that PPS does as the "front-end" work for public space and downtown revitalization can be immensely valuable in addressing the apparent widespread discontent with the current state of affairs of the residents of smaller places caused by social and civic disengagement. This kind of effort is especially important today where population density is lower because in those places, people are physically farther apart. As a result, making connections and having opportunities to share concerns and values are likely more logistically difficult there.

The social changes being wrought by the internet probably have a more isolating effect in less dense cities and towns and in rural communities because they create opportunities for a kind of faux social experience. On the internet, you can get engaged in what feels like social interactions with other people without having to actually ever get to know them or deal with issues of difference with them. If you don't like the conversation, you just end it (often after delivering an insulting, personal attack). This is much more difficult when you are sitting next to someone.

As we all have experienced, social media has an addictive quality—crowding out other activities that involve real, satisfying social interaction. As a result, we become more isolated from other people through our internet experiences rather than more engaged with them. The kind of vitriol and false information that have become the meat and potatoes of the online experience for millions of Americans would be unlikely to have taken place between two people actually talking to each other over the backyard fence or at the neighborhood bar.

Bringing the process of community engagement to less dense communities could provide significant improvements in the quality of life of their residents. Creating social spaces that draw people together over farther distances would likely also improve feelings of being a part of the larger community and lower the anger and sense of alienation of those who don't live in cities. Creating and drawing attention to great places in less dense areas might also attract college-educated creative young people to live in those less expensive, depopulated cities and towns. The positive side of the internet is that, along with the vast package delivery systems of Federal Express, UPS, and Amazon, most of the world's culture and goods are available to people anywhere in the United States. People who want or need less expensive space can have the walkable, authentic community outside of the coasts without giving up access to independent films, books, and stinky cheese—all of which are now deliverable to their homes.[5]

Great places are likely to attract well-educated, talented, entrepreneurial creative people. There is a chemistry that we don't fully understand that generates powerful economic forces of value creation. This process occurs when attractive places bring together creative people. It is the kind of thing that has happened in SoHo and Williamsburg in New York City and in Silicon Valley and SoMa in San Francisco. As Tony Goldman demonstrated in his real estate development activity in SoHo, South Beach, and Wyn-wood, placemaking practice is replicable and transferable—not unique to any particular place. The key element is the creation of places where people want to be—places so interesting and enjoyable that people elect to move to them.

I'm certainly wary of proposing an elite "coastal" approach to a problem people outside of coastal cities may not even think they have. But place-making practices have proven to be so successful in large urban communities across the country that it seems to me very likely that they have great potential for enriching the lives of those who live outside of the major urban centers as well. We might spend more time thinking about how community engagement and public space improvement can be adapted to less dense communities. Vehicles for introducing placemaking practice in rural communities need to be crafted so that those to whom the ideas might seem alien won't dismiss them out of hand. We also need to create scalable programmatic funding and implementation strategies that can bring this work to places where it has not previously existed.

This is going to take some serious rethinking by those of us in the field. In less dense places, cars are a necessity. Walking and biking are not realistic options in many if not most of these places. Some of the "hipsterish" veneers and the kind of "eat your peas (or arugula)" moralism that placemaking has taken on that reflect the sophisticated consumer preferences of some college-educated folks will need to be stripped away in order to introduce placemaking to a new audience of nonurban residents. The basic work of bringing people together, listening to them, and having them listen to each other and leave the process feeling that they have been deeply heard could be essential in addressing some of the anger and alienation that have become such a potent political force. This kind of engagement will also be essen-tial in integrating new residents with different experiences and values into depopulated traditionally insular rural and exurban communities.

The creation of lively social spaces in small towns and suburban com-munities is likely every bit as important in those places as it is to big city life—if, perhaps, very different in form. When people are not connected to folks outside of their immediate families, it is easy to understand how they might become isolated and disengaged from larger social networks and resistant to newcomers. Without firsthand experience of people from different backgrounds and points of view, how can we be expected to understand and appreciate those differences? I suspect that the frustration becomes even more potent when people feel like no one either in their own communities or nationally is paying attention to their concerns. Placemaking is about the things we can do to create vital public spaces where people can have fulfilling social interactions. Those interactions are a basic human need. Bringing such spaces to neglected places can revitalize them and attract new people who have the capacity to add economic value to them. This is important work.

An example of a small place hundreds of miles from any big city is Gloversville, New York, which is an hour from Albany. In Gloversville, placemaking as local policy seems to be showing great potential for economic revitalization—but it also at one point encountered the predictable resistance from a few local property owners. We need to figure out how to win those folks over—and this book is certainly intended to be part of that solution.

THE PARABLE OF GLOVERSVILLE, NEW YORK

Gloversville, New York, is about fifty miles northeast of Albany at the edge of the Adirondacks. For 150 years, it was the center of American glove manufacturing and a thriving commercial hub. Being Gloversville was not unlike being, say, "Buggy Whipville," and by the last quarter of the twentieth century, its classic Main Street had become hollowed out with limited economic activity as the glove manufacturing business collapsed. Today, Gloversville has a population of about fifteen thousand (while at its peak, it had a population of thirty thousand), with a median household income of about $35,000. The downtown has a dollar store, a large number of social service providers, and a lot of empty space. There are a few small industrial firms located in county-sponsored industrial parks outside of the downtown and several longtime retailers on the Main Street. There are more than a half-dozen empty multistory former glove factories in or immediately adjacent to the downtown (all of which will require some level of environmental remediation in order to be repurposed).

Glove making must have been a highly lucrative endeavor for many, many years because the architecture and design of the commercial buildings in Gloversville are mostly of very high quality, and a good deal of that built legacy remains, waiting to be reused. The elegant, private Eccentrics Club is well maintained and is in the middle of the downtown—evidence of the wealth that was generated and at least some of which remains there.[6]

What brought Gloversville to my attention—and one of the things that makes it distinctive—is that the local economic-development authorities have made placemaking a central part of their strategy to revitalize the town. The Fulton County Center for Regional Growth (CRG) hired local resident Jennifer Jennings as Gloversville's "downtown development specialist." Jennings is energetic and imaginative about the possibilities for the downtown. She also knows her placemaking stuff and has brought a range of new programs to the town—including collaborating with the local BID on a micropark on Main Street.[7] She has developed a series of events for the downtown—featuring a regular twilight market.[8]

What the town has going for it is an unusually attractive, intact turn of the twentieth-century physical environment and lots of low-cost, potentially available commercial space. It's in a beautiful, even spectacular part of New York State—the Mohawk Valley, site of the historic Erie Canal—with great access to outdoor recreation and an active local agricultural economy. With so much attention being paid to urban housing costs, a town with the character of Gloversville, four hours from New York City and less than an hour from the rail station and the airport in Albany that has a great deal of inexpensive living and working space, should be very attractive to current big-city dwellers who are finding their current

Figure 22. Main Street in Gloversville, New York, has remarkable integrity and vernacular architecture but features a great deal of empty space—creating great opportunity.

arrangements not worth the money. What with the internet and the expansive reach of national delivery services, Gloversville is practically adjacent to Brooklyn—but with space renting for only around $7 per square foot.

At the center of Gloversville on Main Street is the seven-year-old Mohawk Harvest Cooperative Market. This well-designed market sells local produce, groceries, and crafts and has a coffee bar. Based on my conversation with its staff, the market has the capacity and need for substantial additional sales. It seemed to me an underleveraged asset for downtown redevelopment.

The placemaking strategy for the repopulation of Gloversville should be focused on drawing a critical mass of college-educated, creative, entrepreneurial folks to live in the downtown near the market. This kind of movement is already underway. Appropriately, a high-fashion glove maker has a workshop and store in the town.

The economic-development officials in Gloversville need to start small to test the market, gain control of some of the upper floors of retail space on the block where the market is, and make it available to rent at very low cost and market it to independent artists and recent college graduates as living/working space. With a few dozen of those folks living and running their own businesses downtown, a critical mass will be established, improving sales at the market and attracting/creating the bars and restaurants that will inevitably follow in their wake. As I have argued, building this kind of critical mass is essential to effective economic-development activity. This is the Goldman Properties' place-based strategy for urban revitalization.[9] The importance of establishing a critical mass of activity to generate secondary economic-development effects is essential to inducing those effects and creating the synergies essential to downtown improvement.

There are places, like Newark, New Jersey, that have implemented a large number of downtown development projects that on their own have been successful. But those projects have not had the kind of transformative impact their creators were hoping for because the projects are not adjacent to—and are, in fact, far apart from—each other. It is adjacency and the creation of a critical mass that makes economic-development projects like the ones we did in Jamaica, Queens, catalytic. Quality projects that aren't physically related become one-offs, with limited impact on the neighborhood as a whole. The creation of a critical mass is key. Spreading out projects around the downtown does not have the same kind of impact. It doesn't create the interaction and buzz that make living downtown fun and draw other people to want to be there.

Once there are a few new people living downtown—perhaps making art, doing website design, providing other professional services, selling on the internet, or coding—the market will draw them. In Gloversville, creating retail continuity and further enlivening the block that includes the co-op market will lead to the organic growth of economic activity—and spread around the downtown as people discover the town and its attractiveness.

The market needs to populate its adjacent sidewalks with movable tables and chairs—building on its already existing assets. Making people who are in the downtown visible to other people creates a virtuous circle. Central to Holly Whyte's philosophy is that visible people draw other people. For example, the CRG-created micropark in the downtown needs to be moved from a site across the street to a parking space in front of the co-op market in order to contribute to building on the existing activity there. It is now not adjacent to any other generator of activity. The micropark is where it is because residents complained that putting it in front of the market would eliminate an important parking space. But in a place with as little downtown activity and as much empty space as Gloversville, how important can one or two parking spaces be? Still, this is the kind of resistance to change and to the counterintuitive ideas that are essential to placemaking that such suggestions for new initiatives frequently encounter.

Many small towns consider trying to build bars and restaurants that will attract visitors. However, this is generally a low-probability enterprise and not a good strategy. Attracting a one-star chef to create a destination restaurant in a disinvested downtown is unlikely. Even if it happens, the track record of such ventures isn't very good. Relying on outside visitors is a high-risk strategy in a place that isn't on the way to anywhere else.

Similarly, attracting existing businesses to relocate to Gloversville is the conventional approach to economic development and creating jobs. However, this approach often requires the expenditure of public funds to attract such businesses, those businesses generally bring employees with them, and there may not necessarily be a skills match with the local labor pool. An organic approach of fostering local economic activity by making downtown a desirable place to live and work is a proven, effective long-term strategy. What Gloversville has to offer is inexpensive space in a walkable, attractive downtown environment—this is the resource on which a successful revitalization program can be based.

Unsurprisingly, Gloversville's placemaking efforts have run into resistance. The downtown has a BID, and a few property owners didn't want to pay the assessment and sought to have it eliminated. There are other property owners who tried to defund Jennings's position with CRG. I have mentioned several times how placemaking tactics can seem counterintuitive to people. In many places, well-meaning revitalization projects are unsuccessful because of the skepticism of local property owners. We certainly faced this in Jamaica, and it was a brake on our effectiveness. Many business people and property owners are unconvinced that money spent on public space improvement will provide any benefit to them. One of the most unpleasant meetings I ever attended was with the then owner of the McAlpin Hotel on West Thirty-Fourth Street. He was opposed to the imposition of the BID assessment on his residential rental property (that also had extensive lower-floor retail space). He was literally enraged at having to pay the assessment. His anger was frightening. He did not see any value added to his investment from the BID's activities. He had no way to directly recover the assessment from his rent-stabilized residential tenants. Of course, since the establishment of the BID, the value of the retail and even of the residential space and the increased cash flow from the property have been greater than the minimal BID assessment that owner paid.[10] But it was hugely frustrating not to be able to make this case prospectively to this owner.

In Gloversville, a downtown revitalization scheme is likely to benefit existing residents and property owners in a number of ways. Service jobs will be created for locals in the businesses created by the new residents. Of course, as the downtown improves, the quality of life improves for everyone as retail options expand and public spaces become more usable and attractive. New residents and small businesses will raise downtown property values and expand the tax base to support municipal service delivery. In addition, having more college-educated residents of child-bearing age in the downtown will bring a demand for higher standards and the energy and resources to improve local public schools. As I hope I have demonstrated throughout this book, the returns from money spent on public space improvement are many orders of magnitude greater than the amounts expended. Most recently, Vince DeSantis, the moving force for placemaking activity in Gloversville, was elected mayor, which bodes well for Gloversville's downtown.[11]

Of course, it is impossible to prove what is going to happen in the future. Good quantitative studies of the economic impact of BIDs and other public-space-improvement efforts are difficult to construct and hard to find. Establishing a viable "control" for purposes of statistical analysis has been found to be hugely challenging. A methodologically solid study of the economic impact of the Hudson River Park in Manhattan that was conducted by the Regional Plan Association in 2005 does provide a significant basis for observing the impact of public space improvement over a material period of time. That study said,

> Based on the analysis of the sales data and the correlation of sales prices with the proximity of the involved properties to the new Park, the value of the properties within three blocks of the completed Greenwich Village section of the Park was impacted significantly by the new Park. Approximately 20% of the value of properties within the first two blocks of the Greenwich Village section of the Hudson River Park can be attributed to the Park. For buildings that actually changed hands in this two-block area between 2002 and 2005 (less than 25% of all buildings) approximately 20% of the value of these buildings—$48.5 million—was attributable to the Park. Projected over the entire area within two blocks of the new section of the Park, the value attributable to the Park would approach $200 million.[12]

The study demonstrates the tremendous economic value added that comes from adjacent public-space-improvement projects.

But it is difficult for many business and property owners to envision the projected improvements from placemaking. Some say that they have seen economic-development efforts fail in the past. Some owners are happy with the return they are getting from their property and don't see the need for making current expenditures for an "uncertain" future potential increase in value. A lot of fiercely independent property owners resent being forced by third parties to do anything. Others don't want to pay for something from which they don't get immediate benefit and the expenditure of which they don't personally control. People often say that what worked in other places won't work in their town—because it is bigger, smaller, in worse shape, or in better shape than somewhere else held up as an example. There is a resentment about consultants from outside the community coming in and "dictating" what to do to local residents and business leaders who have lived and worked in the community for decades. I personally experienced some of this during my visit to Gloversville in 2017 as well as in hostile material that was posted online about my visit there.

But there is a rational case to be made for the relationship between placemaking and increased economic value—certainly there is a qualitative one. The RPA Hudson River Park study provides a sound quantitative one, even if it is about a particular place at a particular time. Placemakers do have to be better at making this case. It is my hope that this book contributes to the discussion. The kind of opposition I describe happens frequently in the face of placemaking efforts and became an issue in Gloversville. I believe there is great potential for Gloversville as a vibrant, attractive place to live and work as well as for and tens of thousands of communities like it across the country. It is important that a credible argument be developed that can persuade these skeptics. If the placemaking going on in Gloversville comes to an end, the town's future will remain much more uncertain.

COMMUNITY ENGAGEMENT AND PLACEMAKING

One final obstacle to the expansion of the success of placemaking is that there haven't been enough successful projects. This is because while many of us involved in public space improvement have become highly skilled at what I call the "front end"—that is, the community engagement and planning work—we're less good at the "back end": implementation, programming, and operations. The general model for placemaking practice—and certainly the one employed by my excellent colleagues at Project for Public Spaces—is to come to town, perform an extensive and thorough community engagement process, write a report based on the findings from that process that includes recommendations for improvements to the subject public space, and then to leave town and not come back. The local community is left with a plan—but usually without the technical capacity to implement it. PPS's mantra has been "The Community Is the Expert." But that isn't exactly right—and it certainly isn't anything Holly Whyte ever talked about. While it is important to involve community members in the process of identifying and designing a programming public space, it is not sufficient.

In the wake of Jane Jacobs and her epic battle, both on the ground and in print, with Robert Moses and the forces of big projects and grand planning, community engagement became the sine qua non of urbanism. The most important flaws in Moses's way of doing things as seen by new urbanists were his arrogance and disregard for democratic processes and the ideas and feelings of residents of neighborhoods. But in the real world, neighborhood residents are just as self-interested as anyone else and generally are unable to anticipate or to articulate how they will actually respond to new public spaces. What people say they want in charrettes and community meetings is very often not how they actually respond to a new park or plaza when the project is completed. The community engagement process can play a vital role. It is important to keep the affected public informed about plans for a public space in a personal way, and the more local residents feel ownership of a project, the more they are likely to support and use it. However, great public spaces and downtowns can be created without an elaborate public engagement process. The plans for Bryant Park were almost entirely rejected by the local community board and vocal community leaders, to the limited extent their views were solicited. The planning for the revitalization of Bryant Park was definitely an elite-led, top-down project.

The really important thing and the great insight that Holly Whyte imparted is that public space managers have to carefully observe how visitors actually behave in the public space and make adjustments accordingly. *This* principle is at the center of what is the opposite of top-down planning. Plans for a public space have to be based on how real, living, breathing human beings interact with the physical and programmatic aspects of a park or plaza and not on some abstract political, philosophical, or aesthetic principle. When the assumptions on a public space redevelopment plan turn out to be incorrect and visitors aren't using parts or features of the space, changes and corrections must be made immediately. This requires continued observation of how people are behaving in the place and the humility to admit your mistake, change tacks, and move on. Robert Moses most certainly did not operate this way. He built grand projects that either worked or didn't. If they didn't, he didn't think it was his job to make them better.

In this book, I've attempted to share with readers what I've learned about effective management of parks, plazas, and downtown spaces. Placemaking "experts" and "consultants" have to get better at the actual implementation of public space improvement. We can't just make recommendations and go home. We need to take ownership of projects and stay with them until they are successful. The real business end of this work is in the everyday—creating a great consulting report just isn't enough. We also need to move beyond the big cities and the flagship parks and places. Placemaking has to expand its reach into neighborhoods and small cities, towns, and public spaces. We need to develop the expertise to coach public space managers and share with them best practices of financing, programming, and operations. When we begin to do this, we will see more successful projects—and perhaps the skepticism about these strategies and tactics will soften over time. While today no one ever says that he or she is opposed to urbanism, not enough people have the knowledge, experience, and patience to get their hands dirty actually operating and managing downtowns, parks, and plazas.

At its essence, our work in public space improvement is about bringing people together into shared space to have experiences that enrich their lives—wherever those spaces are. Not only is there no reason that this should be a uniquely urban experience, but it may be an essential corner-stone to a high quality of life (as well as to the strengthening of democratic values) everywhere people live.

ACKNOWLEDGMENTS

I am grateful to Mayor Bill de Blasio; Deputy Mayor Laura Anglin (and her wonderful staff); Commissioner Jessica Tisch; and Michael Pastor, general counsel of the New York City Department of Information Technology and Telecommunications (DoITT), for giving me the rewarding opportunity to continue my work in public space and working to provide affordable access to technology to all New Yorkers—including free, high-quality, secure Wi-Fi service across the city's neighborhoods. It is an honor and a pleasure to be part of a city administration whose values I so deeply share. However, the opinions expressed herein are solely mine and not of the City of New York.

I have been able to have the satisfaction of working in public spaces and disinvested communities thanks to Dan Biederman, president of 34th Street Partnership and executive director of Bryant Park Corporation, and to Carlisle Towery, the now retired president of Greater Jamaica Development Corporation. Both are legendary, pathbreaking leaders in urban revitalization, and both were generous in enabling me to learn so much from each of them. Dan has the remarkable ability to persuade real estate owners and investors to provide sufficient resources for programming and operating public spaces. He also has the brilliant ability to deconstruct and then rethink service-delivery systems so as to provide them more efficiently and often at a lower cost, thereby transforming downtowns and public spaces. Carlisle, a white native of Birmingham, Alabama, came to a community of color in New York City and gained the respect and lifelong friendship of the leaders of southeastern Queens. He and his wife, Susan Deutsch, along with their colleague Helen Levine, pioneered creative means of repositioning, refinancing, and adaptively reusing distressed real estate assets to improve the quality of life for all who live, work, and visit Jamaica, Queens. Peter Malkin, the founding board chair at Grand Central and 34th Street Partnerships, has been an important mentor to me. Suzanne Davis of the J. M. Kaplan Fund and later J. C. Decaux was also an unstinting mentor.

I am grateful to colleagues like Jerome Barth and Dan Pisark at Thirty-Fourth Street and Bryant Park and Max Musicant and Gary Steinberg, Esq., at Greater Jamaica from whom I learned so much and from whose friendship I so greatly benefitted. N. David Milder was a thoughtful, provocative sounding board during the writing of this book and is an incredible resource to all of us working in downtown revitalization. My friends at Project for Public Spaces are a constant source of ideas and inspiration. Phil Myrick, Bob Bass (without whose reliable support there would be no PPS), Jon Zagrodzky, David Burney, Dr. Minnie F. Johnson, Phillip Winn, Meg Walker, Cynthia Nikitin, and most especially Gary Toth are all great placemakers. Vanessa and Michael Gruen and Al Butzel were my coconspirators at the Municipal Art Society on its Streetscape Committee. I could not have better friends and exemplars in public service than Frank Addeo and Deborah Bershad. Frank was doing placemaking from inside city government before anyone in New York.

I had many great community partners in Jamaica, including Archie Spigner, Seth Bornstein, Father Darryl James, Rev. Floyd Flake, Bishop Charles Norris, Tom Crater, Charlene Joseph, Isa Abdur-Rahman, Glenn Greenidge, Kerri Edge, Bill Scarborough, Larry Cormier, Melva Miller, Rhonda Binda, Shanie Persuad, Cathy Hung, Ronald Thomas, Emile Korori, Steve Stowers, Larry Sokol, Tameka Pierre-Louis, and Delicia

Davis. Jim Vaccaro, Richard Eaddy, and Dan Cohen were both wonderful friends and supportive colleagues in my work in Jamaica.

I've had the good fortune to be influenced in my reading and conversations by so many interesting and intelligent people like Justin Davidson, Mitch Dunier, Hakim Hassan, Rosanne Haggerty, Heather Macdonald, and Aaron Renn.

I could not be more appreciative of my publishers at Rutgers University Press, who have been so supportive of this project. Micah Kliet, director; Peter Mickulas, executive editor; and intern Blake Ritchie have been as helpful and supportive as any author could hope for. Peter challenged me to sharpen up the manuscript, both intellectually and in its writing. It's so much better as a result—but the errors are all my own.

I studied political philosophy and learned to write as an undergraduate at Oberlin College from Professor Harlan Wilson—who has been patient with me for years. Counselors Mary Davis and Jane Zimmerman were the catalysts that encouraged me to put my experiences and thoughts on paper. Michael Goodman, Jeff Stone, and Conrad Bahlke supported me along the way. My friend Andra Marx kept me from going off the rails on many occasions.

And I cannot thank enough my daughters Lily and Hannah as well as my wife, Heidi Waleson, who challenges my ideas and makes them better every day. Heidi's position as opera critic at the *Wall Street Journal* (thanks to her brilliant editors, Ray Sokolov and then Eric Gibson) gave me the opportunity to travel with her to cities all over the country, from Boston to Los Angeles, with stops in Cooperstown, St. Louis, Charleston, Omaha, and Santa Fe, among many other places in between. She was endlessly tolerant of my taking photographs of light poles, turning over trash cans to see who manufactured them, and visiting outlying neighborhoods and parks to see what was up in them between opera performances. Most of the ideas here arose out our conversations on those trips. I am endlessly grateful for the decades of our partnership.

A P P E N D I X

To: The Rockefeller Brothers Fund   November 26, 1979

From: William H. Whyte

Revitalization of Bryant Park-Public Library front

Gist:Bryant Park and the front of the Public Library are
now dominated by dope dealers. But they are not the cause of
the problem. The basic problem is under-use. It has been for
a long time. It ante-dated the invasion of the dope dealers
and in part induced it.

Access is the nub of the matter.Pyschologically, as well
as physically, Bryant Park is a hidden place, and so,to a
surprising degree, is a large part of the Library's space.
Relatively few people use these spaces, nor are they invited
to.

It is the thesis of this report that the best way to
meet the problem is to promote the widest possible use and
enjoyment by people. To this end there is reccomended a major
program with concurrent action on four components: (1) structural
changes to open up access;(2) programming to induce use and
build a constituency; (3) A beefed up maintenance effort with supple
-mentary crew;(4)A broadened policing effort,to include supplemental
guards and other full time personnel.

There is a great opportunity for action. The situation is bad,
yes, but so bad it's good, and from this level even modest
actions can have a dramatic effect on these spaces and peoples'
perception of them. It's not just a matter of reclamation. Both
of these spaces have potentials that have never been realized
and there is every reason they should be among the greatest
and most enjoyable of spaces.

- -

First, let me document the charge of under-use.

Back in 1971 and 1972 --comparatively good years
for Bryant Park-- my group was doing a comparative study
of public spaces. At that time the average number of people to
be found at Bryant during the noon period on a nice sunny day
was about 1,000, with peaks up to about 1400.In 1974,
as the very thorough Wentworth-Nager study showed, usage was
at about the same level.

The figures are lower today. I have no summer counts but
to judge by the sightings over a number of very warm and
pleasant days in October, usage is off by a third to a half.
Interestingly, so is the proportion of females--always a
valuable indicator. In the early and mid seventies it was

-2-

about 42%. Now it's about 29%. Conversely, the number of
undesirables has risen, but in absolute terms by not so very
much. As a very rough estimate, I would put the hard core
of regulars at about 100. But they sure look like more. They
are the constant and when nobody else is in the park they
are very, and menacingly visible.

Let's go back to the comparatively good days. A thousand
people sounds like a lot. For a place the size of Bryant it
is not. In our comparative study of space use we found that
the bottom end of the scale for little used places was about
five people per thousand square feet. In Bryant's 237,000
square feet , a thousand people on a good day comes to about
that density.While the comparison may be extreme, it is in
order to note that Paley Park has a density of about forty per
thousand feet, and for a very high quality experience. Were
Bryant"s space to be put to the same density of use, there
would be about 9,500 people at lunchtime. Big spaces, I hasten
to note, generally have lower densities than small ones, but
the comparisons are worth thought.

Clearly, the carrying capacity of Bryant Park is
enormous. To make a rough calculation, I would put 2500
people as the very minimum that should be expected at peak
use times on ordinary summer days. As the constituency builds
up, the number could easily be doubled, and with no over-
-crowding.

There has been some   concern that easier access
would under-cut the sanctuary and refuge quality that
people cite as a reason for coming. I see no merit in this
charge. In the first place, if people really wanted a walled
off sanctuary, Bryant would be a great success. It's a walled
off sanctuary.But it isn't a success and there's some fairly
obvious evidence that they come,say, to enjoy the lawn because
of the lawn, and not because there's a wall and iron fence
around the outside.

Well used places accomodate all sorts of use, all sorts
of people, and in varying moods. Because of the many good
elements in its design, Bryant offers many different kinds of
experience; for the rather raffish group of young swingers
who brave the place now there is the lawn; for the contemplative,
a spot under the plane trees to read a book; for the chess
players, the north end of the upper terrace. When the squalid
crew that now encircles it is gone, the fountain should function
as an activity area much like Grand Army Plaza.

The Library front has had a more consistent use. In
1971-72 the number of people sitting on the steps averaged about
78 at peak use times, sometimes going up to 100--110. Today, the
usage is about the same, though there has been a marked drop
in the proportion of women. As with Bryant, carrying capacity
is much greater. With the kind of improvements reccomended,
the number of sitters on good days ought to be at least triple
the current figures

-3-

STRUCTURAL: PROBLEMS

If there's one lesson to be learned from studying how
people use space, it is that the key factor in whether a
place is used or not is it's relationship to the street. Bryant
Park has a very bad relationship.

In the first place it is unseen. Here and there across
the country there are a number of hidden parks and plazas
and without exception they are little used. Most are hidden
inadvertently. In the case of Bryant Park, however it was
by design. When the plan was drawn up in 1934, it was done
so with the idea of walling off the park as a sanctuary. The
intentions were of the best and the design was widely praised.

Now we know better. If you were to apply the principal
findings of research in reverse and strive to create a park
that would be little used you would:

1)   elevate it four or five feet above street level
2)   put a wall around it
3)   put a spiked iron fence atop the wall
4)   line the fence with thick shrubbery

This was exactly the kind of design Frederick Law
Olmsted warned against. He believed the streets around a
park should be concieved as an "outer park". When the
Commisioners of Central Park asked him to put a wall around
it he responded vigorously."It is not desirable," he said,
"that this outer park should be seperated by any barrier
more than a common stone curb from the adjoining roadways.
It is still more undesirable in the interest of those who
are to use it that it should be seperated more than is
necessary from the inner park...The two should be incorporated
as one whole, each being part of the other."

At Bryant Park the two are quite seperate. So are they
at Union Square, and with the same effect. The problem is not
merely the walls but the excrescences above: the shrubbery
and the iron fences. They block what view there is, and, like
the "NO" signs posted on them they do not invite but deflect.

Olmsted hated them. "I consider the iron fence to be unquestion-
-ably the ugliest that can be used." he said, "In expression
and association it is in the most distinct contradiction
and discord with all the sentiment of a park. It belongs to
a jail or the residence of a despot who dreads assassination."

What is tantalizing about Bryant is how close it comes
to being seeable. Another foot or so of elevation and it would
be beyond redemption save at tremendous cost. But it's close.
If you are just over six feet tall you can see over the top
of the steps on the Avenue of the Americas; if you are five
feet eleven inches you can get occasional glimpses along 42d
Street. Only for want of a few inches is it hidden from most
people.

Bryant Park is so cut off from the street as to accentuate
another defect. There is a very meager pedestrian flow through
the park. The eastern and western steps on 42nd Street, for
example, average only 540 and 480 people per hour respectively

-5-

at lunch time. Again, this is the result of a definite design decision. Various recommendations made for paths to
encourage pedestrian flow were rejected, it being felt that
this would detract from the sanctuary aspect of the place.
But we now know that healthy pedestrian flow is a great asset;
it enhances the activities and acts as something of a magnet.
Characteristically, the most favored places for sitting, reading, shmoozing, are apt to be athwart to the main pedestrian
flow, rather than isolated from it.

For lack of openings, the long balustrades confine the
walls and bar easy pedestrian flow; they also give the park
a labyrinthine quality. It's not an easy place to get out
of in a hurry. You get a certain sense of entrapment here,
and a shuffling wino coming at you poses a menace that he
would not out on the street. On the attached plan note that
in certain spots you have to take a very circuitous route to
reach the street. This lack of easy exit has had a definite
effect on usage, and it is one of the reasons certain areas
have been shunned.

Now let's turn to the library. In contrast to Bryant
Park, it has a good relation to the street. It is elevated
from Fifth Avenue but in easy, inviting stages and the sidewalk functions as part of the over all space. The pedestrian
flows on the sidewalk run around 4500 people per hour at lunchtime. As our timelapse studies demonstrate, even on days when
the library is closed, any kind of event or attraction will
quickly draw a big crowd from the street. On the upper terrace
pedestrian flows are fairly meager. One reason is the gauntlet
of dope-dealers almost permanently stationed on the northern
end of the terrace. Another is the simple fact that access
to the terrace from 42nd Street involves a complicated dog-
leg.

But the cardinal problem is that half of the upper terrace
lies unused, sealed off by the privet hedges in front of the
unused flood lights. This now functionless space is dark and
gloomy.

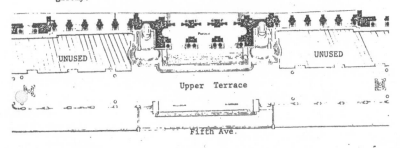

-6-

STRUCTURAL: Reccomendations

Bryant Park : with top priority to access along 42d. Street

1) Remove the iron fences atop the walls.

2) Remove the shrubbery.

3) Open up access with new steps midway between the
   existing ones on 42d Street. They should be inviting:
   broad and of an easy pitch.The broad steps on
   the Avenue of the Americas are a good model; a step
   or two too many,yes, but their low risers and long
   treads seem just right.

4) Provide ramps for the handicapped. The new steps
   should have a ramp,and eventually there should be
   ramps on all sides of the park. As Andrew Heiskell
   has suggested, there might be no better way to
   dramatize the issue of access. The handicapped can
   be helpful allies. In the campaign for new open
   space zoning they helped obtain easier steps,ramps,
   clearer pathways--i.e. easier access for everyone.
   And ramps are also useful in providing access for
   special maintenance equipment, such as vacuum trucks
   and snow plows.

5) Open up access to the upper terrace with new steps.
   This could not only induce more pedestrian use, but
   provide an avenue vista that the design seems to
   call for but leaves unresolved. The upper terrace
   is the best used part of the park and changes here
   would be building on strength.

6) Rehabilitate the restroom structures. There are
   are several new uses they could be put to, such as
   a cafe adjunct. Revolutionary as it might seem now,
   it is possible the undesirables problem can be
   cleaned up enough that the structures can be considered
   for another much needed use: restrooms.

7) Improve the visual access from the steps on Avenue
   of the Americas.This is the best, most inviting view
   of the park,but just out of sight. Bronson Binger
   wants to explore the possibility of raising the sidewalk
   level to open up the sight lines.

8) Rehabilitate the fountain. When this territory is
   reclaimed, it should be a fine gathering place --
   like Bethesda has and can be, with flows and counter
   flows.

-7-

9) Cut openings in the balustrades for easier pedestrian circulation within the park. Done well, the openings would look part of the original design and would not disturb the axial layout. The point would be to provide choices. People like short cuts. The more choices, the easier the flow.

Library

1) Open up the terrace. Remove the privet hedges, the floodlights, and the trees at the rear; plant new trees on the front of the terrace. This is the reccomendation of the landscape architects in the Cambridge Seven proposal. To the basics of it, Amen.

2) Promote use of the terrace with chairs and tables and an attractive food facility.

3) Clean the front of the Library. It would be a grand thing to do in any event, but now there is particular reason. With the cleaning of Grand Central and the new amenitieswin the area there is going to be a dramatic transformation in the feel of the area. It would be great if the Library could anticipate this, and strengthen it, with its own clean=up. Since it would be part of a larger effort to revitalize the area it would be no cosmetic move, but an act of affirmation.

There are a number of other projects to be considered: for the proposed new entrance to the Library on 42d Street, with provisions for the handicapped.

This is fine, but could not some thought be given to a connection between Bryant Park and the rear of the Library? Obviously, the constraints are enormous now and the location of the stacks would seem to preclude any such entry. But must this always be so? Some imagination seems called for. Even trompe d'oeuil would be better than the present bleak back the Library turns to the park.

The fountains on either side of the steps are splendid. The Cambridge Seven proposal bespeaks the restoration of their "sound,effect, and ambiance, but put in no budget item for this. Is something in the works?

There are other worthwhile projects; cutting additional steps to provide through access from 42d and 4oth to the Library terrace; improvements to the constricted defile along the 42d Street side of the Library.

-8-

What gives one pause is the enormous differential in
costs between many of these projects and the basics
that are called for. The basics are relatively inexpensive.
Take the terrace. Of the $415,000 estimated in the Cambridge
Seven proposal for the exterior, the basics of the
terrace re-do come to $45,000. It's the paving and the
stone work that are the costly items -- some $155,000
for the terrace re-do. Granite is great , but at $13 a
square foot it does seem deferable.

First things first. A few thousand dollars worth of chairs
and tables and food facilities would do more to liven up
the front than hundreds of thousands worth of marble and
paving, And they can be immediate.

The experience of the Metropolitan Museum of Art is
relevant.   Its front space is inherently no more attractve
than that of the Library, and the pedestrian flows on
Fifth are lower there. But usage is much higher. At a
time when there will be about a hundred people sitting in
front of the Library, there will be three to four hundred
or more at the Museum.

They are there because the Museum invited them there.
Among other inducements, it puts out up to 200 movable
chairs--and leaves them out 7 days a week,24 hours a day.
It finds it cheaper to buy replacements than cart them
in and out every day. The Museum welcomes musicians and
entertainers. It does not ask cops to shoo away food
vendors. It is a most congenial place and there are
remarkably few problems of security or vandalism.

It could be argued that Fifth Avenue and 42d is a much
more difficult location and that a similarly hospitable
approach wouldn't work there. There is evidence quite
to the contrary. A block nearer Times Square is the New
York Telephone building. For several years after it was
built nobody sat on its plaza. They couldn't. There was
no place to sit. But bums liked it and there would usually
be one or two lying up against the sloping walls. After
he became president of the company, the late John Mulhearn
decided to liven things up by turning the plaza into an
outdoor cafe with movable chairs and tables and a food
buffet. It was an immediate success, well used by employees
and passersby. But not by the bums. As John Mulhearn was
happy to note, the cafe proved the best of security measures.
(Thought: it would be fitting indeed if one of the
improvements to Bryant were named in his memory. He felt
it highly salvageable.)

-9-

PROGRAMMING:

The Parks Council has drawn up an excellent set of proposals and is ready to provide the supervision to carry them out. They propose an upgrading of the present food concession, the possible addition of a cafe concession, flower and plant stalls, book carts and stalls, information and ticket booths. They plan to develop a schedule of enter--tainments, with particular attention to afternoon and evening performances to broaden the hours of use. They propose a full-scale marketing and promotion campaign to build a large constituency for the park in the surrounding area.

They also propose an activity that is generally left out of programming projects -- evaluation. They want to have the changes and activities monitored to find out which work, which don't, and what the lessons are for the next steps. Such evaluation will be equally important for the structural changes. Since they will be incremental there's a great opportunity to learn from each step. People are very quick to show what works for them; through such techniques as time lapse photography, and direct, systematic observation the lessons can be quickly learned. If I may stick in a commercial for my colleagues, a group well qualified for such a task is the Project for Public Spaces.

There has been some apprehension that the structural work reccomended may undercut and dilute support for the programming effort. It is more likely that it will strengthen it. While there has been no programming effort of the breadth the Parks Council is reccomending, there have been some excellent programs in Bryant Park in the past. But they haven't taken. The effect on park use has been transitory. While the band is playing, splendid. Lots of people. Few undesirables. Twenty minutes after the band has packed its instruments, they're all back. The place reverts. And it will continue to unless basic changes are made.

The improved access and stronger pedestrian flows that structural changes can bring about are crucial to the programming attractions reccomended. Bookstalls, for example. Who's going to buy the books? As the experience at Grand Army Plaza has demonstrated, it takes time to build a market and strong pedestrian flows are vital. True, amenities like bookstalls and food kiosks help induce pedestrian flows. But there's no need to get hung up on the chicken-or-egg argument. The structural improvements and the programming efforts should be concurrent, and they should be mutually supporting.

MAINTENANCE   -10-

A good word is in order for the job being done by
the Park Department people. Considering the odds they are working
against, it is a very creditable one. But there are not enough
of them; they lack first rate equipment. The addition of a small
supplemental force would lead to significant improvement and
there is an excellent precedent at hand.

At Madison Square Park Donald Simon has set up,with
Ford Foundation backing, a revitalization program. Operating
as Urban Parks Plaza, his group has enlisted the support of
the neighboring business community in a program to make the
park a safe, comfortable, and enjoyable place. One of the
components is a small supplemental force to work with the
park people and provide them specialized equipment and supplies.
The program works and the park people are enthusiastic supporters.

For Bryant Park Simon proposes two additional service
employees to work on weekdays from March to November; one man
on weekends from April through October. The estimated budget
includes $47,000 for personnel; $2,000 for supplies; $5,000
for overhead, and $12,000 for management and supervision.

There are economies of scale in a program which embraces
several parks; availability of special equipment on a rotation
basis, for example, such as vacuum trucks and motorized snow
plows. Most important, management and supervision should be more
effective on a joint basis.This would be all the more so if, as
reccomended below, a supplemental guard force is also included.

POLICING

It is clear that there is a severe policing problem.
But it is also clear that the police alone will not resolve it.

If a strong police prescence were the answer, there
would be no problem in front of us. Right now the police are
all over the place. They walk up and down the pathways in
Bryant. They stand at the entrances. They walk up and down
in front of the Library. And so, just as obviously, do the
dope dealers. In the films I've been taking of the activity
you can usually see in the same scene both the cops and
the dealers, the latter often openly soliciting trade as they
go from person to person. Time lapse coverage of entrances
indicates thatdealers will move away when cops stand there,
but as soon as they leave, it's only a matter of minutes
before the dealers are back.

To say this is not to denigrate the importance of police;
they have plenty of problems of their own-in the courts, the
cumbersome processes of bringing anyone to book, and the like.
Certainly they are necessary. There is a truly vicious element
in the park and night will pose special dangers for a long time
to come.

-11-

It is in order, then, to press for stronger police
efforts and undoubtedly when a joint program is announced
there will be a great flurry of police activity, vows to
really crack down, and so on. These seem to come along in two
or three year cycles and it's time for another go.

But improvement of the policing of the park--in the
broad sense of the term-- will most likely be achieved by
by an increase in the number of full time regulars in the park.
Most successful places have "mayors"; they can be building
guards, maintenance people,people who run food concessions.They
are familiar faces, a point in one's journey, reassuringly
there.

The most effective would be supplemental guards. They
would operate much as do the uniformed guards of Rockefeller
Center: friendly types who like to keep everything normal but

who are in walkie-talkie communication with a security base
and thence to the police. At Bryant Park it might be possible
to tie in with the security set-ups of New York Telephone
and the City University Graduate Center.

Initially, there could be two on duty for the
March-November period; with,perhaps, additional guards for
special occasions. Personnel cost would probably be in the
range of $60-65,000 ..Management and supervision costs would
be integrated with those for the supplemental maintenance people.

Choice of personnel for the various installations
planned will be important. Their job is not fighting crime,
but along with the guards and the maintenance men they
will greatly affect peoples perception of crime --and that's
a big part of the battle.

LANDMARK STATUS

Bryant Park has been declared a landmark by the New York
City Landmarks Preservation Commission. It has been assumed
by a number of people that the Commission would consider
structural changes such as we contemplate a violation and
would not grant the necessary permit. I made an informal
presentation of the possible changes to Commission Chairman
Kent Barwick. He was most sympathetic;indeed, enthusiastic.
It happens he has been a long time user of the park himself
and is well aware of the isolation problem. He feels the changes
proposed are a case of making a landmark more accessible. He
believes the other members of the commission might be
positively disposed also,but emphasizes that it will be important
to present the changes in the context of the full programming,
maintenance,and policing effort.

Preservation groups should be sought as allies. The board
of the New York Landmarks Conservancy, the leading private
group, has been briefed on the proposals and responded
affirmatively. Testimony by the memebers at the hearings
should be most helpful.

-12-

The Case for Immediate Action

The funds needed for launching a broad program
are relatively modest, and, indeed, could be justified
as a hard-headed business investment that will be repaid
many times over in a better employee environment, property
values, and human values. The programming effort is
estimated at about   ; the maintenance, security
and supervision component, about $150,000. These efforts
will probably stimulate the provision of many additional service
services in kind by the various sponsoring organizations.

The largest costs will be those of the physical
rehabilitation of the park. But government funds should
be available for this. Within several weeks it is likely
that the Park Department will announce that it is embarking
on a major capital improvement program for the revitalization
of Bryant Park. The funds to be committed will be upwards
of $ million dollars over a three year period. In addition
to the changes discussed here, many other projects are under
consideration for the long term. (Among them; a glass walled
cafe proposed by Robert Zion for the fountain area.)

Cranking up such a program will take time. In the
meanwhile, there are high priority projects that do not
require large sums and which ought to be undertaken now.

. To recapitulate:

          Library: Clean out the upper terrace and
                   liven it up with amenities

          Bryant Park: Remove the iron fences and shrubbery
              -             Cut a new set of steps on 42d St.

The Park Department has had a budget of $400,000 for
1979-80 improvements for Bryant Park. Until recently, all
of this was earmarked for rehabilitation work on existing
features. As an earnest of its long range plans, the Park
Department should consider allocating some of its current
funds to the removal of the fences and shrubbery, along 42d
Street at least,

There is another possibility for immediate action. Why
not go the permit route? If the design is in consonance with
the Park Department's plans, a donor can give a project
directly: hire the designer, hire the **contractor**, and set his
own deadlines. This procedure has cut the usual project time
by a half or more and has been successfully used for the
Delacorte sculpture in Central Park, fountains and the like.

If a corporation of the community or a consortium
of them wanted to get things going a set of steps would be
a high leverage gift. They don't have to cost a great deal;
the important thing is that they be broad and easy and they
can be made this way in concrete as well as granite. And
they can be made soon; if a good head of steam is built up,
by June first.

So many things are in place. Even the dope dealers
are helping. If you went out and hired them you couldn't
get a more villainous crew to show the urgency of the situation.
Most importantly, by a fortuitous set of circumstances
some very good people are in most of the key spots --a
constellation that was not in place several years ago.
They understand the breadth of the problem and they are keen
for action. It is a great moment to be seized.

NOTES

CHAPTER 1 — JACOBS, WHYTE, BRYANT PARK, JAMAICA, QUEENS,
AND THE RETURN TO THE CENTER

1. Whyte, *Organization Man.*

2. Whyte, *City.*

3. Whyte, *Social Life.*

4. Lydon and Garcia, *Tactical Urbanism.*

5. Rockefeller Brother Fund, https://www.rbf.org/about/our-history.

6. Wharton, *House of Mirth*, chap. 13.

7. That brilliant study, which is reprinted in the appendix in this book, is the foundational document for the park's restoration.

8. New York Public Library, "Stephen A. Schwarzman Building Facts."

9. Weber, "After Years under Wraps."

10. Goldberger, "Architecture View."

11. Now called Bryant Park Corporation.

12. There will be an extensive discussion of BIDs—what they are and how they work—in chapter 4.

13. Regional Plan Association, *Second Regional Plan.*

CHAPTER 2 — THE BASIC STRATEGIES OF PLACEMAKING

1. Flint, *Wrestling with Moses.*

2. The case for this kind of thinking in evolutionary psychology is made in Wright, *Why Buddhism Is True.*

3. Fried, "Jamaica (Note: Not South Jamaica) Mounts a Revival"; James, "Police Shift Drug Teams"; Marriott, "New York's Worst Drug Sites"; *New York Times*, "Butcher in Queens Is Killed."

4. Jacobs, *Death and Life of Great American Cities*, 70–71.

5. In *Uneasy Peace*, chap. 3, Sharkey notes the national impact on crime reduction that the change in perception about the safety of public spaces produced.

6. Pavlick, "No News(rack) Is Good News?"

7. New York City v. American School Publishing, Inc., 69 N.Y.2d 576, 509 N.E.2d 311, 505 N.Y.S.2d 599 (1987).

8. Section 19-128.1 of chapter 1 of title 19 of the Administrative Code and Section 2-08 of chapter 2 of Title 34 of the rules of the City of New York. See also http://www.nyc.gov/html/dot/html/infrastructure/newsracksintro.shtml.

9. Schmidt, "New York City May Double Number."

10. Our vending proposal for New York City can be found at http://legistar.council.nyc.gov/LegislationDetail.aspx?ID=430534&GUID=4CE1810C-8F2A-4489-B3D3-BD5FE9A23ADC&Options=ID%7cText%7c&Search=110. I still think it is a good one.

CHAPTER 3 — WHY BRYANT PARK IS IMPORTANT

1. *Encyclopedia Britannica*, s.v. "Josephine Shaw Lowell," last modified October 8, 2019, https://www.britannica.com/biography/Josephine-Shaw-Lowell.

2. Florida, *Rise of the Creative Class*, 6.

3. Whyte's 1979 paper for the Rockefeller Brothers Fund containing the recommendations for the park's restoration is included in the appendix.

4. Wilson and Kelling, "Broken Windows."

5. Kelling, along with coauthor, Catherine M. Coles, expanded on these ideas in a book-length work, *Fixing Broken Windows*.

6. The original idea being that the restaurant would generate revenue for the park's ongoing operations. See chapter 5.

7. New York State General Municipal Law, Article 19-A, Business Improvement Districts, https://law.justia.com/codes/new-york/2006/general-municipal/idx_gmu0a19-a.html.

8. The majority of Bryant Park's operating funds are now self-generated from the restaurant, the skating rink, the winter market, and other concessions and events. How earned income can be used in public spaces is discussed in chapter 6.

9. Collins, *Good to Great*.

CHAPTER 4 — THE ROLE OF BUSINESS IMPROVEMENT DISTRICTS IN
URBAN REVITALIZATION

1. New York State General Municipal Law, Article 19-A, Business Improvement Districts, https://law.justia.com/codes/new-york/2006/general-municipal/idx_gmu0a19-a.html.

2. Carmody, "Questions about Restaurant Stall"; Anderson, "Chronicle"; *New York Times*, "Operator for Bryant Park Named."

3. Purnick, "Panel Approves Restaurant Plan."

4. Lueck, "Group Plans to Spruce Up Area."

5. Those lamps used the preferred white, metal halide luminaire rather than the standard orange sodium vapor light. Using white light was part of our "broken windows" approach—with white streetlight creating a warmer and safer atmosphere in the public space. White lighting was also a key element to making Bryant Park feel safe at night. BPRC placed a bank of lights on the New York Telephone Company Building that gave the park a warm glow after dark. Banks of lights were also placed on the Ship Central (now demolished for One Grand Central Tower) and Lincoln Buildings to highlight the facade of the Grand Central Terminal.

6. I was on vacation at the time of that meeting and did not attend. I did receive a call at the beach from the chief of staff to a deputy mayor, who told me that after the meeting, an ash tray was thrown, and he asked me "if my guys were out of their fucking minds."

7. Elstein, "Shaping a Neighborhood's Destiny."

8. MacDonald, "BIDs Really Work."

9. In fact, while the Bryant Park restroom was being designed, we held a charrette in our office with a number of individuals we knew to be homeless to inquire of them as to what amenities they thought would be most useful to them.

10. Jealousy about this journalistic labeling was the source of some of our problems. Others, like the head of the largest Broadway theater chain and the patriarch of one of the city's old-line real estate families (whose staff later publically led our ouster from GCP), had long claimed the title for themselves.

11. See Manshel, "Public Oversight."

12. Furman Center, *Benefits of Business Improvements Districts*.

13. The following are some *New York Times* stories from the period discussed: Howe, "Neighborhood Report"; Lambert, "Neighborhood Report"; Lueck, "Public Needs, Private Answers"; Lueck, "Neighborhood Report"; Lambert, "Ex-outreach Workers Say They Assaulted Homeless"; Lambert, "Hearings Set on Claims of Beatings"; Lambert, "District Attorney to Review Homeless"; Lambert, "Claims

of Homeless Abuse"; Lambert, "Officials Reallocate Money"; Firestone, "3 Tell Council They Beat Homeless"; Lueck, "Private Review of Homeless Program"; Lueck, "Business District Vows to Fight"; *New York Times*, "Abuse of the Homeless Proves Costly"; *New York Times*, "The Grand Central B.I.D. War"; *New York Times*, "After Giuliani Foes Quit"; *New York Times*, "Finance Commissioner to Head Grand Central"; *New York Times*, "For Improvement Districts"; Dumpson, "Partnership Has Done Much"; Stout, "For Troubled Partnership"; Levy, "City Prohibits Borrowing"; Barry and Lueck, "Control Sought on Districts for Businesses"; Firestone, "An Admirer of Giuliani"; Bagli, "Business Group Fails"; Pristin, "Charges Fly as Mayor Is Accused."

14. *New York Times*, "For Improvement Districts, Restored Alliance with City."

15. New York City Council, *Managing the Micropolis*.

16. Thompson, *Audit Report*, https://comptroller.nyc.gov/reports/audit-report-on-the-operating-practices-and-procedures-of-the-grand-central-partnership-business-improvement-district/.

17. Kessler v. Grand Central District Management Association, 158 F.3d 92 (2nd Cir. 1998).

18. The Pershing Square public space, closing the block of Park Avenue between Forty-First and Forty-Second Streets finally opened in 2019—ironically under the GCP management installed by Mayor Giuliani.

19. Those individuals continue to run GCP at the time of this writing.

20. Grand Central Partnership v. Cuomo, 166 F. 3rd 473 (2nd Cir. 1999).

21. Archie v. Grand Central Partnership, Inc., 997 F. Supp. 504 (SDNY 1998).

22. Furman Center, *Benefits of Business Improvements Districts*.

23. There will be a further discussion of creative placemaking in chapter 11.

CHAPTER 5 — OPERATING PUBLIC SPACES

1. The initial problems with managing the lawn are discussed in detail in chapter 2.

2. Blau, "Pigeons on the Pill."

3. Price, "These Are the Top 10."

CHAPTER 6 — PROGRAMMING PUBLIC SPACES

1. Seigel, "Reclaiming Public Spaces."

2. Pétanque happened because Dan Biederman loved seeing it in public spaces in France and Hans Jepson, the spouse of my wife's colleague, was the best pétanque player in the city. He introduced me to the New York pétanque hierarchy, with

whom I had a number of lovely wine-fueled meals to plan how to teach the game in Bryant Park. Chess happened because I walked in off the street into a midtown chess club and got friendly with the guy who ran it. He offered to set up tables in the park and run games there. Both of those activities continue in the park today.

CHAPTER 7 — LEARNING FROM YOUR MISTAKES

1. Hawthorne, "French Landscape Firm Wins."
2. Gregor, "Bryant Park Office Rents Outperform."
3. The "free riders" in a voluntary scheme for supporting programming and maintenance are those property owners and tenants who get the benefit from park improvements without having contributed to their cost.
4. http://www.eggslut.com, anyone?

CHAPTER 8 — IMPROVING DOWNTOWN STREETS AND SIDEWALKS

1. Scruggs, "How Much Public Space Does a City Need?"
2. Ryan, Greil, and Sarver, "Downtown Economics."
3. Roberts, "Black Incomes Surpass Whites."
4. Underhill, *Why We Buy.*
5. New York City Department of Health, *Rules and Regulations.*
6. Hicks and McShane, "Food Poisoning."
7. New York Consolidated Laws, General Business Law, GBS § 35-a. Veterans of the armed forces who vend in cities having a population of one million or more.
8. Pace, "Mixed Reviews on 5th Ave."
9. Hostetter, "Artists Fight to Sell on the Sidewalk."
10. New York City Council, Intro 0110-1998.
11. New York City Council, Intro 1303-2016.
12. Milder, *New York City Council to Introduce.*
13. Goodman, "In Speaker's Final Days."
14. Kim, "State Senator Jessica Ramos."
15. New York City has developed a comprehensive set of storefront guidelines: New York City Department of Small Business Services, *Façade.*
16. Karsenberg, *City at Eye Level.*
17. General Services Administration, "Urban Development."

CHAPTER 9 — SUBURBAN MAIN STREETS

1. Kotkin, *Next Hundred Million*.

2. Kolko, "How Suburban Are Big American Cities?"

3. United States Census Bureau, "Larchmont Village, New York."

4. Milder, "New Normal."

5. Milder, "Let's Get Real about the Arts."

6. United States Census Bureau, "Sleepy Hollow Village, New York."

CHAPTER 10 — HOMELESSNESS AND EQUITY IN PUBLIC SPACES

1. Unfortunately, today there *has* been some backsliding in the area of public order in Midtown Manhattan.

2. Gregory, "Renaissance Theater."

3. Furman Center, *State of New York City's Housing and Neighborhoods*.

4. The one such study of which I am aware is Friends of Hudson River Park, *Impact of Hudson River Park*. I was involved in the design of this study, which was based on extensive data sets from the New York City Department of Finance.

5. Adams, "End of Black Harlem."

6. See Hanna-Jones, "Choosing a School."

7. Sharkey, *Uneasy Peace*.

8. Florida, *New Urban Crisis*.

CHAPTER 11 — ARTISTS, DOWNTOWNS, AND CREATIVE PLACEMAKING

1. First Night began in 1975 in Boston as a family-oriented, alcohol-free New Year's Eve event. At one time, more than two hundred cities had First Night events.

2. Lauinger, "Artist Lishan."

3. Bagcal, "'No Longer Empty' Invigorates Jamaica."

4. Davidson, "The Beauty (and Limitations)."

5. New York City Department of Housing Preservation and Development, "HPD Commissioner Wambua."

CHAPTER 12 — REAL ECONOMIC DEVELOPMENT

1. Professor Steven Deller of the University of Wisconsin is perhaps the leading researcher in this area. A sample of his recent research results can be found here: https://www.researchgate.net/publication/272415711_Regional_Growth_and

_Development_Strategies_Business_Relocation. His extensive list of publications can be found here: https://aae.wisc.edu/faculty/scdeller/.

2. Bartik, "New Panel Database."

3. GJDC is otherwise a typical New York nonprofit entity, exempt from federal income and capital gains taxes under section 501(c)(3) of the Internal Revenue Code like most other charities.

4. Matter of Greater Jamaica Dev. Corp. v. New York City Tax Comm., 25 NY3d 937 (2015).

CHAPTER 13 — DOWNTOWN JAMAICA

1. Regional Plan Association, *Fourth Regional Plan*, http://fourthplan.org/places/new-york-city/jamaica.

2. Bockmann, "H&M Inks 35K."

3. Dan Biederman used to say that "pioneers had their noses in the mud and arrows in their back."

4. Prior to the implementation of the Green Cab program, over the course of ten years working in Jamaica, I saw three cabs available for hire. This was particularly notable because many cab drivers lived in the neighborhood!

5. Ehrenhalt, "Rise of Brooklyn."

6. Ehrenhalt, 11.

7. Regional Plan Association, *Fourth Regional Plan*; the executive summary is at http://library.rpa.org/pdf/RPA-4RP-Executive-Summary.pdf.

8. Regional Plan Association, 17.

9. Regional Plan Association.

10. I participated in the plan as a member of the program committee on economic development.

CHAPTER 14 — REVITALIZING SMALLER TOWNS AND SPACES

1. Florida, *New Urban Crisis*.

2. Vance, *Hillbilly Elegy*.

3. Nottage, *Sweat*.

4. Citizens' Institute on Rural Design, http://www.rural-design.org/.

5. Anderson, "Going to Your Dying Hometown."

6. The Eccentrics Club, Gloversville, New York, http://www.eccentricclub.com/wordpress/.

7. Gloversville micropark website, https://www.facebook.com/gvillemicropark/.

8. Gloversville Twilight Market website, https://www.facebook.com/gloversville twilightmarket/.

9. Kaufman, "Tony Goldman."

10. Horsley, "Herald Towers."

11. Vince is the author of *Toward Civic Integrity: Re-establishing the Micropolis,* a thoughtful and serious discussion of the importance of small towns and their civic and economic revitalization. The book is out of print but available from PPS, https://www.pps.org/product/toward-civic-integrity-re-establishing-the-micropolis. Vince has also given a TED talk on the topic, which is equally terrific: https://www.youtube.com/watch?v=-1qEpNWJGSk.

12. Friends of Hudson River Park, *Impact of Hudson River Park.*

BIBLIOGRAPHY

Adams, Michael Henry. "The End of Black Harlem." *New York Times*, May 27, 2016. https://www.nytimes.com/2016/05/29/opinion/sunday/the-end-of-black-harlem .html.

Anderson, Michele. "Going to Your Dying Hometown." *New York Times*, March 8, 2019. https://www.nytimes.com/2019/03/08/opinion/sunday/urban-rural-america .html.

Anderson, Susan Heller. "Chronicle: Bryant Park Seeks Two Restauranteurs." *New York Times*, June 19, 1990. http://www.nytimes.com/1990/06/18/style/chronicle -254990.html.

Bagcal, Jenna. "'No Longer Empty' Invigorates Jamaica, NYC's Art Scene with Jameco Exchange." Untapped Cities, June 24, 2016. untappedcities.com/2016/ 06/24/no-longer-empty-invigorates-jamaica-nycs-art-scene-with-the-jameco -exchange/.

Bagli, Charles V. "Business Group Fails to Mollify Giuliani." *New York Times*, September 24, 1998. https://www.nytimes.com/1998/09/24/nyregion/business-group -fails-to-mollify-giuliani.html.

Barry, Dan, and Thomas J. Lueck. "Control Sought on Districts for Businesses." *New York Times*, April 2, 1998. https://www.nytimes.com/1998/04/02/nyregion/ control-sought-on-districts-for-businesses.html.

Bartik, Timothy J. "A New Panel Database on Business Incentives for Economic Development Offered by State and Local Governments in the United States." W. E. Upjohn Institute for Employment Research, 2017. https://research.upjohn .org/cgi/viewcontent.cgi?referer=&httpsredir=1&article=1228&context=reports.

Blau, Eleanor. "Pigeons on the Pill Bring Cleaner Bryant Park." *New York Times*, May 28, 1994. https://www.nytimes.com/1994/05/28/nyregion/pigeons-on-the -pill-bring-cleaner-bryant-park.html.

Bockmann, Rich. "H&M Inks 35K sf Lease in Jamaica." *The Real Deal*, September 21, 2016. https://therealdeal.com/2016/09/21/hm-inks-35k-sf-lease-in-jamaica/.

Carmody, Deirdre. "Questions about Restaurant Stall Bryant Park Redesign." *New York Times*, December 1, 1986. http://www.nytimes.com/1986/12/01/nyregion/questions-about-restaurant-stall-bryant-park-redesign.html.

Collins, Jim. *Good to Great*. New York: HarperCollins, 2001.

Conroy, Tessa, and Steven Deller. "Regional Growth and Development Strategies: Business Relocation." ResearchGate, 2015. https://www.researchgate.net/publication/272415711_Regional_Growth_and_Development_Strategies_Business_Relocation.

Davidson, Justin. "The Beauty (and Limitations) of El Barrio's Artspace PS 109." *New York Magazine*, February 5, 2015. http://nymag.com/daily/intelligencer/2015/02/beauty-and-limitations-of-artspace-ps109.html.

DeSantis, Vincent. *Toward Civic Integrity: Re-establishing the Micropolis*. Troy, N.Y.: Troy Bookmakers, 2007.

Dumpson, James R. "Partnership Has Done Much to Help Homeless" (letter to the editor). *New York Times*, September 18, 1995. https://www.nytimes.com/1995/08/18/opinion/l-partnership-has-done-much-to-help-homeless-409695.html.

Dunier, Mitchell. *Sidewalk*. New York: Farrar, Straus and Giroux, 1999.

Ehrenhalt, Alan. "The Rise of Brooklyn, What's Wrong and What's Right." *New York Times Book Review*, February 1, 2017. https://www.nytimes.com/2017/02/01/books/review/new-brooklyn-kay-hymowitz.html.

Elstein, Aaron. "Shaping a Neighborhood's Destiny from the Shadows." *Crain's New York Business*, September 18, 2016. http://www.crainsnewyork.com/article/20160918/REAL_ESTATE/160919896/shaping-a-neighborhoods-destiny-from-the-shadows.

Firestone, David. "An Admirer of Giuliani Feels His Wrath." *New York Times*, July 31, 1998. https://www.nytimes.com/1998/07/31/nyregion/an-admirer-of-giuliani-feels-his-wrath.html.

———. "3 Tell Council They Beat Homeless to Clear Out Business District." *New York Times*, May 11, 1995. https://www.nytimes.com/1995/05/11/nyregion/3-tell-council-they-beat-homeless-to-clear-out-business-district.html.

Flint, Anthony. *Wrestling with Moses: How Jane Jacobs Took on New York's Master Builder and Transformed the American City*. New York: Random House, 2009.

Florida, Richard. *The New Urban Crisis: How Our Cities Are Increasing Inequality, Deepening Segregation, and Failing the Middle Class—and What We Can Do about It*. New York: Basic Books, 2017.

———. *The Rise of the Creative Class: And How It's Transforming Work, Leisure, Community, and Everyday Life*. New York: Basic Books, 2002.

Fried, Joseph P. "Jamaica (Note: Not South Jamaica) Mounts a Revival." *New York Times*, December 12, 1988. https://www.nytimes.com/1988/12/12/nyregion/jamaica-note-not-south-jamaica-mounts-a-revival.html.

Friends of Hudson River Park. *The Impact of Hudson River Park on Property Values.* 2008. https://hudsonriverpark.org/assets/content/general/Property_Values_Full_Report.pdf.

Fulton County Center for Regional Growth. *Downtown Gloversville.* https://downtowngloversville.org/.

Furman Center. *The Benefits of Business Improvements Districts, Furman Center Policy Brief.* July 2007. http://furmancenter.org/files/publications/FurmanCenter BIDsBrief.pdf.

———. *State of New York City's Housing and Neighborhoods in 2015.* 2015. http://furmancenter.org/files/sotc/NYUFurmanCenter_SOCin2015_9JUNE2016.pdf.

General Services Administration. "Urban Development / Good Neighbor Program." October 15, 2019. https://www.gsa.gov/real-estate/design-construction/urban-development-good-neighbor-program.

Glaeser, Edward L. *Triumph of the City: How Our Greatest Invention Makes Us Richer, Smarter, Greener, Healthier, and Happier.* New York: Penguin, 2011.

Goldberger, Paul. "Architecture View; Bryant Park, an Out-of-Town Experience." *New York Times*, May 3, 1992. http://www.nytimes.com/1992/05/03/arts/architecture-view-bryant-park-an-out-of-town-experience.html.

Goodman, J. David. "In Speaker's Final Days, City Council Votes up a Storm." *New York Times*, December 17, 2017. https://www.nytimes.com/2017/12/17/nyregion/new-york-city-council-melissa-mark-viverito.html.

Gregor, Alison. "Bryant Park Office Rents Outperform the Rest of Midtown." *New York Times*, October 2, 2012. https://www.nytimes.com/2012/10/03/realestate/commercial/bryant-park-office-rents-outperform-the-rest-of-midtown-manhattan.html.

Gregory, Kia. "Renaissance Theater Is at the Crossroads of Demolition and Preservation." *New York Times*, December 19, 2014. https://www.nytimes.com/2014/12/21/nyregion/in-harlem-renaissance-theater-is-at-the-crossroads-of-demolition-and-preservation.html.

Hanna-Jones, Nikole. "Choosing a School for My Daughter in a Segregated City: How One School Became a Battleground over Which Children Benefit from a Separate and Unequal System." *New York Times Magazine*, June 12, 2016. https://www.nytimes.com/2016/06/12/magazine/choosing-a-school-for-my-daughter-in-a-segregated-city.html.

Hawthorne, Christopher. "French Landscape Firm Wins Pershing Square Competition with Call for 'Radical Flatness.'" *Los Angeles Times*, May 12, 2016.

http://www.latimes.com/entertainment/arts/la-et-cm-pershing-square-winner
-20160512-snap-story.html.

Hicks, Nolan, and Larry McShane. "Food Poisoning, 'Hopeless' Lack of Regulation Cited at NYC's Street Carts." *New York Daily News*, November 17, 2014. http://www.nydailynews.com/new-york/food-poisoning-lack-regulation-cited-street -carts-article-1.2013238.

Horsley, Carter. "Herald Towers, 50 West 34th Street." City Realty, 2019. https://www.cityrealty.com/nyc/midtown-west/herald-towers-50-west-34th-street/ review/3708.

Hostetter, Martha. "Artists Fight to Sell on the Sidewalk." *Gotham Gazette*, January 5, 2004. http://www.gothamgazette.com/index.php/city/2263-artists-fight-to -sell-on-the-sidewalk.

Howe, Marvine. "Neighborhood Report: Midtown; Homeless Program Suspended." *New York Times*, March 6, 1994. https://www.nytimes.com/1994/03/06/ nyregion/neighborhood-report-midtown-homeless-program-suspended.html.

Jacobs, Jane. *Death and Life of Great American Cities*. New York: Random House, 1961.

James, George. "Police Shift Drug Teams in Queens." *New York Times*, November 17, 1988. https://www.nytimes.com/1988/11/17/nyregion/police-shift-drug-teams-in -queens.html.

Karsenberg, Hans, Jeroen Laven, Sander van der Ham, and Sienna Veelders. *The City at Eye Level*. Wageningen, the Netherlands: Blauwdruk, 2017.

Kaufman, Leslie. "Tony Goldman, SoHo Pioneer, Dies at 68." *New York Times*, September 15, 2012. https://www.nytimes.com/2012/09/16/nyregion/tony-goldman -real-estate-visionary-dies-at-68.html.

Kelling, George, and Catherine M. Coles. *Fixing Broken Windows: Restoring Order and Reducing Crime in Our Communities*. New York: Touchstone, 1997.

Kim, Elizabeth. "State Senator Jessica Ramos." Gothamist, November 4, 2019. https://gothamist.com/food/state-senator-jessica-ramos-wants-lift-cap-street -vending-permits-food-carts.

Kolko, Jed. "How Suburban Are Big American Cities?" FiveThirtyEight, May 21, 2015. https://fivethirtyeight.com/features/how-suburban-are-big-american-cities/.

Kotkin, Joel. *The Next Hundred Million*. New York: Penguin, 2010.

Lambert, Bruce. "Claims of Homeless Abuse Lead to Program Revisions." *New York Times*, November 6, 1995. https://www.nytimes.com/1995/11/06/nyregion/ claims-of-homeless-abuse-lead-to-program-revisions.html.

———. "District Attorney to Review Homeless Abuse by 'Squads.'" *New York Times*, April 19, 1995. https://www.nytimes.com/1995/04/19/nyregion/district -attorney-to-review-homeless-abuse-by-squads.html.

———. "Ex-outreach Workers Say They Assaulted Homeless." *New York Times*, April 14, 1995. https://www.nytimes.com/1995/04/14/nyregion/ex-outreach-workers -say-they-assaulted-homeless.html.

———. "Hearings Set on Claims of Beatings." *New York Times*, April, 16, 1995. https:// www.nytimes.com/1995/04/16/nyregion/hearings-set-on-claims-of-beatings.html.

———. "Neighborhood Report: Midtown; between the Food Lines: Feuding over Homeless Aid." *New York Times*, July 31, 1994. http://www.nytimes.com/1994/07/ 31/nyregion/neighborhood-report-midtown-between-the-food-lines-feuding -over-homeless-aid.html.

———. "Officials Reallocate Money for Grand Central Homeless." *New York Times*, February 2, 1996. https://www.nytimes.com/1996/02/02/nyregion/officials -reallocate-money-for-grand-central-homeless.html.

Lauinger, John. "Artist Lishan Chang Uses Road Kill in Art to Highlight Tension between Man, Nature." *New York Daily News*, April 15, 2009. http://www .nydailynews.com/new-york/queens/artist-lishan-chang-road-kill-art-highlight -tension-man-nature-article-1.363067.

Levy, Clifford J. "City Prohibits Borrowing by Improvement Districts." *New York Times*, September 14, 1996. https://www.nytimes.com/1996/09/14/nyregion/city -prohibits-borrowing-by-improvement-districts.html.

Lueck, Thomas J. "Business District Vows to Fight City's Order to Shut It Down." *New York Times*, July 31, 1998. https://www.nytimes.com/1998/07/31/nyregion/ business-district-vows-to-fight-city-s-order-to-shut-it-down.html.

———. "Business Improvement District at Grand Central Is Dissolved." *New York Times*, July 30, 1998. https://www.nytimes.com/1998/07/30/nyregion/business -improvement-district-at-grand-central-is-dissolved.html.

———. "City Council Orders Review of 33 Business Improvement Districts." *New York Times*, April 19, 1995. https://www.nytimes.com/1995/04/19/nyregion/city -council-orders-review-of-33-business-improvement-districts.html.

———. "Group Plans to Spruce Up Area around Grand Central." *New York Times*, October 30, 1987. http://www.nytimes.com/1987/10/30/nyregion/group-plans-to -spruce-up-area-around-grand-central.html.

———. "Neighborhood Report: Upper East Side; Homeless Sue over Wages." *New York Times*, February 5, 1995. https://www.nytimes.com/1995/02/05/nyregion/ neighborhood-report-upper-east-side-homeless-sue-over-wages.html.

———. "Private Review of Homeless Program Is Planned." *New York Times*, June 10, 1995. https://www.nytimes.com/1995/06/10/nyregion/private-review-of -homeless-program-is-planned.html.

———. "Public Needs, Private Answers—a Special Report; Business Districts Grow, at Price of Accountability." *New York Times*, December 20, 1994. https://

www.nytimes.com/1994/11/20/nyregion/public-needs-private-answers-special
-report-business-districts-grow-price.html.

Lydon, Mike, and Anthony Garcia. *Tactical Urbanism: Short-Term Action for Long-Term Change*. Washington, D.C.: Island, 2015.

MacDonald, Heather. "BIDs Really Work." *City Journal*, Spring 1996. http://www
.city-journal.org/html/bids-really-work-11853.html.

Manshel, Andrew. "Public Oversight: Business Improvement District Accountability." *City Law*, December 1995. https://www.nyls.edu/center-for-new-york-city
-law/publications/citylaw/.

Marriott, Michael. "New York's Worst Drug Sites: Persistent Markets of Death." *New York Times*, June 1, 1989. https://www.nytimes.com/1989/06/01/nyregion/
new-york-s-worst-drug-sites-persistent-markets-of-death.html.

Milder, N. David. "Let's Get Real about the Arts as an Important Downtown Revitalization Tool Redux Part 1." http://www.ndavidmilder.com/2017/06/lets-get-real
-about-the-arts-as-an-important-downtown-revitalization-tool-redux-part-1.

———. "The New Normal for Our Downtowns Cheat Sheet." http://www
.ndavidmilder.com/2017/02/the-new-normal-for-our-downtowns-cheat-sheet.

New York City Council. *Managing the Micropolis: Proposals to Strengthen BID Accountability: Staff Report to the Committee on Finance*. November 12, 1997.

———. *New York City Council to Introduce "Street Vending Modernization Act."* October 11, 2016. https://council.nyc.gov/press/2016/10/11/124/.

New York City Department of Health. *Rules and Regulations for Mobile Food Vending*. June 2017. https://www1.nyc.gov/assets/doh/downloads/pdf/rii/rules-regs-mfv.pdf.

New York City Department of Housing Preservation and Development. "HPD Commissioner Wambua, Artspace Projects, Inc, and Operation Fightback Announce $52.2 Million for Construction of 90 New Affordable Apartments in East Harlem." July 5, 2012. https://www1.nyc.gov/site/hpd/about/press-releases/
2012/07/07-05-12.page.

New York City Department of Small Business Services. *Façade: Guide to Storefront Design*. 2008. http://www.nyc.gov/html/sbs/downloads/pdf/neighborhood
_development/sbs_documents/sbs_facade_guide.pdf.

New York Public Library. "Stephen A. Schwarzman Building Facts." 2019. https://
www.nypl.org/about/locations/schwarzman/facts.

New York Times. "Abuse of the Homeless Proves Costly" (Editorial). December 12, 1995. https://www.nytimes.com/1995/07/12/opinion/abuse-of-the-homeless-proves
-costly.html.

———. "After Giuliani Foes Quit, Business Group Drops Plan to Reorganize." December 24, 1998. https://www.nytimes.com/1998/12/24/nyregion/after-giuliani
-foes-quit-business-group-drops-plan-to-reorganize.html.

———. "Butcher in Queens Is Killed in a Robbery near His Shop." December 23, 1990. https://www.nytimes.com/1990/12/23/nyregion/butcher-in-queens-is-killed-in-a -robbery-near-his-shop.html.

———. "Finance Commissioner to Head Grand Central Business Group." February 21, 1999. https://www.nytimes.com/1999/01/21/nyregion/finance-commissioner -to-head-grand-central-business-group.html.

———. "For Improvement Districts, Restored Alliance with City." February 19, 2002. https://www.nytimes.com/2002/02/18/nyregion/for-improvement-districts -restored-alliance-with-city.html.

———. "Operator for Bryant Park Named." October 15, 1988. https://timesmachine .nytimes.com/timesmachine/1988/10/15/811688.html.

———. "The Grand Central B.I.D. War" (Editorial). August 1, 1998. https://www .nytimes.com/1998/08/01/opinion/the-grand-central-bid-war.html.

———. "Strong-Arming the Homeless" (Editorial). April 15, 1995. https://www .nytimes.com/1995/04/15/opinion/strong-arming-the-homeless.html.

Nottage, Lynn. *Sweat.* New York: Theater Communications Group, 2017.

Pace, Eric. "Mixed Reviews on 5th Ave. to Veterans' Peddling Curb." *New York Times,* July 4, 1991. https://www.nytimes.com/1991/07/04/nyregion/mixed-reviews-on -5th-ave-to-veterans-peddling-curb.html.

Pavlick, Michael A. "No News(rack) Is Good News? The Constitutionality of a Newsrack Ban." *Cas. W. Res. L. Rev.* 40, no. 2 (1989). http://scholarlycommons .law.case.edu/caselrev/vol40/iss2/5.

Price, Emily. "These Are the Top 10 Highest Grossing Independent Restaurants." *Fortune,* October 31, 2017. http://fortune.com/2017/10/31/top-independent-restaurants/.

Pristin, Terry. "Charges Fly as Mayor Is Accused of Dismantling Grand Central Civic Group." *New York Times,* December 4, 1998. https://www.nytimes.com/ 1998/12/04/nyregion/charges-fly-as-mayor-is-accused-of-dismantling-grand -central-civic-group.html.

Purnick, Joyce. "Panel Approves Restaurant Plan for Bryant Park." *New York Times,* April 23, 1985. http://www.nytimes.com/1985/04/23/nyregion/panel-approves -restaurant-plan-for-bryant-park.html.

Regional Plan Association. *The Fourth Regional Plan.* New York: Regional Plan Association, 2017. http://fourthplan.org.

———. *The Second Regional Plan.* New York: Regional Plan Association, 1968. http://library.rpa.org/pdf/RPA-Plan2-Draft-for-Discussion.pdf.

Roberts, Sam. "Black Incomes Surpass Whites in Queens." *New York Times,* October 1, 2016. https://www.nytimes.com/2006/10/01/nyregion/01census.html.

Rockefeller Brother Fund. "Our History." 2019. https://www.rbf.org/about/our -history.

Ryan, Bill, Amy Greil, and Dayna Sarver. "Downtown Economics, Ideas for Increasing Vitality in Community Business Districts." *University of Wisconsin Extension*, no. 180 (2015). cced.ces.uwex.edu.

Schmidt, Samantha. "New York City May Double Number of Food Vendor Permits." *New York Times*, October 10, 2016. https://www.nytimes.com/2016/10/11/nyregion/new-york-city-may-double-number-of-food-vendors-permits.html.

Scruggs, Emily. "How Much Public Space Does a City Need?" Next City, January 7, 2015. https://nextcity.org/daily/entry/how-much-public-space-does-a-city-need-UN-Habitat-joan-clos-50-percent.

Seigel, Fred. "Reclaiming Public Spaces." *City Journal*, Spring 1992. https://www.city-journal.org/html/reclaiming-our-public-spaces-12701.html.

Sharkey, Patrick. *Uneasy Peace*. New York: W. W. Norton, 2018.

Stout, David. "For Troubled Partnership, a History of Problems." *New York Times*, November 8, 1995. https://www.nytimes.com/1995/11/08/nyregion/for-troubled-partnership-a-history-of-problems.html.

Thompson, William C., Jr. *Audit Report on the Operating Practices and Procedures of the Grand Central Partnership Business Improvement District.* May 12, 2006. https://comptroller.nyc.gov/wp-content/uploads/documents/MG06_076A.pdf.

Underhill, Paco. *Why We Buy*. New York: Simon & Schuster, 1999.

United States Census Bureau. "Larchmont Village, New York." American Fact Finder, https://factfinder.census.gov/faces/nav/jsf/pages/community_facts.xhtml.

———. "Sleepy Hollow Village, New York." American Fact Finder, https://factfinder.census.gov/faces/nav/jsf/pages/community_facts.xhtml?src=bkmk.

Vance, J. D. *Hillbilly Elegy: A Memoir of a Family and Culture in Crisis*. New York: Harper, 2016.

Weber, Bruce. "After Years under Wraps, a Midtown Park Is Back." *New York Times*, April 22, 1992. https://www.nytimes.com/1992/04/22/nyregion/after-years-under-wraps-a-midtown-park-is-back.html.

Wharton, Edith. *The House of Mirth*. New York: Charles Scribner's Sons, 1905.

Whyte, William H. *City: Rediscovering the Center*. New York: Doubleday, 1988.

———. *The Organization Man*. New York: Simon & Schuster, 1956.

———. *The Social Life of Small Urban Spaces*. New York: Ingram, 1980.

Wilson, James Q., and George L. Kelling. "Broken Windows: The Police and Neighborhood Safety." *Atlantic*, March 1982. https://www.theatlantic.com/magazine/archive/1982/03/broken-windows/304465/.

Wright, Robert. *Why Buddhism Is True*. New York: Simon & Schuster, 2017.

INDEX

Page numbers in *italics* refer to figures.

ABOUT THE AUTHOR

For ten years ANDREW M. MANSHEL was associate director and counsel at the Bryant Park Restoration Corporation (conceptualizing and successfully implementing many of its most noted programs including its performances, the film series and the construction and leasing of the Bryant Park Grill) and general counsel and director of Public Amenities to the Grand Central and 34th Street Partnerships (where he created the horticulture, street vendor and newsrack programs). Later, he became executive vice president of Greater Jamaica Development, in Jamaica, Queens. Mr. Manshel blogs about downtown and public space revitalization at theplacemaster.com. He is a long-time director and the treasurer of Project for Public Spaces, Inc. He holds Juris Doctor and Master of Business Administration degrees from New York University and a BA in Government from Oberlin College in Ohio.